Lifting a Ton of Feathers:
A Woman's Guide for Surviving in the Academic World

Lifting a Ton of Feathers is not only a survival guide, it is also a destroyer of academic myths about women's career chances in the university, and a revelation of the catch-22 positions in which women find themselves. Paula Caplan demonstrates that while many women believe that when they fail it is their fault, their fate is more likely to be sealed by the barriers they face within the male environment. She aims to help women avoid self-blame and understand the real sources of their problems. Readers will find the information about the mine-field of academia for women infuriating, but the means of telling it highly entertaining.

Women account for more than half of all undergraduate students in the United States and Canada, yet they make up only 10 per cent of faculty members at the level of full professor. What keeps women out of the highest levels of academia? Caplan is a veteran of the academic career struggle, and she explores this question with her own observations and those of many women she has interviewed, and with a strong backing of established research. She provides a clear assessment of what women who have embarked on an academic career, and those who are considering it, may expect.

Forewarned is forearmed, and Caplan presents a list of the forms that the maleness of the environment take: two are the conflict between professional and family responsibilities, and sexual harassment. In addition, her book offers advice on practical techniques of how to prepare a curriculum vitae, handle job interviews, and apply for promotions and tenure. A final chapter is a unique checklist which serves two purposes: to provide guidance in a search for a woman-positive institution and to give suggestions for ways individual women, and women in groups, can work to improve the situation at their own institutions.

PAULA CAPLAN is Professor of Applied Psychology at the Ontario Institute for Studies in Education. She is the author of *Between Women: Lowering the Barriers; The Myth of Women's Masochism;* and *Don't Blame Mother: Mending the Mother-Daughter Relationship.*

A project of the Council of Ontario Universities Committee on the Status of Women.

Lifting a Ton of Feathers:
A Woman's Guide
For Surviving in the
Academic World

PAULA J. CAPLAN

UNIVERSITY OF TORONTO PRESS

Toronto Buffalo London

© Council of Ontario Universities
Toronto
Printed in Canada

Paperback reprinted 1994

ISBN 0-8020-2903-5 (cloth)
ISBN 0-8020-7411-1 (paper)

Printed on acid-free paper

Canadian Cataloguing in Publication Data

Caplan, Paula J., 1947–
    Lifting a ton of feathers : a woman's guide for
    surviving in the academic world

    Includes bibliographical references.
    ISBN 0-8020-2903-5 (bound)   ISBN 0-8020-7411-1 (pbk.)

    1. Sex discrimination against women — Canada.
    2. Sex discrimination against women — United States.
    3. Sex discrimination in employment — Canada.
    4. Sex discrimination in employment — United States.
    5. Sex discrimination in education — Canada.
    6. Sex discrimination in education — United States.
    I. Title.

    LB2332.3.C3 1993   378.1'2'082   C93-093082-7

Contents

To the memory of my dear Uncle Billy,
William Herschel Karchmer,
who gave me so much love
and so much love of learning

Prologue

In her now famous 1927 lecture to the women of Girton College, novelist and feminist Virgina Woolf asserted that a woman who wished to be a successful writer required £500 a year and a room of her own.

Today's woman who aspires to a career in the academy will certainly need a more generous stipend, but a room of her own – both actual and metaphorical – remains an essential, if not sufficient, requirement for success.

What else will she need to survive in the university – that wonderful and terrifying, inspiring and discouraging institution of medieval lineage? And, once she knows the tools she will need, how can she acquire and use them? The Council of Ontario Universities Committee on the Status of Women sponsored this book to provide some strategic information and survival skills.

These questions assumed sharpened focus for members of the Council of Ontario Universities Committee on the Status of Women in 1990–1. Still mourning the murder of fourteen young women colleagues at Ecole polytechnique in Montreal, we were appalled by a year in which each day's news seemed to bring forth another incident demonstrating how tenuous was the progress we thought we had made on women's issues in Canadian universities. What we were learning was a more ancient truth: change comes hard and slowly, and those who have disproportionate power are loathe to balance the scales.

Since its founding in 1985, the Committee has underpinned its advocacy work with strong baseline studies. We have pressed for policy change within the Ontario university system and, for the most part, the policies we sought are in place. The time has come, we believe, to balance our efforts in support of institutional change with an effort in support of individual action. We decided to develop a guidebook for aspiring women academics – a conceptual map for surviving the agonies of university life in order to enjoy its many personal and professional rewards.

We were fortunate that our enthusiasm for this project intersected with an upcoming sabbatical year for Dr Paula Caplan, well-known feminist academic and psychologist. While literally hundreds of women contributed to this book informally through letters, conversations, and memoranda, fourteen women deserve special thanks for helping initiate the formational process for this book through a weekend of reminiscence and advice in June 1991: Carol Agócs, Helen Breslauer, Patricia Gentry, Eleanor Irwin, Madelaine Lennon, Marilyn Marshall, Janet Mays, Elizabeth Miles, Kathryn Morgan, Mary Powell, Lois Reimer, Cecilia Reynolds, Mary Frances Richardson, and Mercedes Steedman.

It says much about the need for this book that each of these highly successful women had experienced being discounted or displaced, had believed it when they were told their scholarship was inadequate and their research or teaching interests were inappropriate or trivial. They had survived and grown in strength through support from other women (and some open-minded men), and by learning to believe in the truth of their own experiences and powers of discernment.

Thanks to Paula Caplan's work, we hope the new generation of women academics will be able to circumvent some of the pain of those who have gone before. In these pages, the reader can learn that she is not alone in questioning older, more patriarchal notions of knowledge and departmental or disciplinary organization. She can learn practical strategies for dealing with boors at committee meetings and for planning the path to tenure and promotion. And, we hope, she will also recognize the power of sisterhood in easing the discomforts of the academic journey.

The usual disclaimers are in order: having chosen Dr Caplan to chart this course, our Committee did not interfere with her navigational decisions. From time to time we offered advice and feedback (with special thanks to Cecelia Reynolds, Dan Madar, and Laura Selleck for their beyond-the-call efforts), but Dr Caplan is the one and true author. True to past practice, the Council of Ontario Universities was strongly supportive of this project, even though they will not agree with all of its tenets and recommendations. Since the Committee was formed, Council members have unfailingly affirmed our role in helping them to be reflectively and constructively self-critical of the university system.

From the perspective of our Committee, this book is one we all wish we could have read at the start of our university careers. Even now – a little wiser and more aware of the pitfalls along our paths – we find we learn from it.

As the present and past chairs of the COU Committee on the Status of Women, we are proud to introduce *Lifting a Ton of Feathers*.

Jacquelyn Thayer Scott, Ph.D.
Director of Continuing Studies, University of Toronto, and
President-designate, University College of Cape Breton
Chair, Committee on the Status of Women in Ontario Universities,
1991–2 to 1992–3

Susan Mann, Ph.D.
President, York University
Chair, 1985–6 to 1987–8

Sandra W. Pyke, Ph.D.
Professor of Psychology, York University
Chair, 1988–9 to 1990–1

November 1992

Preface

This book is intended to be a handbook, a source of suggestions, ideas, perspectives, and many other references that might be useful to women academics. The focus is on graduate students and faculty, although much of the material is also applicable to other staff.

Some women in academia say that they have faced gender-based and other kinds of discrimination, and some say they have had no such trouble. It is important for the latter to respect and empathize with the former, and it is also important for women who have dealt with discrimination to respect the different reports of those who say they have not.

Women academics also vary widely in terms of the number of educational institutions they have observed first-hand, the mix of good and bad experiences they have had there, the degree to which they feel they could use some support or suggestions, their knowledge about academia as a system, and the extent to which they are familiar with, interested in, and sympathetic to the women's movement. In light of these differences, two extensive appendices and a detailed bibliography have been included. Readers who are interested in or want to learn more about the statistics relevant to women in academia can therefore inspect appendix 1 in detail, and readers wishing to read women's stories and some research about the maleness of the academic environment can have a look at appendix 2.

This book is based on the wealth of existing literature on women in academia, on interviews and discussions with hundreds of ac-

ademic women, and on my own experiences. The interviews and
discussions include those that took place before this book was
conceived and those that took place afterward. The idea for the
book came from the 1990 Status of Women Committee of the
Council of Ontario Universities and was funded by the COU. To
kick off my work for the book, that committee arranged a wonderful, 1½-day storytelling and advice-giving session of a group
of senior women faculty and administrators from across Ontario.
No book like this can be all things to all women, and the decision
was made that the focus of this one should be on what women
can do to strive, survive, and, hopefully, thrive in academia. I
interviewed some women of colour,[1] indigenous women, immigrant women, older women, women with disabilities, and lesbian
and bisexual women, as well as some white, younger, native-born,
able-bodied, and heterosexual women. To locate writings in the
field, I used in-person searches, a computer search, and direct
consultations with numerous experts on the topic. If you notice
gaps in the information (for instance, in the statistics on women
with disabilities and lesbians in academia), that is because my
efforts to find such data were unsuccessful.

Based on these various materials, I have assembled some background information, but the bulk of the book consists of suggestions and advice. I have tried to include a variety of suggestions,
since each of you readers will no doubt find only some of them
relevant to your own situation, only some will suit your personal
style, current energy level, and interests. What you find relevant[2]
will probably depend to a great extent on such factors as whether
you work at a more teaching- or more research-oriented place,
whether the student body is all-female or mixed, whether you
teach at a historically Black college or not, whether you teach at
a junior-community college or a four-year college or a university,
and whether you work in a traditionally female, male, or mixed
department; however, even in some non-male or non-white realms,
the traditional styles and values of white, middle-class, North
American male academics can hold sway.

A bibliography divided into topic areas is located at the end of
the book. Readers should consult its introductory text, in which I
outline its divisions and explain the reference system used in the

endnotes. Although the bibliography is extensive, the wealth of fine material available on women in academia is so great that I am quite sure I must have inadvertently omitted some useful sources, and for this I apologize. Most of the references included are focused on specific topics that apply to women academics regardless of their discipline area. In spite of a computer search, as well as checks of lists of references from many of the books and articles I was able to obtain, the number of new sources never did dry up, and finally I had to stop because it was time for this book to go to press. My apologies, therefore, to those authors whose works I was unable to include.

The impact on academia of women, as well as people of both sexes from other non-dominant groups, has been limited, as will be seen in the course of this book. As a result, the scope and richness of both the work produced and the lives lived in academia have been more limited and constrained than they might otherwise be. Just as men often have a great deal to learn from reading the words of women, so white or heterosexual or able-bodied or young women have a great deal to learn from reading the words of racialized, lesbian, bisexual, and old women and women with disabilities. Accordingly, it is important for readers to read items from sections in the bibliography that may not seem at first glance to apply to them. None of us can afford to avoid the possibility of learning about ourselves from the experiences of others and of finding common ground and foundations for solidarity both among those we think of as similar to ourselves and among those we think of as different.

Acknowledgments

I want to thank Kathryn Morgan for suggesting to the Council of Ontario Universities (COU) that I write this book and for urging me to do it; Laura Selleck of the COU for the many times she helped me in doing the work for the book; Sandra Pyke, who headed the COU Status of Women Committee when the idea for this book was born; and Jacke Scott, who headed that committee and provided feedback while I was writing this book. Thanks, too, to the COU Status of Women Committee members, especially Cecilia Reynolds, who provided feedback on the manuscript. June Larkin gave me invaluable, detailed, and thoughtful feedback, plus stacks of reference materials and moral support every step of the way, and Veronica Horn of the Ontario Confederation of University Faculty Associations (OCUFA) also provided voluminous articles. A meeting I had with Linda Briskin, Rebecca Coulter, Mary Frances Richardson, and Veronica Horn of the OCUFA Status of Women Committee early in the process was absolutely inspirational. I also wish to express my appreciation to a number of women whom I interviewed (including those brought together in a full-day storytelling session by the COU to kick off the work on the book) but whose names cannot be listed here, in order to protect their privacy; as well as to the following people, who provided various forms of technical or personal support: my children, Emily and Jeremy Caplan; my parents, Tac and Jerry Caplan; my grandfather, Nathan Karchmer; and Monique Bégin, Helen Breslauer, Peggy Bristow, Sheila Cannon, Frieda Forman, Julie Fung, Nikki Gerrard, Margaret Grant, Ella Haley, Arlene Levine, the OCUFA Status of Women Committee, Donna Sharon, Mary Roth Walsh, and Amy Zelmer. Suzanne Rancourt, John St James, and Carolyn Wood of University of Toronto Press have made it a pleasure to work on this project.

Lifting a Ton of Feathers

*Men make the rules that determine who gets tenure. Because they
have been socialized differently from men, women are ill-equipped
to see the kinds of hurdles that must be overcome in order to be
allowed into the select fraternity. The rules are seldom verbalized,
but the politically naive woman discovers them all too often in the
breaking of them.*

Ellen Henderson (reported in *Newsletter*, 1982)

*While an individual woman may see herself as simply another
member of the group, her male colleagues are likely to perceive her
as being quite different from themselves.*

Angela Simeone (*Academic Women*, 1987)

*Although women have participated in American higher education
for over 150 years, academic women are still pioneers, carving out
a place for themselves in an unwelcoming, nonsupportive, and frequently hostile environment. Their energy and persistence in the
continuing struggle is a source of inspiration.*

Angela Simeone (*Academic Women*)

*There can be no question that women ought to have social, eco-
nomic, political, and cultural equality with men in our society. But
they do not. Universities ought to be in the forefront of change in
respect to the status of women in our society. But they are not.*

Thomas Symons and James E. Page
('Some Questions of Balance,' 1984)

1 The Good, the Bad, and the Perplexing

Visions of the academic life draw us women toward it, picturing an intellectual community whose members search with passion and integrity for Truth and Knowledge. We imagine that in academia we shall find freedom from bias, freedom from worldly struggles for power and wealth, freedom to choose what to study and what to say, and an environment characterized by tolerance and openness, where everyone's energy is focused on the open exploration of ideas.

For women, these images are especially attractive, because most of us have felt intense pressure to think and say what others want, to try to please and avoid upsetting them. Thus, the prospect of choosing what to study and what to say in the classroom is exhilarating. Most women consciously or unconsciously know that the band of behaviour that is acceptable for females is extremely narrow:[1] many of us constantly monitor our behaviour, realizing that, with every step we take, we are in danger of being labelled either as cold, rejecting, castrating, and bitchy or as smotheringly warm, overly emotional, hysterical, and intrusive. But perhaps on the university or college campus, we think, 'academic freedom' and respect for ideas and debate will provide a haven where we shall be free to say what we believe is true and to do what we believe is right, without worrying about such constraints.

Furthermore, since most women have been taught to schedule our lives around other people's needs, there have likely been stringent limits on our time for ourselves and our own work. The prospect of choosing when and where to do some of our work, of spending long hours in the library (no telephones, no family members or friends to demand that we meet their needs now!), of researching what we choose to research at our own pace, is tantalizing.

Many women who believe that they would not be welcomed or feel comfortable in the traditionally male worlds of big business, medicine, or law, for instance, believe that the world of academia will be more congenial. It is clear, though, that in few workplaces of any kind are women treated as well as men, and in most colleges and universities, women do *not* find, in all respects, the sanctuary for which they yearn. Still, there are some powerful pluses of academic life for women, and we need to see clearly both the pros and the cons of the academic environment for women.

This realistic view is especially important for women in academia. Because so many people have the impression that colleges and universities are welcoming and safe for women, the woman who enters that world but encounters barriers is in great danger of not recognizing the systemic sources of those barriers; instead, she is likely to blame those problems on herself, to feel – as 'good' women are trained to feel – that she must be doing something wrong, not doing enough, or both. Even women who enter clearly male-dominated fields, such as engineering firms, tend to blame themselves and themselves alone when they are underpaid or denied promotions; this tendency is all the more dangerous for women who encounter obstacles in fields that are supposed to be bias-free. Since so few workplaces are truly safe and secure for women, we simply cannot avoid every setting that is not completely safe; but we *can* go into academia with our eyes open, with a clear view of *both* the benefits and the obstacles we are likely to encounter.

Understanding the terrain is an essential first step, but understanding alone does not equip us to cope. We need to keep the advantages of an academic life clearly in view, and with respect to the problems, we need to know what steps we can take to minimize them at various times – in choosing a college or university, in preparing ourselves for the problems we are likely to encounter, at the specific moments when we are being demeaned or stymied, soon after such moments, and in the long run. Women who have blazed and are blazing the trails into academia for other women have accumulated a wealth of helpful information, and while this book cannot provide you with all the answers, its aims are to share some of the experiences of women academics, provide some practical suggestions for dealing with common situations, and offer some leads about where to find further information on and more detailed analysis of specific topics. For the latter purpose, an extensive bibliography, organized by topic area, is included at the end of this book.

The benefits

Most women academics report that at least some aspects of the ideal image of academia *are* matched by their reality, although these good features tend to come and go, even within a given day. For instance, a lecturer may spend an inspiring hour in an early-morning class with an intellectually passionate group of students; be patted on the bottom by a male colleague as she checks her mail; open a letter notifying her that her article based on her dissertation has been accepted for publication; and then rush to a meeting of a committee where she joins the other five members – all of whom are male – and most or all proceed or ignore or dismiss the occasional comments she ventures to make. Many women thrive on the variety of the good events in such a day, although they could happily do without the presumptuousness and the put-downs. Since in most academic positions one is expected to combine teaching, research, writing, and service to one's department, institution, profession, and wider community, women have the chance to use and develop a wide range of skills, meet a variety of people, and avoid a great deal of the boredom that characterizes one-note jobs. (The downside of this variety – fragmentation – will be examined later.)

One of the greatest attractions academia holds for women is the opportunity of receiving a salary for spending time indulging their sheer love of learning, thinking, debating, reading, researching, modifying ideas, and discovering new materials or connections among known ones. Many relish the solitude of such work, and many also greatly value the fact that, in an important sense, the university is *about* interpersonal interactions for the purposes of teaching and learning. At least sometimes, that *is* the bottom line – learning and teaching together, with colleagues, with students, and with administrative staff.

For women who value the life of the scholar or teacher, a college or university faculty position may represent the pinnacle of success and achievement. They may be the first people, or the first women, in their families to acquire a university education, never mind becoming a professor.

Many academics are energized by the process of working with students who are young or new to academia and who, therefore, bring zest and freshness to their work. Most relish the fact that sometimes there *is* genuine intellectual debate, that at least the *principle* of openness to disagreement and difference is a stated or implicit claim on campuses, that academia is supposed to be the place where we push back the frontiers of knowledge and thought. Although that principle is certainly not consistently upheld in academia, the very existence and prominence of the principle can sometimes work to our advantage.

The college or university environment is often characterized by energy and vitality, due in part to the sheer numbers of different programs and departments and in part to the wealth of intellectual and cultural events that universities tend to host. The academic setting often has considerable impact upon the town or city in which it is situated, and that impact tends to be most positive when the interaction between town and gown is mutual, when the academic setting's talents and resources are used to help the wider community *and* the wider community participates in college-related events and reminds academics of the realities of living outside the campus.

Many women value the chance to interact with other faculty women and men and to enjoy and learn from their considerable talents, to be challenged to stretch their thinking and imagination and to increase their abilities. Some take great pleasure in watching younger or newer faculty move up the academic ladder, seeing their interests change or expand, noting their developing competence and, sometimes, self-confidence.

Another benefit is the chance to work on interdepartmental committees or in informal groupings to organize events or even work for changes in the institution itself. Increasing numbers of women are choosing to channel some of their energies into making their campus a more congenial place for women and for members of other groups that have been excluded from or made to feel unwelcome in academia.

Some academic settings are physically beautiful, pastoral campuses, and others are vibrant ones in bustling, urban environments. Many also have splendid libraries and cultural activities, as well as low-cost athletic facilities – swimming pools, workout rooms, and so on. Often, conferences in interesting locations, plus subsidies from one's institution, bring the chance for enjoyable travel.

Although most academics will tell you truthfully that they feel pressured and harried much of the time, there is some flexibility built into a teaching job that is hard to find in other kinds of work. On a day when you have no classes, you can *not* go in to work. You can stay at home to read, write, mark papers, or work on your computer, even take the phone off the hook or turn on your answering machine and work without interruption. You can meet with students when and where you and they find it convenient. Sabbatical leave can be taken in tranquil or fascinating locales away from your home institution. Some work you might want to do anyway in your community can sometimes be counted as part of your scholarly or service work, for which you can receive credit for tenure, promotions, or merit increases. Depending on your contract, you may have few or no requirements for classroom teaching in the summer, and you do tend to have longer vacations than employees in other kinds of work, even than other kinds of workers at your academic setting. (You may feel that this is not fair to the others and wish to work to change their working conditions, but nevertheless you will likely be pleased to have some flexibility yourself.) The degree of flexibility depends on your particular institution and department, especially in regard to which subjects you may choose to study and teach, but rarely will you be given absolutely no choice.

In terms of financial benefits, despite the gender-based inequities that still plague most academic institutions, some have clear or reasonably clear guidelines for merit increases, and many have good medical, dental, and disability insurance plans, as well as pension plans. Some have day-care centres – of widely varying availability, cost, and quality – and a few have housing that is subsidized in various ways.

Keeping in mind the positive aspects of a life in academia, in later chapters we shall examine some of the difficulties there for women. To put these various aspects in perspective, let us listen briefly to a sampling of voices of women academics.

Women speak

Women academics are extremely heterogeneous in terms of race, class, age, sexual orientation, physical condition, academic and personal style, academic discipline, location of academic setting, and the nature of that setting in terms of its emphasis on research versus teaching, the value it places on diversity, and the closeness of its connections with the corporate world and with governmental agencies. Therefore, our attitudes and opinions are extremely heterogeneous as well. Women's words are woven throughout all of the chapters in this book, but before examining the belief structures and the daily practices that perpetuate their second-class status, we need to hear some of the themes that academic women say matter the most to them.

THE PLEASURES

Nearly every woman I interviewed described the exhilaration she regularly feels about some of her work. Such comments as 'It's such a wonderful feeling to help students learn and to learn from them' and 'I love nothing better than hunkering down in the library and finding pieces of research that help me fit together a theoretical puzzle.' A dean of women said, 'I have great freedom. I modified my already general job description from Dean of Women Students to Dean of Women Students, Faculty, and Staff. Women from all those groups know they can talk to me, and that will have no influence on the students' grades, the staff's raises, or the faculty's tenure and promotion decisions. I am an advocate for women.'

Many women reported that both formal and informal women's groups had been sources of great joy and support. Some simply 'get together and talk about everything and nothing – maybe play squash,' while others 'deal with the dirty political stuff.'

THE DILEMMAS

The enormous number of dilemmas and challenges academic women face – what one woman has called being hit by 'a ton of feathers'[2] – is in a sense the subject of this entire book. Some of the dilemmas frequently mentioned are reflected in the following comments from women I interviewed:

–   'I know I'm supposed to play the academic game, use the jargon, make political moves, etc., but I really, desperately want my work to speak for itself.'
–   'I also feel torn between feeling I should be tough on students in order to prepare them for graduate school and giving them grades for opening their souls to me, especially in courses that resonate with their own lives and feelings. I want to allow students to connect personally to the course material, but I also feel that I have to make sure they meet high academic standards in their assignments.'
–   'As a woman academic, should I support other women and feminists, no matter what? Is it OK to do research that is *not* about women or *not* about feminist women?'
–   'How do I reconcile my contempt for "academic games" with my obligation to give students marks?'
–   'Men seem to feel comfortable covering up their failures and weaknesses in the name of theory, of academic freedom, of being an absent-minded professor, or of being eccentric. I don't feel right about doing that.'
–   'I feel I have to be on guard all the time, careful not to say anything about my private life in front of male faculty, because otherwise they will find it hard to take me seriously as a work-

ing colleague. At the same time, as a woman, I find it unnatural to have to be so closed-mouth about things that matter to me.'[3] This is a particularly poignant and difficult dilemma for lesbian faculty: 'It *is* an extremely heavy burden to be continuously on guard to prevent people gaining knowledge about one's intimate life; a very powerful separation between the public and the private must be maintained; every word and every action carefully monitored.'[4]

And Aisenberg and Harrington report that women teachers both want, more than men do, for their students to like them and also fear that their authority won't be respected.[5] Thus, they are torn between wanting to be well-liked and not wanting to fear their students' evaluations of them, on the one hand, and wanting to be highly regarded for their teaching abilities, on the other.

THE ROLE CONFLICT

It is not unusual for women academics to describe feeling, even in the 1990s, a role conflict between doing work of the intellect and being 'a real woman.' A highly respected philosophy professor told her story in a particularly vivid way: 'When we were both in graduate school, my husband had lots of confidence that he was writing a path-breaking thesis. I thought I could never do that, but what I could do was support him. So I went out and ordered the Jell-O cookbook. When I was awarded my Ph.D. with honours, this so startled me that I went right out and bought myself an apron. And when I was promoted to Full Professor, I bought a sewing machine. I felt such tension between the academic and the female roles.'

Women also described themselves as sometimes being slotted by others into female stereotypes, such as the graduate student in wildlife biology whose professor told her, 'The reason women go into wildlife biology is *always* to find a man.' Not uncommonly, such stereotypes are hauled out as a way to justify mistreatment of women. One interviewee, for instance, said, 'I researched and wrote a whole grant proposal, and when it was funded, my supervisor put a man in charge. I asked him why, and he said that

I was only upset because I was too sensitive. He never gave me a legitimate answer to my legitimate question.'

ABOUT INSECURITIES

Women academics not uncommonly experience both emotional insecurity and the actual insecurity of not having firm, long-lasting contracts for work.

Women often say they got into academia 'almost by accident,' that they lacked the self-confidence to believe that they could qualify for places in those hallowed halls. Many told me such stories as, 'I didn't enter academe because of my self-confidence and single-mindedness but because someone else saw my ability and thought of me when a professor fell ill (or suddenly decided to emigrate to another country or to work in the private sector).'

A full professor said she has always felt she is 'a fraudulent presence in the university. I remain terrified of speaking in public and never spoke at all in classes in graduate school.' This is a woman who won a prestigious teaching award after her students wrote a glowing nomination brief about her. Another senior woman reported her 'constant fear of being unmasked, because I'm not a *male* physicist.'

Other women, once in campus jobs, assumed they would 'never make it as an academic' and accordingly made other plans for the future. One woman with a Ph.D. from a high-status university in the humanities began a master's program so that when she was unable to find academic work she could do family therapy.

Many women told me that their insecurity makes them drive themselves hard to 'overproduce' at work; because of their certainty that *they* are unworthy, they feel that their *work* had better be damned good. After canvassing large numbers of women, Feldman as well as Sandler (with Hall) reported that women graduate students are less likely than men to see themselves as scholars or scientists rather than as students.[6] Similarly, women are less likely than their male classmates to feel confident about their preparation for and ability to do graduate work[7] in almost all major fields, class years, and colleges, even when the sexes are matched for grade average and plans after graduation.[8]

Women are often blamed for their own insecurity, but in fact the combination of female socialization to feel inadequate and the very real sexist aspects one finds in most academic settings are the major culprits. As a consequence, even women who are secure in the knowledge that they have excellent intellectual abilities may feel emotionally insecure because their work has been dismissed or minimized; as one high-achieving woman told me, 'It didn't matter how smart I was or how good the work – because I was short, brown, and female.'

In addition to this emotional insecurity, many women experience the concrete insecurity that comes from not having a long-term job contract or tenure. A woman who is now in a secure position described the earlier years of her career in this way: 'I spent eight years during which I alternated among one-year contracts, no job at all, one-third of a women's studies position, etc. I had credentials in both philosophy and women's studies. Finally, I was hired for a three-year, part-time, women's studies job, but the philosophy department at the same institution would only give me a one-year contract. Every year, I was spending months developing teaching materials for both new and old courses knowing that each course could be the last of my career.'

THE VISIBILITY / INVISIBILITY TRAP

Women in academia, especially those who belong to one or more other non-dominant groups, find that sometimes they are treated as though they are invisible, and sometimes they are made to feel too visible. As Nellie McKay writes in her article, 'Black Woman Professor – White University,' 'one constantly feels the pressure of a double-edged sword: simultaneously a perverse visibility and a convenient invisibility. The small number makes it easy for others to ignore our presence, or be aware of it.'[9] On the one hand, for instance, a Black, female medical student described an instructor in a small-group learning situation who never looked at her and responded only to the people on either side of her;[10] on the other hand, the only female in her department 'observed ironically that when she was first hired in her department, the chair would often say at the beginning of each departmental meeting, "Well, we can start now, our woman has arrived!" '[11] and an interviewee told me, 'My colleagues are always saying to me, "You're Black – What do you people think about this issue?" '

A type of heightened visibility is reflected in the fact that students tend to treat women from racialized groups differently from other faculty, as illustrated by one Black woman faculty member's observation. She writes that, if you are 'a minority instructor,' 'the students make assumptions about you and about who you are ... You are tested more; you are challenged more.'[12]

Invisibility of women – especially racialized and older women – can result in part from their falling through the cracks; even when institutions have programs aimed at helping 'women' and programs aimed at helping 'members of ethnic minorities,' the compounded and complicated forms of discrimination against people who are simultaneously members of both groups are often not addressed by any programs.[13]

Older women report faculty ignoring them or speaking to them in patronizing ways in class, suggesting in class or in advising sessions that they ought to be home with their children, and making disparaging comments in class about older women.[14] They also say that some faculty seem to feel uncomfortable working with students older than themselves, and a common story told by older women students is that admissions officers make negative comments about their 'irregular academic history,' which was irregular because they were raising children. Some have described being grilled by search committees about why they should be hired for a position when they will work fewer years before retirement than a younger candidate.[15]

Another form invisibility can take is the bypassing of women in authority: 'One Black woman administrator explains, "I have noted that Black males here tend to go to the white man when they need something in my area of responsibility, even though I'm in charge." '[16] And women's abilities are often treated as though they are non-existent, as when women are unjustifiably said to have been hired because of others exercising undue influence on their behalf or because they allegedly slept with someone in power.[17]

The isolation of feeling invisible is poignantly reflected in the

words of a Black lesbian academic: 'What would help me is this:
That those of us who are Black lesbians in academia at least would
start a survival and support network – newsletter, once-a-month
chain letter, union, whatever, so we won't feel so alone and isolated. In other words, establish some sort of system for mutual
survival and *celebration*. A system to prevent our being individually devastated and individually neglected.'[18]

The positive and negative feelings of current women academics
are products not only of the women's individual experiences and
backgrounds but also of the centuries-long story of academia.

A brief record of women in academia

Academic institutions have a long record of failure to welcome
women with open arms, partly because the monastic life gave rise
to universities,[19] which were intended to be places for study and
quiet thought and were tailored to the needs of men, since they
were designed to serve men. And so it went, for the most part,
for centuries.

In her classic work on women and universities, Adrienne Rich
describes how resistance to the admission of women has been
'justified' since the beginning of the last century: 'The major educational question for the nineteenth and earlier twentieth centuries was whether the given educational structure and contents
should be made available to women. In the nineteenth century
the issue to be resolved was whether a woman's mind and body
were intended by "nature" to grapple with intellectual training.
In the first sixty years of our own century the "problem" seemed
to be that education was "wasted" on women who married, had
families, and effectively retired from intellectual life.'[20] In the previous century and in this one, many have claimed that women's
physiology makes us unable to endure the strains of higher education and that our presence in universities is socially inappropriate.[21] It was often alleged, for instance, that studying draws
the blood necessary for menstruation and for pregnancy away
from the womb and into the head, thus interfering with our pro-

creative abilities. And most women today can recall having been taught outright or insidiously that intellectual achievement makes us unattractive to men. Because of some religious beliefs that physical separation of the sexes is essential to allow men to engage in 'pure' prayer, until the 1950s it was commonly claimed that co-education led to sexual promiscuity.[22]

Rich explains that the various attempts to justify barring women from higher education were often not based on sincere beliefs but rather were rationalizations aimed at keeping women out of power: 'These issues ... really veiled (as the question of "standards" veils the issue of nonwhite participation in higher education) the core of politics and social power. Why women gave up their careers after marriage, why even among the unmarried or childless so few were found in the front ranks of intellectual life were questions that opened up only when women began to ask them and to explore the answers.'[23] In earlier times as well as today, it has certainly been hard for women both to fulfil the traditional nurturer's role and to find their place in academia. One woman's college president, noting the potential for education to lead women to question our subordinate position in society, has said that 'to educate women to take themselves seriously at all is, in itself, a subversive act.'[24] There have been long-standing beliefs that men represent the mind, women represent the body, and the mind is superior to the body.[25] In this context, to acknowledge that it is legitimate for women to develop their minds raises the spectre of women leaving their 'natural,' inferior place. It is only a short step to such contemporary, familiar remarks as, 'No man will want to marry you and have you bear his children if you show how intelligent you are.'

In recent years, economic constraints as well as concern about the tenure system providing job security for too many unproductive people have led most academic institutions to toughen their requirements for renewal of contracts and for tenure and promotions. As a result, for both women and men, the standards they have to meet (such as number of publications) are much higher now than, say, fifteen or twenty years ago, and many senior people who make these decisions about the careers of junior faculty have records that would not qualify them for tenure or promotion today.

Furthermore, as financial resources become more scarce and universities feel more pressured to justify every new hiring, tenure, or promotion as well as every new program, they often tend to become more conservative, less willing to recognize achievements in non-traditional research and teaching – where women are often found – and less inclined to fund programs such as women's studies. Still another consequence of economic constraints is that increased proportions of academic positions are part-time or short-term contracts with low pay and few or no benefits, research resources, secretarial assistance, and so on. Since women are disproportionately likely to be hired for such positions, we may see what looks like a positive move toward hiring more women, where those increased numbers of faculty women do not represent secure or substantial gains.

Some people believe that, as a result of the women's movement or other social changes, women are no longer excluded from academia. Well, everything is relative. Of course, women are now admitted as students at nearly every institution of higher education, and most higher-education faculties include at least some women. Even some administrators of such institutions are women, and there is the occasional female college president. But, the higher one goes in academia, the smaller the proportion of women one finds there (see appendix 1). Furthermore, the vast majority of faculty are white; even the few members of non-dominant groups who receive doctorates are not hired in proportion to their numbers for faculty jobs; and among 'minority' faculty, women are less likely than men to be hired.[26]

Women faculty who do not look able-bodied or who are openly lesbian are also rare. For instance, a senior faculty woman at a small university told me that, of the approximately eighty female faculty members there, she is the only 'out' lesbian, although statistically there must be many more. And after spending three years in a large graduate and professional institution, an openly lesbian assistant professor was asked to recommend other lesbian or lesbian-positive faculty for a doctoral dissertation committee; she replied, 'I can't think of any. And I think it is significant that, although I am an out lesbian, I have no idea who else on our faculty might fit your description.'

The inclusion of women also varies greatly among departments and fields of study. Thus, for instance, some fields include large numbers of women (see appendix 1), but 'despite a variety of efforts starting in the 1970s to narrow the gap, men still vastly outnumber women in science and engineering. Even more disturbing ... colleges and universities are losing the female students whose interest they had piqued by special recruiting efforts, and they lack data that could help them stem the losses.'[27] Indeed, the American Chemical Society's women chemists committee finds it can't yet stop publishing its intermittent list, known by some as the 'Dirty Dozen,' which identifies major chemistry departments, some with dozens of faculty members, that still have no women in tenure-track positions.[28]

Even when progress is made, there can be backsliding. For instance: 'In 1978 no women (and approximately 100 men) were invited to talk at the prestigious International Congress of Mathematicians, held every 4 years. Before the next meeting, in 1982, women protested, and a few were invited. In 1986 only one woman was invited and she spoke on the history of math. "We didn't make a fuss, and here they go again," recalls Linda Keen, president of the AWM at the time. Keen organized a protest, and, according to Marina Ratner, Berkeley's only woman mathematics professor, "at the last minute three women were grudgingly invited." Ten women were invited in 1990 after the American delegation "reminded" the organizing committee to invite women.'[29]

It is important to remember that the mere admission of *some* women to most institutions has not meant the elimination of subtle forms of exclusion or mistreatment of them. Indeed, typically, when any form of prejudice (such as sexism or racism) is labelled as unacceptable, it does not simply vanish; rather, it tends to take increasingly subtler forms, thus protecting the prejudiced person from both social and legal accusations of prejudice. For instance, at universities that have affirmative action offices, it can seem that, because the officer is assigned to look after, for instance, 'women' and 'indigenous peoples,' therefore 'indigenous women' are well looked after. But that is by no means necessarily so: 'Minority women are not often viewed as a group with specific concerns. Some programs aimed at recruiting minority faculty and students may focus primarily on minority men; similarly, programs aimed at helping women may overlook minority women.'[30] In fact, when women from non-dominant groups point out the minuscule numbers in which they are hired and promoted, they have often been asked disingenuously, 'Do you want us to hire fewer white women and men of colour?' – as though only a small proportion of faculty should be other than male and white. In the following section, you will see many examples of the quantifiable aspects of the mistreatment or second-class treatment of women, and in chapters 2 through 4 and appendix 2 you will read about some of the features of the academic atmosphere that make it less hospitable for most women than for most men.

In this section, however, we consider from a longitudinal perspective some of the less blatant forms into which differential treatment of the sexes has been transformed in academia. Compare the percentage of university women faculty at many institutions today, for instance, with that of 200 years ago, and there is no doubt that women's situation has improved. However, numbers can be deceiving. For instance, university presidents have been known to announce the creation of what sounds like a substantial number of new positions earmarked specifically for women – without disclosing that those positions would only be filled if departments wanted them filled and put up the money to finance part or all of the costs!

In uncovering relatively subtle bias, the specific point of comparison can make a great deal of difference. For instance, at one Canadian university that recently received an award for its allegedly wonderful strides on behalf of women, the numbers of women faculty actually peaked in 1944 at 19.9 per cent;[31] by 1958 that percentage was down to 11 per cent, and by 1985 the figure had only climbed to 17 per cent of the full-time teaching staff. As in most colleges and universities, at that institution 'men hold most of the permanent senior positions, while women are confined to the temporary, low-status positions.'[32] Progress has also been slow in the United States, where 73 per cent of higher-education faculty are male, and only 27 per cent are female, compared with 25 per cent female ten years earlier,[33] and this is despite the striking increase during that time in the proportion of doctorates awarded to women.

The marginalizing and mistreatment of women, then, remain substantial, and these are increased geometrically for women who are not white, born in the country where they teach, heterosexual, able-bodied, or older than the average woman at their academic level.

Often, what seem to be significant steps forward in higher education only mask a real or pervasive lack of progress. Symons and Page report that the appointment of 'Women's Affairs Officers,' for instance, 'has often proven to be little more than a gesture, an exercise in tokenism or window-dressing. In some instances, indeed, the existence of such Women's Affairs Advisors and offices has provided an excuse for the rest of the university or college to carry on with its general neglect of the status of women and to continue practices that are effectively discriminatory.'[34]

Thus, in both the distant and recent past, women have been excluded from academia on baldly sexist grounds, and in spite of some exciting, positive changes, we still cannot truthfully say that equal treatment of academic women and men today is the norm. Having seen that reflected above (and in appendix 1) in concrete percentages, it is instructive to look at a qualitative example of a historical shift from blatant to less obvious sexism. When I spoke recently to a group of first-year undergraduate women, one of them, looking exceedingly uncomfortable, told me the following story to illustrate her claim that people in the engineering program had stopped demeaning or humiliating women: during orientation week, the engineering orientation organizers used male and female plastic blow-up dolls in simulated sexual activities. The woman student smiled nervously and said she guessed that they had gotten rid of their sexism, because formerly they had used only female dolls. Clearly, this young woman was feeling that her unease about this experience was unreasonable. After all, wasn't she supposed to be glad that they had stopped using only female dolls?

This story illustrates one of the subtle ways in which academia is made less comfortable for women than for men: the use of female figures in visual sexual 'jokes' resonates with our lifelong experiences of women being regarded as 'good for nothing but sex,' as objects of debasing jokes, whereas men have been far less likely to be regarded in these ways. Thus, to see a female doll being sexually used reminds us of the way we ourselves have been regarded, raising the distressing prospect that, even as engineering students, we shall be considered objects of intensely sexual interest rather than as capable scholars. It is upsetting to feel that, in spite of having fine minds, it is our bodies that are the centre of attention. As Jennifer Nedelsky writes: 'The special tensions for female academics in their sense of themselves as knowledge seekers and as sexual beings seems captured in one of our most pervasive myths: Eve (usually depicted as sexually alluring) committing the sin of eating from the tree of knowledge [Nedelsky credits Mary Becker for pointing out the connection to the myth]. We violate multiple, intersecting taboos and are drawn into hopeless, ultimately self-destructive, efforts to be related to as pure minds. And we are punished for our inevitable failure to be pure minds in ways that range from sexual harassment to the manifest envy of male colleagues for the "advantages" female attractiveness is thought to bring. No matter what we do, our female bodies make us feel somehow wrong.'[35]

The engineering orientation story also raises in women a well-founded fear for their own safety as they attempt to live a full academic life, which may include late nights in the laboratory, walking home in the dark from the library, and so forth. Men students are simply less likely to have such feelings and less apt to feel threatened if they see a male doll being sexually used.

Another hard-to-pin-down form of unfair treatment is the public announcement of progressive, new procedures followed by the reversion of those procedures to less progressive ones. For instance, a senior woman administrator reported that many years ago, her university established a 'peer pairing' system, pairing each woman with someone *she* accepted as her peer in order to match them for salaries. Over the years, this procedure was quietly changed, so that an administrator now decides who will be classified as a woman's peer. The initial peer pairing significantly reduced the sex differences in salaries, but now the gap has again grown to as great as $10,000. In a special section on 'Women in Science,' *Science* magazine editor John Benditt notes the persistence of both subtle and blatant forms of mistreatment of women in scientific fields within academia: 'In many fields the era of out-front discrimination is fading as women enter research in growing numbers. But that doesn't mean women are zooming straight to the top ... In Neuroscience outspoken gender-based discrimination has largely disappeared, to be replaced by invisible obstacles. In Mathematics, by contrast, sexist ideas are pervasive, and women often feel isolated and embattled. Chemistry lies somewhere between the extremes.'[36]

One of the most explosive issues related to the progress of women and other disadvantaged groups concerns affirmative action. Opponents of affirmative-action programs have effectively conveyed the erroneous impression that affirmative action is about *lowering standards* in order to hire women, racialized people, people with disabilities, and so on, and that quotas are set that unfairly exclude white, able-bodied males. The fact often missed is that, historically, overwhelming numbers (unspecified quotas) of less-qualified, white, able-bodied men have been hired in preference to women, racialized people, people with disabilities, or members of other disadvantaged groups. Consider the words of mathematician Lynn Butler, who says that of the three women mathematicians she knows who were hired under an affirmative-action plan, one 'was better than almost all of the men they hire ... and is a hell of a lot better than I am,' another was equal to her in mathematical talent, and one would have been hired without affirmative action.[37]

In later chapters you will read other stories about the variety of subtle and not-so-subtle factors that evolved from earlier, more blatant exclusion of women and continue to make academia a less-welcoming place for most women than for most men. Now, however, it is time to look at gender-biased patterns that are reflected in some of the hard data from institutions of higher education.

Gender-biased patterns in the date

As you experience the ups and downs of life as a woman in academia, it is important to have an overview of some of the quantifiable forms that gender bias takes in colleges and universities.[38] Women are taught to assume the best about people and institutions, to cope uncomplainingly even with the worst that life brings our way, and to overlook unfairness in the ways we are treated. It's the Rose-Coloured Glasses Syndrome. But seeing, for example, how much less women are paid than men – and seeing it in cold, hard, black-and-white print – moves this unfairness out of the realm of an individual woman's situation and thus makes it that much harder for you to forget to negotiate for a decent salary, to assume that the people who hire are concerned about your financial situation (rather than that of the institution that employs them to save money). The following is a brief summary of the quantitative forms of bias. For ease of reading, most of the numerical data are omitted from this chapter but are reported in detail in appendix 1, which you are urged either to skim or to inspect carefully.

A general notion about the proportions of women at various levels in academia, financial support for them, and so on is essential for you to have, so that you won't mistakenly believe you are unjustifiably 'paranoid' about the genuine, gender-based inequalities that characterize most academic settings. As you read, keep in mind that the precise facts for your current institution or a prospective academic home ought to be available from its administration.

1. **The academic funnel**: Although women account for more than half of all undergraduate students in the United States and Canada, the proportion of women drops at each step from undergraduate enrolment to master's to doctoral programs, and from there onto and right up the faculty ladder. By the time one reaches the level of full professor, the proportion of women is about 10 per cent. In fields that have traditionally been mostly male, the percentage of women at the full-professor level may be minuscule or non-existent, and this pattern is even more pronounced for women from non-dominant groups. As part of this same pattern, women faculty tend to be less likely than men to receive tenure and promotions.

2. **Part-time vs. full-time**: Women are disproportionately likely to be part-time students and faculty, and concomitant with

part-time status go a host of disadvantages, ranging from scarcer financial resources to difficulties in getting to know the politics of the department.

3. **Women are severely underrepresented in administrative positions**, especially the upper-level ones – those with real power.

4. **Women graduate students in many fields are disproportionately unlikely to receive financial support.**

5. **Faculty salaries tend to be lower for women than for men, and this is even worse for racialized women.**

6. **Women are disproportionately likely to work in lower-status institutions.**

7. **Women faculty tend to have heavier teaching loads and family responsibilities than do male faculty.**

The plan of this book

The next four chapters of this book provide essential background material aimed at enhancing your understanding of the workings of academia, especially as they affect women. This background material is included because the greater your familiarity with the system, the less likely you will be, in times of stress or trouble, simply to blame yourself in the traditional and often-misguided 'feminine' way. Indeed, your two most potent and helpful sources of support and ideas are likely to be your understanding of the system and the support you can obtain from other women. Chapter 2 (and the related, detailed appendix 2) is a description of some of the key features of the maleness of the academic environment. Chapter 3 deals with the many unwritten rules that are the basis for the functioning of most colleges and universities. Chapter 4 is a listing and discussion of myths about women and academia, and chapter 5 is a presentation of some of the Catch-22 situations most frequently encountered by academic women.

I hope you won't feel daunted when you see how much of this book is about problems and how to overcome them. You don't *need* a guide to recognize and take advantage of many of the good things. What you need to know about in considerable detail are the dangers, so that you won't become caught up in them without recognizing what is happening – or, if you do get caught up, you'll be less likely to believe that your trouble is due to your own, personal, individual failings. Misplaced self-blame is enormously draining of your time, energy, and self-confidence. In later chapters, you'll read suggestions about what you can do to deal with many of the problems. The helpful suggestions don't take nearly as long to describe as the problems, but they can be enormously, lastingly important. For instance, once you come to believe that there is *no* great moral value in trying to tough out the difficult times in academia all on your own, once you recognize how helpful it can be to link up with other women, the alternative of reaching out to others will spring to your mind more readily and in a wide variety of problematic situations.

As you read, though, if you start feeling overwhelmed by the prospect of the barriers you may confront, do flip back to this chapter's description of the benefits, because there certainly can be a great deal of joy, interest, and reward in academic life for women.

In chapters 6 and 7, we look at some highly specific ways to deal with particular situations and incidents that come up. Some of those methods, such as forming supportive connections with other women, will be helpful in a wide variety of situations, and some that we suggest are tailored to particular situations or occurrences. Included in these chapters are suggestions for necessary events, such as preparing your curriculum vitae, attending job interviews, and applying for tenure or promotions; although these are obstacles that academics of both sexes have to surmount, there are special pitfalls for women that we address in some detail. We also include hints about how to deal with aspects of academia that *ought not* to be part of college and university life but that you will no doubt encounter; thus, for instance, we include suggestions for dealing with sexist comments or 'jokes' and with the tendency of departments and institutions to dump disproportionately burdensome workloads on women. Chapter 8 is a checklist designed to help you identify relatively woman-positive institutions as you look for jobs, and you can use the same checklist for considering what changes you may want to work for once you are ensconced in a college or university.

2 Why Can't a Woman Be More Like a Man? or The Maleness of the Environment

We are angry because for a brief moment we believed that if the law allowed for women to be hired in the workplace, and if we worked hard for our educations and on the job, equality would be achieved. We believed we would be respected as equals. Now we are realizing this is not true. ANITA HILL[1]

Men and women academics operate in almost separate worlds within the academy. JOHNSON, TIMM, and MERINO[2]

I am with a friend in a restaurant, and we see two long tables filled with men. He says, 'Must be from the university.' I readily nod my agreement – not for a few minutes does it hit me how naturally and unquestioningly, for both of us, the maleness of university faculties came to mind. INTERVIEW

The maleness of the academic environment, described by Hall and Sandler in their ground-breaking paper (1982) on the chilly climate in academia, remains pervasive and often powerful, even while it is undergoing significant, positive changes. In spite of that maleness, the joys of working in academia also persist, and many of the drawbacks are similar to the maleness of most work environments. So, throwing up our hands and forsaking academia won't be the answer for many of us. What *can* we do about the maleness of the environment?

1. Realize that, at those times when that maleness gets to us, we are *not* paranoid if we feel upset. We need to understand that, whatever we are feeling, it is extremely likely that any woman in our position would feel the same. Every time I have believed that my own experience was bizarre or my own reactions were a product of too much sensitivity, if I have ventured to talk to another woman about it, I have learned that my experience and my reaction were very similar to hers or that she knew someone who had felt that way. Furthermore, 'Women aren't the only ones who perceive sexist attitudes. Jerry Marsden of Berkeley, winner of the 1990 Norbert Wiener prize – the top prize in applied math – says, "I had a female graduate student who wrote a fine thesis. Around the time it was being completed, a graduate student told me that it was "common knowledge" that I wrote her thesis for her in exchange for sexual favors – which of course was not true.'[3]

2. **Remember that many women and some men are working on ways to cope with and change this maleness, and we can learn a great deal from them.** Some of you will want to be part of the movement to transform the maleness of academia in the ways that so many women are now working to make 'the workplace' in general less impersonal, more flexible, and more consistent with the real needs of people who want to work in an environment where they can retain as much of their humanity as possible.

3. **Realize that, if we like, we ourselves can work to change this maleness and that, in important ways, our very presence in an academic institution is a part of that change.**

4. **Put some of the material in this book to use. It was written for you.** Chapters 6 and 7, in particular, include many suggestions for ways to cope with the maleness of the academic environment.

5. **Consider studying/teaching at an all-women's institution.** According to journalist Michele Landsberg, writing about Mount Saint Vincent, 'Canada's only women-focused university,' 'In the United States, where 94 women's colleges are still going strong, the research has shown them to be a bastion of women's intellectual attainment, a sanctuary for women's self-affirmation.'[4] The all-woman nature of an institution does not, of course, guarantee that all your problems in academia will be solved,[5] but in many obvious ways it will reduce the physical maleness of the environment.

It is such an interesting time to be a woman in academia. In

most departments and at most places, we are likely still to be in
a gender minority – even those who are white, heterosexual, able-
bodied, and 'just the right age' – but with little effort we can
probably find women in our department and discipline, or at least
on our campus, with whom to share our feelings, experiences, and
concerns. In the words of a woman dean, 'Women are talking
more, revealing more, empowering each other, and there are some
enlightened men.'

Women in areas traditionally considered female – such as library
science, education, nursing, nutrition, and home economics – will
find today a buzz of activity as some of their colleagues organize
seminars and conferences and write papers about the ways in
which femaleness has been good for them and the ways in which
it has been used to limit and demean their work.

Women in the increasingly rare woman-student-only institutions can be found debating both sides of such questions as 'Should
we start admitting men students? And if we do, what changes
would that be likely to bring, and how would we feel about
them?'

The fact that academic institutions are generally expected to
encourage open debate has meant that, in certain respects and on
some campuses, it has been possible to hold frank and open discussions about the harm done to women students and faculty by
the maleness of the academic environment. On the good side, the
wishes of some university administrators to take the lead in implementing new programs and policies – or, viewed more cyni-
cally, some administrators' fears of losing government funding if
their institutions are shown to be biased – have led many colleges
and universities to respond positively to women's lobbying. This
has brought the appointment of status of women, affirmative action, employment equity, and sexual harassment officers and the
creation of women's studies programs and women's centres. This
is *not* to say that the struggles to make these changes and to combat
the frequent, consequent backlash are easy but that it is a period
of ferment and foment in regard to women. Furthermore, unlike
in many workplaces, in academia increasing numbers of women
and men are devoting some or all of their paid work time to
researching and teaching about these issues.

One exciting example of the work being done to reduce the maleness, as well as the other uniformities, of courses is Brown University's Odyssey Two program. In that program, funding is provided for students to work with faculty in revising course content so that it incorporates more diversity, including sessions about sex and gender and writings by women. At this writing, an astonishing 40 per cent of Brown faculty have requested such student assistance.

Keeping these points in mind, we have to recognize that, according to the most recent research, the environment in the majority of colleges and universities tends to be more welcoming and comfortable for males than for females.[6] Some of the factors that contribute to this involve style, and some involve substance. Where men say, 'I have a theory,' women are more likely to say, 'I wonder if, maybe ...' Where many men are socialized to relish the cutthroat nature of some campus politics, most women are socialized to avoid or at least not to enjoy them. And, in the words of a senior woman administrator I interviewed, 'male faculty and administrators pontificate and hog the floor. They announce, "I have three points to make," and that paves the way for them to hold the floor until they've made all three. They've claimed the floor. Women usually don't feel they have the right to do that.'

Some of the specific factors that contribute to the difference in the degree to which academia is welcoming for women in contrast to men include the following:

–   The relative lack of incentives for women
–   The frequency of sexist language, 'jokes,' and comments
–   The frequency of sexual harassment and the lack of safety for women
–   The devaluing of women
–   The devaluing of much of women's work
–   The exclusion of women
–   The even greater harassment and exclusion of women from non-dominant groups and of feminists
–   The existence of a double standard
–   The expectation that women will fit feminine and racial stereotypes

–   The general maleness, racism, and heterosexism of the envi-
     ronment

Many women are disarmed or confused because, seeing other
women on campus, they assume that they will feel as at home in
academia as men do. As a result, every time they are ignored,
patronized, or excluded, they think it is due to their own failings.
They are undergoing culture shock that is all the more perplexing
because they do not realize they are in a somewhat alien, or even
hostile, culture. In this regard, forewarned is forearmed.

Since readers vary in the degree to which they are familiar with
and interested in each of the ten factors listed above, each one is
treated in much greater detail in appendix 2. You are encouraged
at least to scan that appendix, even if some of the sections strike
you as covering material you already know, since you may experience a 'click' of recognition of upsetting experiences that you
have had, have blamed on yourself, or simply haven't been able
to understand. Thinking about them in the context of the maleness
of colleges and universities may be helpful to you.

Imagine you're a woman academic

Since the maleness and heterosexism of academia are manifested
in a wide variety of ways, beyond the overarching ones described
above, it is instructive to imagine how it would feel to be a woman
who

–   has been sexually harassed, tells her academic vice-president
     about it, and later hears him claim publicly that there is no
     chilly climate for women at his university (interview)
–   learns that her university has suppressed their own research
     data that reflect the sexism there[7]
–   as a lesbian in academia, discovers that 'academe has been al-
     most entirely silent on lesbian and gay issues' and that when
     she raises lesbian issues in class, she is met with tense silence[8]
–   encounters outright homophobia in class[9]
–   as a lesbian graduate student, has an 'apparently well-mean-
     ing, but ill-informed and heterosexist professor who mentions

homosexuality, but negates any positive potential through het-
erosexist assumptions such as attempting to explain homosexuality in the absence of explanations for heterosexuality'[10]
- has a professor who, in a lecture on sexuality, raises male
  homosexuality only in the last five minutes of the lecture and
  lesbianism only in the last two minutes, and then only to talk
  about lesbian sadomasochism[11]
- as a racialized or disabled or old woman, overhears the head
  of her department saying, 'Thank God we don't have to hire
  another one.'
- learns that birth control is not covered in her graduate student
  health-insurance plan[12]
- discovers that the recreation and athletic facilities for women at
  her institution are markedly inferior and more limited, compared with those for men[13]
- tries to write simply and straightforwardly but is told her writing is simplistic – and knows that, if she wrote in a more flow-
  ery way she would be regarded as overly feminine and
  unscholarly, and if she wrote in a more obtuse way, she would
  be told she isn't making herself clear[14]
- shows intense excitement about someone's work and has this
  misread as flirtatiousness or sexual excitement[15]
- is denied, by two different institutions, her requests to have
  her degrees reissued in her maiden name following her divorce
  (interview)
- learns that, when she had applied to be dean, a male administrator had warned the hiring committee, 'I think she's a lesbian,' and another had replied, '*That's* not so bad – but I *think*
  she's a feminist!' (interview)
- doesn't know what to do when, during her interview for a faculty position, the men became involved in a lengthy discussion
  of hockey trades (interview)
- realizes, as a woman academic, that even in her own mind the
  word 'professor' evokes a male image[16]
- realizes that, although as an 'out' lesbian she did obtain a job
  in a university, if she included many readings about lesbian issues in her courses' that would jeopardize her chances of getting tenure (interview)
- is at a meeting to provide support and encouragement to new
  scholars and looks 'around the room at the pictures on the

wall. The great, late men of the University smiled down upon
her. There was not even the spirit of another woman in the
room.'[17]

– prefers cooperative to competitive learning, but finds that that
  is mocked and demeaned in one's department[18]

– hears senior professors in her program making negative gener-
  alizations about women based on a single negative experience
  with one woman[19]

– as a woman administrator, has her ambitions mocked, and is
  described as unfeminine and aggressive – and if she ventures
  to work for women or on any women's issues at all, is said to
  be 'biased' and 'too feminist'[20]

– is told that 'since even deferential women are potentially
  threatening, ... all-women subcommittees are contravening the
  law, or at least should have male members because otherwise
  they carry no weight [in contrast to the typical academic committees, which are mostly or entirely composed of men]; that it
  is inadvisable for three female members of staff to see Professor X about problem Y because the poor man will be alarmed
  by a feminist delegation ...'[21]

Effects

The effects that the maleness and heterosexism of the environment
have on women academics range from mild irritation to complete
devastation. They include interfering with their ability to concentrate, hampering their freedom to work, and destroying or thwart-
ing the creation of a supportive environment, as well as 'using up
women students' energies in conflict, anger, and self-doubt.'[22] In
spite of these devastating consequences, the existence of such
problems 'most often goes unacknowledged. The feelings that it
provokes in women are denied (doesn't she have a sense of humor?), ridiculed (what's *your* problem, honey?) or minimized.'[23]

It is essential that we not minimize the seriousness of the harm
that this type of academic environment can do to women. Theodore writes: 'For most, the years of training in a predominantly

male environment and under conditions that refused to take them seriously had left an indelible mark on their aspirations and self-concepts – "the psychological scars I received from trying to be a scholar." '24

In an important study, exit interviews with faculty leaving a major university revealed that 'a disproportionate number of those faculty *opting* to leave were women,' and when those women were questioned about their reasons for leaving, they said such things as, "the academic environment was uncomfortable and inhospitable." '25 In fact, only three of the eighty-one faculty participants in the focus-group sessions and individual interviews said they had had very positive experiences in academia, and 'women of color were more dissatisfied than other women ... due to their perceptions of deep-seated racial insensitivity on the campus.'26

As you wait for the maleness of academia to change, or strive to help it change, I hope that you will use this book to make your way through an environment that can be liberating and fulfilling for women in some ways but inhospitable in others. The next chapter is designed to familiarize you with the extent to which colleges and universities function on the basis of unwritten rules.

3 Unwritten Rules and Impossible Proofs

The University runs with very little self-examination. The University lives the unexamined life. It has unwritten rules, and those who can 'read' them are the most like those in power – white, male, etc.; others are least likely to know what the words AND the silences mean. INTERVIEW

Rules are so vague, it is often difficult to find out who has the power to make decisions, how decisions are made, who sets agendas (if you are lucky enough to have agendas), how to use university structures to make change etc. LINDA BRISKIN[1]

Anyone who spends much time in academic settings learns that they are riddled with unwritten rules, and this can make for a great deal of bewilderment and frustration for all kinds of academics. For any oppressed group, this situation is particularly dangerous, since rules can be made and broken in order to keep them in their place. Furthermore, the unwritten nature of so many rules means that people who are treated unfairly may find it nearly impossible to prove that any rules were broken. In the words of a woman I interviewed, 'At university, the employer is invisible. You're never sure who has what authority over you. How do things work? What are the levels and the sequence of power?'

It is difficult and crazy-making to try to follow the rules when we don't really know what they are, an even more hazardous predicament for women than for men. This is because, first of all, women are more likely to have been raised to be rule-followers

and, combined with our generally poor self-esteem, to blame ourselves when we discover we are not following the rules, *even if
we aren't sure what they are*. In addition, since academia is already
a more congenial atmosphere for men, in order to feel at home
and secure, women even more than men need to figure out what
the rules are. Those people most likely to know – or to be able to
sense correctly – what the unwritten rules are are most likely to
be the most similar to those who use those rules to run the university, and they are mostly white males. And finally, since women
are supposed to wear rose-coloured glasses and not be suspicious
about hidden motives and rules, it often doesn't even occur to us
that there *are* unwritten rules. So, we diligently press on, carefully
following those rules we know about and feeling stunned and
foolish when we learn that others have expected us to know and
follow the unwritten ones.

Aisenberg and Harrington note that unwritten rules arise from
various sources, including 'tradition, ... governing instruments of
particular colleges and universities, [and] union [or association]
contracts.[2] They sometimes come also from government policies
or pressures. First, we shall look at some examples of how those
unwritten rules operate, then at the function they serve, and finally
at how this situation affects women academics.

How they operate

GRADUATE STUDENTS

One of my interviewees observed, 'When I was a graduate student,
I found that the more unlike the supervisor you are, the harder it
is to know what the words mean – and what the silences mean.'
Graduate students report terrible dilemmas with respect to figuring
out the rules for virtually every phase of their work: How often
is too often to consult your thesis supervisor about your thesis
proposal and project – and how often is not often enough? To
what extent can you become friends with your professors? Without
sounding like you are trying to get off easily, how do you find

out whether a file of sample questions for comprehensive (or 'pre-liminary' or 'general') examinations is available to students as a study guide? How, in general, do you know whether or not you are being treated 'normally' or whether your adviser, supervisor, professor, or other graduate students are especially critical or ne-glectful of you?

A woman I interviewed told me: 'In all the years I worked on my thesis, not until my final year did I get one written comment.' She went on: 'I never knew who was supposed to call a meeting of my thesis committee or how often such meetings should be held. I never knew what I could ask my supervisor and what he didn't want to hear. His interpretation was, "If you have to ask, you shouldn't be here." '

Another woman told me that her whole cohort of graduate students in her program spent the first year of their training know-ing they would have to take comprehensive examinations in their second year but having no idea about when they would be given, how or whether to prepare for them, and what the format would be. In fact, they weren't even sure whom to ask about all of that: Was it a program function or a departmental function, and, there-fore, should they ask the program director or the department head? Would they look overly anxious or ridiculously clueless if they asked? But would they be totally unprepared if they didn't ask?

Several women informed me that their thesis advisers were ex-tremely critical of their theses – to a point that might have been called harassment – and they learned through various routes that it was because the advisers had been angry that the women hadn't consulted them 'enough' before writing their initial drafts. Some of those women said they had been reluctant to bother their ad-visers because they hadn't wanted to be regarded as too depend-ent, and the rest said they had pulled back when their advisers seemed preoccupied or irritated about having to spend time dis-cussing their thesis proposals.

Similarly, a woman who had had some mental blocks about writing her thesis had been terrified to 'impose' on her supervisor by 'burdening' him with discussions of her blocks. When she fi-nally overcame the obstacles on her own and handed in a first draft of her first two chapters, her supervisor made sarcastic comments about the delay. She found out that he hadn't been upset about the delay itself, since he had other students who had taken far longer to complete their work. What really irritated him was that she had not let him know the reason for the delay. 'But,' she said, 'how was I to know? He never laid down any ground rules for how we would work as supervisor-supervisee.'

HIRING

The written rules for hiring do not always match the actual process. For instance, in many academic settings vacancies in administrative positions are supposed to be offered first to qualified candidates already working at that institution, but 'in practice well-qualified women are passed over.'[3] Even when the job search is formally completely open, the old boys' network can still operate in powerful ways; for example, unwritten rules give members of a search committee great leeway in the ways they evaluate various items on the curriculum vitae of any particular female or male applicant (for instance, Is it a good thing that the candidate published two articles about older lesbians in science programs?).

For administrative positions in particular, an unwritten rule my informants frequently mentioned was that, in order to be hired – or even seriously considered – for an administrative post, you are supposed to have had administrative experience already. The unwritten aspect is that that requirement may not appear in the job description, and you may not even be told at any point that you cannot possibly be hired because of your lack of experience. And, obviously, it is a catch-22 that in order to get an administrative job, you have to have previous administrative experience, for if every administrative job has that requirement, it is extremely hard to get that previous experience. (Some women have gotten around this problem by pointing out specific administrative *tasks* that they have carried out, even though their previous jobs did not have administrative titles.)

Many women feel so grateful to be hired at all, and then so pleased to be given what seems like a high salary, that they never stop to wonder – or to ask – who decides where on the salary grid an assistant professor should start *or* how that decision is made.

Many assume that the decision is made objectively, based on the employee's years of education, experiences, and publications. But the truth is that in most institutions one or more administrators have some degree of leeway in making that decision. The results of that leeway are documented in appendix 1, in the statistics that show that when women and men are equally qualified and equally experienced, the women still tend to receive lower salaries. Breslauer and Gordon point out that 'the initial salary is usually determined in discussion or negotiation with the Chair of the unit doing the hiring,'4 and women – as well as some men – are unaware of the unwritten rule that such discussion and negotiation are expected features of the hiring process.

I once felt I had been shabbily treated during a search to fill a tenure-stream position and then was asked at the last minute whether I would help the department by accepting another one-year contract. Having learned that negotiation was expected, I decided to pretend I was brave, took a deep breath, and bluffed, 'I could make two or three times my salary here if I went into private practice next year,' knowing all the while that it takes two to three years to build up to a full-time practice and knowing that I had two children and myself to support. I went on, 'To help you out, I'll accept another one-year contract on two conditions: I want a promotion from assistant to associate professor, and I want a raise.' I had to stand my ground, because the administrator looked offended and exclaimed, 'But then you'd be earning more than I earn!' I told him I was sorry about that but perhaps he, too, should request an increase in his salary. He then left the room briefly and returned with the message that the director of our institute wanted me to know that, if I were promoted, the search committee for the tenure-stream job that had botched its hiring procedures this year might consider me overqualified for the job. I said quietly that I appreciated the director's concern, but I would take my chances. I got the promotion and the raise, and I got the tenure-stream job the next year. The outcomes are not always so felicitous, of course, but if one doesn't know that it is all right to negotiate, the outcome is likely to be to one's disadvantage.

Around the time of hiring, a decision has to be made about which courses we will teach. One woman told me that she had 'really blown it' at that stage because 'I was always searching for someone who was gonna say, "This is how the system works," someone to interpret the codes for me, because I was not good at that.' When hired to teach, she had been asked, 'What courses do you want to teach?' She says that she answered their question honestly, and they let her teach the courses she requested, but they became *very* angry and punitive toward her. The unwritten rule she had not known was that she was expected to ask, 'What do you *want* me to teach?' and then to agree to do it – to show that she was collegial, a team player, 'a good woman.'

ORIENTING NEW FACULTY

There was little concrete evidence to suggest that the academic infra-structure was not supporting her.   DEBORAH HAY[5]

At most colleges and universities, there is no comprehensive system for orienting newly hired faculty in important ways.[6] Although most institutions make sure that new instructors fill out personnel forms and tour the library, it is rare that anyone takes them to lunch and informs them about the informal, unwritten rules, such as to whom one turns for help or support of various kinds, the best ways to avoid irritating the department head, and the real criteria for decisions about tenure and promotions.

In the face of this information vacuum, one newly hired woman specifically requested a meeting with the head of her department to discuss the tenure review process. However, when she asked what was expected he said vaguely that she should just work hard, and when she asked how she would get feedback on her progress, he dismissed her question by saying that she would be notified if there was any problem. She was never notified, and her contract was not renewed.

If you are lucky, you may be hired into a department in which yearly, written appraisals are sent to you, but even then, most such appraisals are brief and provide minimal information. Furthermore, if the person designated to write the appraisal fails to do a conscientious job, including carefully investigating whether or not your work is heading toward qualifying you for advancement, there is no guarantee that you will be warned in your appraisal of anything that might stand in your way.

Ideally, a department chair – or a designate – would help to guide new faculty in the process of learning the ropes, finding out the unwritten rules, and simply figuring out how to do the job. However, as Johnson et al. report, 'Lacking direction from the chair in many cases, several women said that the process of learning how to balance the different components was slow, painful, and needlessly confusing. Indeed, several faculty recalled not knowing, as junior members of their department, what goes into a personnel dossier or that the department chair has a responsibility to inform them of the process.'7 When a junior faculty woman had taught for two years in our department, I felt terrible when I realized that she had received no more orientation about the written rules than I had received twelve years earlier. As a result, when the time came for her to apply to have her three-year contract renewed, she hesitated to ask me how to go about it. And even after I gave her that advice, I neglected to check with her later on, so I found out months later that she had heard absolutely nothing from her committee and had no idea what point the review had reached. Still worse, none of us had told her that she had a right to ask the department chair to expedite the process and to be given a firm schedule for each step. She had been reluctant to make such a request, for fear of being regarded as pushy and over-anxious.

EVALUATION

Whether we are evaluated as graduate students or for hiring, promotion, or tenure, we need to be aware of some of the most common cloudy areas, where the lack of written rules leaves us uncertain about what to do. We also need to be aware of some of the procedural problems that arise in trying to appeal evaluations that are based on unwritten rules. No attempt is made in this section to be comprehensive, but it will be helpful to keep in mind that nearly every source of bias or trouble mentioned in chapters 2 through 5 and appendices 1 and 2 is partially or entirely made possible by the lack of clear, written rules.

The areas of uncertainty include all of those mentioned so far in this chapter, including not knowing whom to ask about what – or when to ask. As for new faculty, typically they are told – or it may even specify in an individual contract or in a faculty union's or association's collective agreement – that they are expected to do teaching, service, and research and will be evaluated on those bases. However, new faculty usually have no way of knowing the *relative* importance placed on each of these aspects currently or in the future by whatever group of people will evaluate them.[8]

To many new and even more seasoned faculty, it is not clear what will be counted as research or as good research.[9] As discussed in appendix 2, people whose research is rooted in the community or in 'real life,' and especially women whose work relates to women's issues or the conditions of other non-dominant groups, are especially likely to be denied jobs, contract renewals, raises, promotions, and tenure because of the nature of their work or because it is not published in the mainstream journals.[10]

Contracts do not usually specify the number of publications you need in order to be considered adequate for hiring, promotion, or tenure, or how your editing of an anthology, contribution to a textbook, or writing of a chapter in a book edited by someone else will be evaluated.[11] Other cloudy areas include such specifications as that you will be evaluated on the basis of your 'quality of mind,' 'intellectual force,' 'future promise,' or 'collegiality,'[12] all of which are impossible to measure and leave wide scope for subjectivity and interpretation. Black women have been negatively evaluated, for instance, on the basis of claims that their work was 'minority-related' and had 'no substance or theoretical value.'[13] Even if you do publish a book that is well reviewed by some of your colleagues or if you publish articles in high-prestige, mainstream, refereed journals, members of the evaluating committee at your institution can argue that the work is actually of poor quality.

Not only a lack of clearly specified, written criteria but also frequent use of irrelevant criteria and criteria that shift from one case to another are further problems.[14] Inappropriate evaluation methods that actually have been used have included the chairperson listening at the door of the candidate's classroom instead of using the classroom evaluations and making decisions based on the 'assumed' health or rumoured vacation plans of an instructor.[15] An example of shifting criteria was told to me by an interviewee, who said: 'In our department, it was known that in order to chair the department, you had to have a Ph.D. A woman, who had the only Ph.D. in the department, was suddenly told she could not be the chair. Suddenly, the administration said (for the first time ever), the requirement for chairing the department was that your work had to be in a particular specialty. The only person in that specialty was a man, and they gave him the position.'

Some women – and men – have taken a special interest in teaching continuing-education courses at their institution, as a result of their commitment to teaching and encouraging mature students. However, what no one tells them is that, at many universities, teaching continuing education or distance education doesn't usually help, or can actually hurt, one's institutional evaluations, since these tend to be considered low-status endeavours.

Compounding the uncertainty about standards of evaluation are a number of procedural obstacles that yield the same outcome: it is extremely hard to prove discrimination in hiring, promotion, and tenure.[16] To begin with, while you are *doing* the work that will be evaluated, there is no way of knowing who will be the personnel committee members, department chairs, or review-committee members when the actual evaluation is done.[17] If you are denied tenure on the grounds of having published in non-mainstream journals, it may do you absolutely no good to say, 'But Professor X was department head when I was hired, and she assured me that those journals would be given equal weight with mainstream ones.' Too bad. You will probably have no proof that she said that. And even if you do, the question of whether the current decision-makers must be bound by the assurances of their predecessors would probably have to be resolved through long, painful, expensive litigation – which you might or might not win.

Furthermore, quite apart from changes in evaluating committees, because of historical changes even standards that have been reasonably consistent at one time may be modified. It is well known, for instance, that at virtually every institution one now needs to have more publications than fifteen years ago in order to be awarded tenure. Thus, older women who were hired years ago

may be told that the standards are higher now and so their contracts will not be renewed or they will be denied tenure.[18] Aisenberg and Harrington have observed that women often do not
realize that they need to plan in advance for the times when they
will be evaluated;[19] however, even women who realize that they
should be planning ahead will be unable to find infallible guidelines about how to plan.

Other procedural problems that perpetuate the uncertainty for
women in academia include the paucity of written rules or procedures for hiring, tenure, and promotion committees to follow.
This allows tremendous scope for jockeying for power among the
committee members and for the following of borderline or frankly
unethical procedures. For instance, people known to be hostile to
the applicant's published work or methodology can be chosen
exclusively by the committee to be external reviewers. Although
some institutions provide for the applicant to participate in the
choice of at least some reviewers, she cannot control the relative
weight given to the various reviewers' comments. Similarly, if all
the members of a given committee keep mum, there is no way to
prove that such comments as 'Why does she need a raise? Her
husband is a full professor in the Engineering School' were made
in closed meetings where no minutes were kept.[20]

Another aspect of procedure that needs to be clarified and cod-
ified is that of the frequent discrepancy between 'evaluational
criteria used at the departmental level and the criteria used cam-
puswide. Some women indicated that they did not know whether
their dean acted as an advocate for the department or as a representative of the administration.'[21] Although a committee set up
by one's department usually makes the initial recommendation
about hiring, renewal, promotion, raises, and tenure, it usually
must go through often multiple levels, and problems may arise at
any level.

In many colleges and universities, there are no clear policies for
reporting and dealing with sex discrimination,[22] and often those
policies that exist are riddled with loopholes. Typically, when formally or informally charged with sex discrimination, officials throw
up roadblocks. They may deny that their staff members have dis-

criminated on the basis of sex; precipitously dismiss the case on the grounds that the accused denies the claim; or stall or use secrecy ('It wouldn't be right to make the deliberations of these committees public!'), distortions, lies, deceit, divisiveness ('You're complaining that we didn't hire you, and you are a woman. We thought you, as a good liberal, would be glad that we hired a black man for that job.'[23]), and/or retaliation through harassment of the complainant (ranging from nitpicking to outright firing and blacklisting through their collegial networks), character assassination, or harassment of one's supporters.

Other procedural steps some administrations have taken with impunity, in the absence of written rules, have included sudden firings or non-renewals with no concrete reasons given; administrators' refusal to allow complainants to bring a lawyer to meetings on the grounds that this should be a 'non-adversarial' process – or even administrators' bringing lawyers but not allowing complainants to do so; firings or non-renewals of contracts when concrete reasons are given but with no time for the people to improve their performance; the holding of 'grievance procedures' in which the complainant's appeal is heard by the same group that already denied her tenure; the failure to keep a list of committee members and a record of votes; the keeping of confidential files, to which the appellant has no access in trying to prepare her case (although through litigation this is now being prohibited in some places); the specification of time limits for filing complaints and appeals that are so short that they penalize the complainant or even make it impossible for her to file a complaint or an appeal if the accused is not found guilty; and delays before deciding about complaints that are so long that the complainant has already had to find work elsewhere.[24]

As a result of all of this, as Backhouse et al. poignantly write, 'there may come a day when those disadvantaged by discrimination feel they can identify themselves without exacerbating the problem. But at present, freedom of speech on these issues seems more like a distant dream. Threats of libel suits, professional stigmatization, and the multiple ways in which colleagues can evidence personal displeasure all combine to silence most discussion of this sort.'[25]

The function unwritten rules serve

Whether you believe it is intentional or unintentional, the plethora of unwritten rules and impossible proofs helps to maintain the traditional power balance within academia, and this includes keeping women down – and keeping women from non-dominant groups down even farther.[26] The most powerful mechanism here is the wearing down of the individual woman through the dominant maleness of the environment combined with the paucity of clear, concrete rules she could use to combat it – or at least to prove that biases and mistreatment exist.

Some women who have been unfairly treated withdraw into silence. Others make formal or informal complaints but may drop them because of exhaustion, fears of recrimination, or lack of financial and personal support. In fact, according to one report,[27] about one-fifth withdraw their complaints at the university level alone. Whether or not women drop their complaints, they may experience any of the following:

- Fears for and threats to their future careers and relationships with academics
- When filing complaints through agencies, 'confusion, disorganization, incompetency, and delays'[28]
- When filing court cases, 'a hostile climate and judges unwilling to set legal precedents favorable to women'[29]
- Being labelled a troublemaker by college and university officials when contacted by outsiders about their case[30]
- Lack of support, cessation of support, or active hurts from their colleagues
- Lack of support from other women, sometimes because of their own internalized sexism, apathy, or fears of retaliation
- Inadequate support or no support from one's own unions, because they tend to be male-dominated, just don't bother to try, or are weak[31]

In fact, according to Theodore's investigation, 'few women who fight academic discrimination encounter victory.' Furthermore, it is demoralizing that typically, when complaints have been filed, 'there is little change in the institution, but the experience of fighting has a strong negative impact on the protestors regardless of whether or not they have "won" their case.'[32]

In an important sense, the most distressing aspect of the unwritten rules is that so many women find it distasteful to follow the 'rules of the game.'[33] Thus, feeling pressured to find out what the unwritten rules are and to follow them in order to acquire and maintain position and status in their institutions, many women feel torn apart when they find that they cannot respect so many of the rules, both written and unwritten. Whether or not they are comfortable in playing the game, women with experience in academic settings have learned much about how to deal with the rules and how to try to increase their clarity and fairness. Some of their suggestions make up chapters 6 and 7. Before moving to these suggestions, however, we shall look briefly at the myths and catch-22s that characterize academia.

4 The Myths

When gender discrimination exists, it is often subtle and systemic. NANCY HENSEL[1]

The more you understand about the real sources of problems that you encounter in academic life, the better prepared you will be to decide how best to deal with them. This chapter and the next one provide some of that understanding, because many women in academia have said that, had they been aware of the myths and the catch-22s, they would have felt better about themselves.

When women find we are having trouble in academia, two major factors usually make it hard for us to see the obstacles that are in our way; one is the learned 'feminine' tendency to regard ourselves as inadequate and blameworthy, and the other is a set of myths that masks the true nature of the obstacles. The two factors interact with each other, since the myths specifically portray academia as an ideal setting and women as deeply flawed. Where people and systems can no longer announce, 'Women are not wanted here,' they can nevertheless use the belief system composed of myths to make us feel uncomfortable, doubt our abilities, find it hard to be productive, or even become convinced that we don't belong in academia, so that we 'choose' to leave.

Through reading the literature, interviewing women academics, and reviewing my own experiences, I collected twenty-seven different myths, and you may think of even more. Of these, twelve are about academia, eleven are about women, and four are about women in academia. Some will be very familiar to you, but others may be new. Taken together, they support the potentially dev-astating system of belief that can be summarized succinctly as, 'Woman, if you don't succeed in academia, it is probably your own fault.' As you read the myths, you will notice that many of them intermingle, and together the Big 27 pack one hell of a wal-lop: believing them means not believing in yourself. This is partly because many of the myths are subcategories of the old, sweeping, but still active – though often subtle – myth of male superiority.

We shall look only briefly at each myth, because many of them will be so familiar to you and will need little or no explanation. Furthermore, many are related to information in chapter 1 and appendices 1 and 2.

Myths about academia

1. **The myth of meritocracy**. The myth of meritocracy is the belief that, in academia, people are formally rewarded (with a degree, a job, promotion, tenure, merit increases, or increases in power and status) simply according to the quantity and quality of the work that they do.[2] In Aisenberg's and Harrington's words, women often have the 'merit dream,'[3] the need to believe academia is a meritocracy, and Reid has found that faculty women in the more male-dominated departments are more likely than other faculty women to believe in this myth.[4]

Believing we will be judged on our merit feels so different from fearing we will be judged according to our physical attractiveness or our willingness to be nurturers and caretakers. Many of us find it painful to recognize that making a place for ourselves in the academy can involve putting on shows of various kinds, being in the right places, saying the right things, knowing the right people. We long to have our work speak for itself.

The academic meritocracy truly is a myth, since many factors other than merit play substantial roles in deciding who receives the rewards. But if you believe that merit is the only criterion, then if one of these rewards is denied to you, you will certainly believe that it is your own fault.

In keeping with the academic meritocracy myth, administrators frequently say they *want* to hire more women – but only if their work is good enough. At one level, that sounds reasonable, but the insidious and misguided implication is that all the men working in academia were hired solely on the basis of merit, without networks, friendships, and so on.[5] A related (and erroneous) implication is that when women are not hired, it is only because their work isn't good enough.

2. The myth of objective standards and neutrality in the classroom and in hiring, promotion, and tenure. In the first place, there is simply no such thing as true objectivity.[6] Furthermore, many committees have denied people tenure on the grounds that the applicants lacked a certain 'quality of mind' or 'intellectual force' or some other amorphous, certainly not objective, standard. Specific examples include such highly subjective grounds as that 'the book wasn't good enough,' a woman hadn't published in the 'right' journals, an applicant had 'no future promise,' and a Black woman's work was just 'minority-related' and had 'no substance or theoretical value.'[7] Similarly lacking in objectivity and neutrality are the use of such labels as 'not collegial' for assertive women when committees wish to deny women tenure or promotions or to avoid hiring them altogether.[8]

3. The myth of non-discrimination and fairness. According to this myth, there are no power dynamics in academia; a person's sex, race, class, age, physical condition, and sexual orientation play absolutely no role in the distribution of academic rewards. This is clearly untrue, since all these factors have been shown to play significant roles in the evaluation of academics.[9]

In her important work, Briskin describes the way that many men in the academy argue 'for abstract notions of non-discrimination'[10] rather than openly naming the various, concrete forms of discrimination that persist. In regard specifically to gender discrimination, Briskin notes that men deny the gender bias in academia in the following ways: 'by challenging the legitimacy of autonomous women's organizing in forms such as union women's committees; by maintaining that introducing gender into the curriculum challenges objectivity ... a refusal to acknowledge male privilege.'[11]

In addition to these specific forms of discrimination, candidates are evaluated, 'either during hiring or later in the career ... against an image of a "model" academic career, and ... this model is more applicable to the lives of male than female academics.'[12] For instance, the tendency to deny tenure to faculty who have not published a certain number of articles within, say, a five-year period is more likely to be a problem for women, who are far more likely to have significant family-related responsibilities, than for men.[13]

4. The myth of democracy. While still undergraduates, we probably hear about departmental meetings, meetings of faculty senates or other representative bodies, and votes about hiring, tenure, and promotion decisions. The holding of so many meetings feeds the myth that universities are run democratically, that everyone has an equal say in important decisions. As noted above, such features as the race, sex, and age of the person being evaluated often play important roles in decisions about her career, but in addition, the 'votes' of those making the decisions tend not to have equal weight. Take, for instance, the understandable timidity of a newly hired, tenure-stream assistant professor about opposing a tenured, full professor in a meeting to decide whether or not applicants to the program should be required to take Graduate Record Examinations. The full professor will likely have some power when the junior person comes up for tenure review. Or, to use a gender-specific example, for women faculty or graduate students to support the introduction of material on women into core courses can be to put their own careers at risk with powerful, male colleagues who will sit in judgment on them at a future time.

5. The myth of collegiality. This is the myth that academia is not about power, that we work as cooperative partners here. Pointing out the serious dangers of this myth, Briskin writes that, in reality, it is used to create an in-group of those who 'belong,' those who constitute 'the colleagues,' and to allow those in power the maximum amount of flexibility.[14] That is, they can always claim that a decision was made 'in a collegial manner,' when what actually happened was that the old boys' network got together and decided what ought to be done. The collegiality myth is related to the myth of objectivity because those in power can deviate from the allegedly 'objective' standards in the name of collegiality. This gives those in power the flexibility to have rules when they choose but also to justify bending them when they deem it necessary. But by asserting the force of 'collegiality,' those who run the academic power structure can convey the impression that they operate fairly and on the basis of 'a broad consensus ... [even when] that consensus does not necessarily assure women candidates a fair hearing in the hiring process.'[15]

So dangerous does Briskin consider this myth that she calls it 'the tyranny of the collegial' and explains that it operates 'because of the invisibility of the employer and the vagueness of institutional rules. Collegiality is invoked as central to the decision-making process, indeed as a positive alternative to decision-making structures found elsewhere. The informality of collegial processes, however, functions as a mechanism of exclusion for those, like women, who are marginal in the institution. Rules are so vague, it is often difficult to find out who has the power to make decisions, how decisions are made, who sets agendas (if you are lucky enough to have agendas), how to use university structures to make change etc.'[16]

Women are particularly likely to be excluded by this myth, because 'collegiality is defined by the cultural characteristics of male sociability,'[17] so that women who do not socialize in certain ways (going out for a beer together, talking at length about hockey and boxing, and so on) are not considered as part of the in-group.

6. The myth of liberalism and openness. Many people in and outside and academia regard colleges and universities as bastions of liberalism and fairness, but the truth is otherwise. As already noted, academia has historically *not* been equally open to hiring and promoting people of both genders and all races, ages, classes, sexual orientations, and types of physical states. Furthermore, this alleged bastion of openness has been notoriously slow to welcome

Black studies, native studies, women's studies, and gay and lesbian studies programs. Because of the myth, many members of non-dominant groups feel confused when they sense they are negatively treated because of their group membership or because they display – or do not display – characteristics stereotypically linked to their group. For example, Wine points out that, as in most workplaces, in the academic community lesbians have often got the clear message that it is *not* acceptable for them to be as open about their sexuality as heterosexuals are allowed, even encouraged, to be. Wine writes: 'In academe ... its liberalism ... holds that people may do what they wish in their private lives as long as they don't talk about it.'[18] The power of this structure is evident to any heterosexual person who tries the exercise of avoiding, for a day or a week, *every* reference to casual, intimate, or long-term relationships with members of the other sex.

7. The myth that, in academia, the primary goal is the search for knowledge. For women academics in particular, their intelligence and search for knowledge may be treated as 'a social problem,' so that female seekers of knowledge are often treated as though they are abnormal: 'Intelligent women who demonstrate superiority simply by being themselves are then particularly likely to be seen as aggressive and sexually unnatural.'[19]

Furthermore, as noted in a report by Aitken and Walker for the Ontario Confederation of University Faculty Associations, 'What is considered important is no longer any work of general interest, creativity or quality, but rather work which will contribute directly to the ability of the university to attract corporate, foundation and government monies'[20] – a far cry from objective and neutral standards.

8. The myth that, in academia, people's search for knowledge is done cooperatively, not competitively, and that this cooperation is rewarded. Much of what is relevant to myth 8 is also relevant to myth 7. Women in particular, being more likely than men to have been socialized to feel that cooperation is good and competitiveness is bad, are often stunned by the dual discoveries that many academics are seeking power rather than knowledge, and that many of them work in fiercely competitive rather than cooperative ways or even in solitary, task-oriented plodding for the sake of the work itself. The myth that cooperative work is highly regarded and rewarded in academia is belied by such practices as tenure committees' devaluing of co-authored work. And one prominent academic woman reports that 'on an NIH study section she was surprised by the attitude of male colleagues, who were much more likely to question whether a woman's work was independent of her advisor than they were to ask the same question about a man's research.'[21]

Stark-Adamec, who chairs an academic department, describes her belief, as a young student, in these myths and her subsequent experiences that revealed their mythological nature:

> Before entering university, and even as an undergraduate Honours student, I thought that academia was an environment in which people worked together, collaborated, to push back the frontiers of knowledge, putting aside self-aggrandisement and personal biases and goals for the greater good and for the excitement of advancing the discipline and the university. It seemed an environment dedicated and conducive to thought and learning and discovery.
>
> As a graduate student a quarter of a century ago, I got the first inklings of doubt in the veracity of my vision. My peers in clinical [psychology] were very competitive and some one or others of them used to cut articles out of the journals so that no one else could read them. Graduate students in physiological and experimental [psychology] behaved a little more like my vision: they spent about 20 hours a day in the lab discussing wild ideas and collecting data ... But the non-clinical students didn't fully live up to my ideal either: they were constantly putting down clinical and claiming that only *they* did *real* research.[22]

9. The myth that 'they' really want you to do service, teaching, and research in equal amounts and that, when it comes time for tenure and promotion, they will count all three as equally valuable. As described in chapter 1, although women and men are about equally likely to express an interest in teaching, women are more likely than men to be given heavy teaching loads, and this makes it difficult to do research and writing for publication. Many find out too late that, at most institutions, publications count far more for tenure and promotion than do teaching and service to the institution, the profession, and the community. And as Johnson, Timm, and Merino found in their research, 'Although the "publish or perish" formula in academia is legendary, few women in the study actually believed it at the beginning. Most described genuine confusion about what was expected of them and took seriously the stated tripartite duties of teaching, service, and research.'[23]

10. The myth of individualism. In a sense, a cumulative result of the first 9 myths is the myth of individualism, that if you just try hard and do good work, you will succeed – and, conversely, that if you fail, it must be your own fault.[24] For instance, anyone who genuinely believes that academia is a meritocracy in which objective standards are used to make democratic, collegially respectful decisions must necessarily believe that a person who fails to 'make it' must be individually deficient. The numerous gender-based and other barriers in academia show that this individualistic attitude is not based in reality.

In this connection, Briskin warns us: 'The documentation of women's experiences in the university has demonstrated that a focus on tenure and hiring decisions, on proving ourselves, on playing by the rules ... has not worked for women. We are rarely considered good enough to hire; our publications are challenged because of both the substance and method of what we study; we face more difficulties and often hostility getting tenure; we are excluded from the informal yet powerful decision making structures even as we sit on endless numbers of committees. Despite this, we take up the role of the dutiful daughters of the academy.'[25]

11. The myth that all teaching and scholarly work, regardless of its content and methods, will be regarded as equally important and valuable, as long as they are of good quality. (See also appendix 2.) This is untrue, because within virtually every discipline there is a 'pecking order,' so that some areas of research and some research methods are regarded as more prestigious and intellectually valuable than others. Furthermore, women are more likely than men to teach courses that deal with emotional and personal issues and feelings, and one prevalent attitude is that the presence of emotional content indicates the absence of academic and intellectual content.

Women's studies, Black studies, Asian studies, and gay and lesbian studies courses in particular – most of which are taught by women and/or members of non-dominant groups – are often regarded as illegitimate offspring of academia, 'fuzzy' in methods, and lacking in discipline and 'real content'; the same often applies to researchers and research in those areas. As Breslauer and Gordon found, 'the nature of academic assessment, particularly its insistence that "excellence" is both objective and measurable, often means that feminist scholarship and publishing outlets are not as highly valued as more traditional ones. Women have problems in this regard when being considered for appointment and when being evaluated for tenure and promotion.'[26]

12. The myth that partial acceptance in academia means full acceptance. When administrators point with pride to the fact that they have doubled the number of women in your department over the past five years, as a 'good woman,' you know you are supposed to feel grateful. But when that doubling means that women now account for 20 per cent of your department rather than 10 per cent, still leaving you clearly in a minority, you realize with a start that partial acceptance is *not* the same as full acceptance. Add to this the patterns reflected in the statistics given in appendix 1, and you realize that women are a long way from full acceptance in academia.

The situation is very much like that of the woman in a heterosexual relationship who feels that, because the man makes breakfast twice a week and takes out the garbage – and, therefore, really *is* better than many men in those respects – she ought to feel simply, thoroughly grateful and to ask for more is unfeminine and selfish.

Myths about women

13. A good woman can ignore it when she is mistreated in the workplace, or, A good woman wears rose-coloured glasses. As we have seen, chances are great that any given woman in academia will be treated worse than a man in a similar job. Most women, however, have been raised to feel that we are supposed to put on our rose-coloured glasses and do the traditional, feminine thing – look on the bright side, interpret in the best possible light the behaviour and motives of those who treat us badly, and hope like crazy for the best. We often believe it is selfish and unfeminine to object when we are demeaned or otherwise mistreated. In the workplace, we face the further risk of being called unprofessional or 'not tough enough for this kind of job' if we do anything about unfair treatment other than ignore it.

Three of the major factors in our culture that encourage women to support this myth are: (1) the well-documented tendency of people of both sexes to learn to attribute females' successes at work to their luck, hard work, or chance, while attributing males' successes to their solid abilities, and to do the reverse for females' and males' failures at work;[27] (2) the tendency to label in demeaning ways nearly everything that is primarily associated with females;[28] and, not surprisingly in light of all this, (3) the tendency for so many females to have abysmal self-esteem.[29]

To understand just how constricting – and how gender-based – this myth is, imagine putting men in an academic workplace, underpaying them, seriously overworking them, mocking them if they can't fully take part in traditionally feminine ways of conducting their interpersonal relationships, and then warning them that we'll label them 'unmasculine' if they can't ignore all of that.

14. A good woman doesn't ask for much. As Karen Glasser Howe has said, nagging is what it's called when a woman asks for something.[30] Historically, women have been not only allowed but actually encouraged to ask for things on behalf of the men or children in their lives, the sick, the poor, the variously disadvantaged – in fact, for anyone *except* for themselves. Asking for more in our culture is asking to be called selfish, demanding, never-satisfied, and unfeminine; asking for more as a woman in academia is asking to be regarded as non-collegial, 'bitchy,' and grasping. Whereas men's demands tend to be regarded as legitimate requests for space, money, assistance, or flexibility, women's demands are more likely to be regarded as unreasonable. Indeed, that is the usual pattern of differential interpretation given to the same behaviour, depending on whether the behaviour comes from someone who is assumed to have full rights or from someone who is assumed to be lucky to be allowed in the setting at all.

15. A good woman doesn't get angry or put herself forward. This is related to myth 14. Whereas a man's anger is considered consistent with the male role, a woman's anger is considered inconsistent with the female role. the same is true for men's, in contrast to women's, proud descriptions of their accomplishments: such men are nicely self-confident, but such women are unfeminine, boastful, and pushy.

16. Women are dangerous when they are powerful. This myth[31] has a great deal of force whether the issue is women's intellectual power or their power through administrative responsibilities in the university. In regard to this myth, too, for males to be powerful is fine, even desirable, but for females to be powerful is to be 'overpowering' or 'engulfing' (and usually compared in a matrophobic way to mothers who are said to be intrusive and engulfing[32]).

17. Women are naturally, endlessly nurturant. Because of the pervasiveness of this myth, an academic woman who is not willing to listen endlessly to her colleagues', students', and employees' personal problems is in danger of being disliked, because these people assume she can effortlessly and naturally provide such nurturance incessantly (in addition to doing the full-time work included in her job description). (See also the catch-22 concerning women and nurturance in chapter 5.)

18. Women are bottomless pits of emotional neediness. Women are assumed to be so emotional that, if allowed free rein, they would drain everyone around them of their own emotional re-sources.[33] For this reason, any display of feeling by a woman can be used as evidence of her emotional neediness. In academia, where the traditional male model of objectivity and rationality holds such sway, displays of feeling are often used as proof that women don't belong in higher-education faculties. It is poignant that, as in many workplaces, women faculty may well have *fewer* emotional needs met than male faculty, whose mothers, female partners or friends, or secretaries are probably meeting many of their needs. Certainly, men's need to feel at home in academia is more likely than women's to be met. If some women faculty then feel emotionally needy, the existence of this myth makes it seem to be the women's fault.

19. Women are intuitive, automatic Reactors, in contrast to men, who are rational, active Thinkers. Similarly, women are subjective, whereas men are objective, and the latter is what constitutes respectability in academia. These beliefs are based on the assumption that women are more tightly tied to their biology – and, therefore, more preoccupied with the life of the emotions – than are men.[34] As a consequence, the roles in an academic setting in which women are most welcomed are as members of what is called the 'support staff' or, possibly, as students, whereas it is considered more fitting for men to be the teachers and those administrators who have real power to make important, 'objective, rational' decisions.

20. Full-time men work full-time, but part-time women only work part-time – and both full-time and part-time male employees work harder than females. When I started my first 'real' job, I was raising four children and, like most women in that position, made absolutely sure that, while at my office, I worked full steam ahead. I was worried that my co-workers might think I wasn't carrying my share of the work because of my home-related responsibilities. I was astonished to see that several men, some married and some single, some with and some without children, spent hours at work reading the newspaper and gossiping (yes, gossiping – an activity that is usually attributed to women).

And a highly respected professor of political science once described how stunned she felt when she, who spent every moment of her time at the university doing work-related activities, discovered that many of the men would close their office doors and 'pay their bills from home or chat with their buddies about things that had nothing to do with work.'

Whether women work part-time or full-time, especially in traditionally male worlds like academia, they tend to try extra hard to prove that the boss was right to have hired a woman. They feel they have to prove their worth. As noted, part-time academic jobs are disproportionately likely to be held by women, and part-timers are lower on the academic ladder than full-timers. In general, lower-status people (part-timers, women) are assumed to be less capable than others, and this is an extra burden. Thus, both women who are employed part-time and those who are employed full-time are assumed to do less work than men – the former because they are 'only' part-timers and the latter because women are assumed to be the ones who take time away from work for gossiping, shopping, and cooking. However, 'As Everett C. Hughes has pointed out, academic men in fact work part-time at their supposed jobs, spending the rest in committee meetings, office sociability, and other activities; but by social definition this is full-time work. The woman, however, who teaches regularly and intensively during the hours her children are in school is defined as a part-time worker, even though she actually puts in as many hours as the men.'[35] (Although some committee work is an essential part of the job, some is make-work or self-serving, and office socializing is not what academics are paid to do.)

21. Married women and mothers do less work in their place of employment than do single women.

22. Single women academics have all the time in the world and thus should carry more teaching and committee responsibilities. Myths 21 and 22 are related to myth 20 and form a dangerous pair, because they justify putting down or imposing on women on the basis of their marital or motherhood status.

In regard to myth 21, a single woman who had no children once told my boss that she was certain that I did less than my share of work. When I was informed of this, like a 'good' woman, I assumed she was right, but when I investigated, I discovered that I was actually doing slightly more work than she. After learning of this, she had the forthrightness to come to me and say, 'I'm sorry, but I just assumed that since you have four kids at home, you couldn't possibly be doing your share.'

And with regard to myth 22, many single women I interviewed had versions of this story: 'My department chair keeps putting me on more and more committees, asking me to do the work of writing our lengthy, detailed reports for tenure and promotion and applications. The reason given is, "You're single and you have no kids, so you've got more time than the rest of us." It is especially ironic when 'the rest of us' includes single men and men who do little or no household-related work.'

23. Women are masochistic and have a fear of success, or, When women fail or feel unhappy, they have brought it on themselves. It is clear by now that women work under the burden of an enormous number of myths that are demeaning to and limiting for them. The negative part of the picture is further revealed by the statistics given in appendix 1. When women are suffering because of these various forms of mistreatment, if they dare to speak up and name that mistreatment and to demand something better, their pain is often dismissed on the grounds that they are masochists, that they *enjoy* suffering, that they – consciously or unconsciously – bring it on themselves.[36] Thus, for instance, a woman who protests the denial of her promotion is told that she must have unconsciously 'sabotaged her chances' through her 'fear of success,' which led her to write an inadequate brief for the promotion, rather than being told that three committee members voted against promoting her because they considered her work on the history of women in mathematics to be 'unimportant.'

The myth of women's masochism is dangerous to women in academia because it provides a rationalization for our difficulties and unhappiness there. Anyone who accepts the myth as though it were true can avoid looking at the actual causes of women's unhappiness and difficulty.

Women in academia

24. Affirmative action gives women and 'minorities' unfair advantages ... which men and members of dominant cultures have *not* had. A historical perspective is helpful in understanding the mythical nature of the above statement, that is, that academia has, in large measure, been one big affirmative-action plan for white men for hundreds of years. Susan Mann, now president of Toronto's York University, has written that, in the nineteenth century,

> 'while [the well-to-do young man] was being educated in an all-boys' school for individual, meritorious achievement an entire social structure of servants and of women family members attended to all other aspects of his life so he could concentrate on becoming meritorious.
>
> 'Now *that* is affirmative action, on a grand scale! And you need only recall hearing the phrase somewhere in the family, "Don't disturb your father, he's working!" to know that all of this is still very much with us.'[37]

When one looks at such current data as those on sex-differential workloads and salaries; sex-differential hiring, promotion, and tenure rates; and sexual harassment on campus, in which the targets are disproportionately female and the perpetrators disproportionately male,[38] it is clear that academia is rife with informal affirmative-action programs for males – and especially for white males. Breslauer and Gordon conclude that, although 'any suggestion that [personnel practices in academia are] unfair or biased meets with wounded cries of outrage and indignation ... there is mounting evidence that here as elsewhere in employment systems systemic discrimination operates to keep women out.'[39] In that context, to claim that formal affirmative-action programs give women in general and members of both sexes from non-dominant groups 'unfair' advantages seems bizarre.

25. The myth that affirmative action and equal representation of women and men at every level of academia are *the* solutions.

In some sense, myth 25 is the other side of myth 24: whereas myth 24 is used by those who wish to keep women down, myth 25 is dangerous because it can lull members of underrepresented groups into believing that changes in numbers are all it will take to create an academic environment where diversity is truly respected. However, it doesn't do women very much good if we constitute half of the faculty but if the kinds of work that many of us do (such as women's studies or applied work rather than theoretical work with no practical applications) are accorded less value and less respect. And hiring women and men in equal numbers helps little if women with children still have more child-rearing responsibilities than men with children, while in order to get tenure both sexes are expected to publish the same numbers of papers in scholarly journals in the same period of time. Furthermore, affirmative action is primarily related to hiring but thoroughly unconnected to curriculum and research, where changes are sorely needed.

Another problem with affirmative-action programs is that they are often implemented on the backs of women and members of other disenfranchised groups. Women who have full-time academic jobs are often asked to add the duties of 'Affirmative Action Officer' to their load, to serve on affirmative-action advisory committees, or to serve as 'the woman' or 'the non-white' person on job search committees. Since women and members of non-dominant groups are already relatively few in number on most campuses, the university's decision to implement such programs puts a disproportionately great burden on these people – all the more so because not all women or disenfranchised people will take on that kind of work. The few who do take it on become the targets for resentment and anger as resistance of affirmative action builds. In addition (with the exception of most affirmative-action officers), rarely, if ever, are those who do such work given release time from their other responsibilities.

26. Women's studies and feminist perspectives restrict the academic freedom of those who are not associated with them. Those who teach women's studies or use feminist approaches in their classrooms are often claimed to be *imposing* those approaches on their students (and even, sometimes, on their colleagues) and thereby restricting their academic freedom[40] – although ironically, the forms often taken by objections to this supposed imposition actually constitute violations of academic freedom, such as students who harass and intimidate both students and faculty when they mention feminist theories or studies. Women who teach in women's studies programs or who use feminist approaches are treated as though they insist that everyone agree with them and as though no one outside women's studies does that. Furthermore, they are often treated as though all feminists or women's studies instructors are rigid and strident (see myth 16, that women are dangerous when they are powerful).

27. An imperfect woman teacher is a bad woman teacher. Just as an *imperfect* mother is often regarded as a *bad* mother,[41] the imperfections of women faculty are often exaggerated into justifications for declaring them bad teachers and therefore for denying them full-time jobs, job security, promotions, or merit increases.[42] Similarly, the performance of women faculty tends to be scrutinized more than that of men.

This myth is related to the expectation for women teachers to be nurturant and caring (with the danger of being regarded as *only* nurturant rather than nurturant and also skilled at conveying information and provoking thoughts – see chapter 5), while there is little or no such expectation for male teachers. It is similar to the expectation that mothers will be endlessly nurturant, in the absence of much expectation for nurturance from fathers. This myth is also related to the frequent assumption that women cannot be both nurturant *and* competent;[43] thus, a male lecturer's warm style is more likely than a female's to be regarded simply as a plus because the assumption from the outset is that males are competent (so warmth is a bonus), whereas females are not (and if they are nice, they cannot be competent, too).

Many of the myths give rise to no-win situations for women in academia. These will be examined in the next chapter. Chapters 6 and 7 offer strategies for dealing with these myths when they intrude on your academic life.

5 Damned If You Do, Damned If You Don't

Many of the academic women I interviewed said that they have not only felt responsible for any problems they have encountered at work but have sometimes even felt quite crazy. We have learned from feminists who have written about women and mental-health issues that many women who feel crazy are suffering not from internal, individual, psychological problems but rather from their attempts to survive in a system that may damn them no matter what they do. Then, when they are upset because they see no way out of their dilemmas, they are labelled masochistic, self-defeating, paranoid, neurotic, premenstrually distressed, meno-pausally plagued, or simply 'depressed.'[1]

Many of the myths described in chapter 4, singly or in various combinations, provide the foundations for the catch-22 dilemmas that academic women encounter. In what follows, I have stated the catch-22s in their most extreme forms. Women subjected to them in their worst forms can feel absolutely devastated, but even the less extreme forms can be crazy-making, because the source of the trouble can be harder to identify. As with the myths, you will probably think of no-win dilemmas besides the fifteen I list here, and I urge you to jot those down in this chapter, so that you can refer back to the entire list as needed. Most of the issues involved in the catch-22s have been or will be discussed in other chapters as well.

First I shall describe the catch-22s that appeared from my reading of the literature and my interviews with women, and then I shall discuss the sociopolitical function served by these impossible dilemmas.

The catch-22s

1. If a woman fails, it 'proves' that women are inferior: but if she succeeds, she becomes 'proof' that nothing stands between women and success in academia and so women have no right to complain. This catch-22 is based partly on the myths related to women's inferiority, unsuitability for the rational, objective work of scholarship, and so on. As Hay has written, 'If [a woman academic] was unsuccessful that would prove that women were not up to the demands of academic life. If she were too successful, it would be obvious that it was "easy" for women to make it – if they really wanted to.'[2]

2. If a woman makes her preferences known, she is demanding, selfish, and non-collegial; but if she asks her department chair or other boss what *they* want her to do, and she then does it, she is considered spineless or lacking in focus. Based partly on the myths that good women are nurturant and don't get angry or ask for things, partly on the myth of collegiality, and partly on the myth of women's unsuitability for academic work, this catch-22 has been used to justify denying women academic jobs, financial support, tenure, promotion, and merit increases.

As described earlier, when a woman makes known her preference for teaching particular courses, she may be allowed her choices but, as a result, later punished for being so 'self-centred' and 'non-collegial.' But, on the other hand, a woman who uncomplainingly took on the excessive teaching load she was given had too little time to produce publications that would have helped her to get tenure and was regarded as having no 'mind of her own' (and, therefore, no mind). Similarly, another woman, afraid of being branded 'too aggressive,' taught two new courses each semester of her one-year contract; this meant spending not only the actual teaching hours but also enormous amounts of time designing the courses, locating appropriate readings, making up examinations and lists of possible paper topics, and so forth. When a tenure-stream position became available, she was not hired, because they said she was a 'typical female, with no real focus and no field of her own.'

3. If you do any nurturing or caretaking – of colleagues, other staff, or students – that work may be invisible or unappreciated, or it can even be used as 'proof' of your lack of professionalism; but if you *don't* nurture, your lack of nurturing behaviour becomes highly visible, and you are considered a 'cold bitch.' This catch-22 is founded partly on the myth of women's endless capacity to nurture and partly on the belief that women can be nurturant *or* competent at work but not both. For many women, the invisible nurturing includes endless hours of committee work or labour to help the university prove that it is implementing affirmative-action or sexual-harassment policies, but women receive little or no credit (or, at worst, are damned) for that work when they come up for tenure, promotions, or merit increases.

A typical story from one assistant professor of chemistry went like this: a senior man on the chemistry faculty suddenly became seriously disabled. The department chair asked the woman to help him teach his course, saying, 'If you don't help him, we don't know *what* we'll do.' Because she liked the senior professor and also wanted to make sure the course would be given, for the sake of the students, she agreed – but it didn't occur to her to get a commitment from the chair that this extra work would count as credit when it came time to her tenure application. Needless to say, the chair never raised that possibility. Because of the overwork, the chemist failed to complete an article she had been asked to revise for publication, and when tenure time came, she was found wanting.

Another form this catch-22 takes is in regard to teaching styles. A man with high standards for students' performance is likely to be respected for his attitude, but a woman with the same standards is likely to be considered unreasonable, rigid, a bad teacher. Male faculty who try to *reduce* the power differential between teacher and students may be considered innovative and humane, whereas women faculty who do this risk 'proving' that, like traditional women, they have no backbone, no concept of the demands of scholarship, or they are simply lazy. If, for whatever reasons, women teachers are well liked, their popularity may be attributed either to their allegedly low standards or to their mesmerizing powers (see the myth that women are dangerous when they are powerful).[3]

Two forms of nurturance whose significance is rapidly growing for women are those of mentoring and thesis supervision, which are substantial drains on the professor's time and energy. As the number of women students and students wishing to do their research on topics related to women has increased, women faculty members have wished to provide them with mentoring support and supervision (see chapter 6 for more details). Many women hate to turn down requests for such help, because they feel selfish for wanting to save time for their own research, even when they desperately need that time. Supervising students' thesis work is another major drain on time and energy, but in order to avoid seeming uncaring and in order to meet the real needs of students who say, 'There's no one else who knows about this topic,' many women faculty report taking on far more students than they can comfortably handle.

4. Women academics are not considered real women if they don't have children and devote a great deal of time to them; but women academics who devote much time to their children are said not to take their careers seriously. Even if you do not have children, you may be taken less seriously because some day you might have them. Here, too, we have a painful, no-win set-up based partly on the myth of women's endless capacity for nurturance. Some childless women told me hair-raising stories of colleagues in staff meetings accusing them of being 'afraid of being a real woman' (especially in departments of psychiatry, psychology, or social work). On the other hand, another woman described a rather lengthy, spur-of-the-moment meeting she had with a male colleague, because he needed a great deal of information from her about a research grant for which he was applying. After she had dropped her own work to give him detailed assistance, he said to her, 'I know you have four kids at home. You *really* ought to be there with them.'

In a related vein, a woman who refuses to take a job that would mean living apart from her partner, children, or elderly family members 'doesn't take her job seriously,' but a woman who is prepared to make such a move is uncaring and unwomanly. As Theodore points out, some hiring committees simply will not believe you if you tell them that you *are* prepared to move.[4] But heaven help you if you 'force' your family to move because of your job.

5. When women academics band together, they are perceived as threatening; but when they do not band together, many remain isolated and powerless or begin to think of themselves as crazy. Related to the myth that women are dangerous when they are powerful, in some ways this dilemma could be called a 'catch-33,' since there is often a third part – that when women band together, they are assumed to *have* to travel in groups because they are too weak on their own. As Cummings et al. note, 'The working of the old-boys network and socialization among males are viewed as natural, while women seeking professional friendship are considered to be showing signs of weakness.'[5] Although it is certainly true that women together are more powerful and effective than each woman alone, the weakness lies in the system that disempowers women rather than in innate, individuals' weaknesses.

In some ways, the most distressing form of this dilemma is that, if you are the only woman or one of very few in a department or program, you may feel isolated, but where women are present in increasing numbers (even though they may still be far from the 50 per cent mark), they are perceived as being too many. How many times have we heard the phrase, 'We don't need another woman. We already have one!' 'Indeed, a few highly visible women ... may lead to the misperception that "women are everywhere." This effect is exacerbated in the case of minority women.'[6]

As noted in chapter 4, women have traditionally been encouraged to work with each other for the sake of others *but not for other women and themselves.* The danger of working together is even greater when the purpose of the work is to improve conditions for women on campus or elsewhere. Dagg and Thompson report that many women fear to talk about or even recognize sexism on campus, because once a woman discovers that she and other women are unfairly treated, she tends to seek out other women who feel the same way – and this is considered threatening.[7] That fear is realistic: you can suffer in silence and nothing will change, or you can speak up and risk being cast out. According to Cummings et al., 'Women seeking support in their endeavours or working to develop a support system for themselves and others are too often perceived as insecure or as troublemakers,'[8] and Backhouse et al. quote a woman who 'didn't join the caucus of women, because I didn't want to be identified that way. Knowing what the grapevine had said about this not being a supportive environment for women, I decided not to be politically active.'[9]

6. If you try to improve the climate for women – including yourself – on campus, you are considered a troublemaker; but if you don't make such an attempt, you go on suffering and are considered a masochist. This catch-22 is closely related to the previous one. Feminist faculty are often charged with disrupting a campus or department or upsetting students through discussing women's issues and working for change. Feminist students risk being labelled as belligerent challengers of the authority and wisdom of traditional faculty members. So much for academic freedom.

If you remain isolated and unhappy, those who stand in the way of improving conditions for academic women will be unlikely to call you a masochist outright, but they may well say that you are miserable because you '*keep yourself* isolated' or that you failed to be promoted because you 'undermined your own chances.' These are simply subtle forms of the myth of women's masochism. So, too, are the urgings of well-meaning friends and family members, who may advise you to search your psyche to figure out how you 'sabotaged your own chances of success,' rather than helping you to focus on the institutional barriers that may have stood in your way. As Dale Spender's important research has shown, women who speak as little as one-third of the time in mixed-sex groups are perceived to have talked the *majority* of the time.[10] So, timid women risk not obtaining the resources or experiences they need and want, but women who make their preferences clear are told that they ask for 'too much.' As June Larkin has observed, 'The dominant groups use the term "reverse discrimination" to refer to any practice that does not benefit them.'[11]

7. A woman who speaks up is aggressive and doesn't know

when to quit; but a woman who remains silent is passive and incompetent and has nothing worth saying. This catch-22 is based partly on the myth that a good woman doesn't get angry and partly on the myth that women are unlikely to be capable of scholarly thinking and speaking. Aisenberg and Harrington write that, when women speak with the voice of authority, they are labelled either as 'shrew/vixen/bitch or talkative, dumb blonde'[12] – a clear no-win situation. At the other end of the spectrum from those who speak up are those women who are silent because, being unaccustomed to expressing their anger but having encountered unfair treatment in academia, they fear just *how* angry they will act if they do begin to speak up.

8. If you do well in your academic work, you are not 'truly' feminine; if you do badly, you will fail for sure.[13] Founded on the myth that women cannot do the kind of thinking that is thought to characterize superior academics, this catch-22 makes women feel that, if they are capable of fine academic work, that somehow proves that they are unwomanly. All too common are the stories of women who have been told outright that their incisive cognitive and lecturing abilities make them 'ballbreakers': 'the old norms dichotomize women's sexual and intellectual natures and, given this split, women are *accused* of being rational and ambitious rather than commended for it.'[14] On the other hand, if they do *not* appear to be rational and ambitious, they are considered too unscholarly and feminine to deserve permanent places in academia.

According to Sandler and Hall, the situation is one of double jeopardy for Black women or for women who come from some of the other disempowered racial or cultural groups, because if they succeed, they may be regarded as exceptions both to their sex *and* to their race or culture.[15] In contrast to this is the pressure on, for instance, Asian women, some of whom report that, if they do *not* graduate with honours or get every paper they write published, they are considered exceptions to their race (though *not* to their sex), because of the stereotype that all Asians are smart.

9. Writing for publication requires concentration; but if you refuse to become overloaded with work other people ask you

to take on, you are considered uncollegial and even 'bitchy.' Based on the myth that women are naturally nurturant and the myth of collegiality in academia, this catch-22 has psychologically paralysed or exhausted many women. Having learned that they have to work extra hard to prove their worthiness, women are likely to deal with this dilemma by accepting teaching or committee-work overloads *while also* working additional hours in order to do the work required to produce publications.

10. An individual woman is told that she is judged on her own merits, as an individual; but an individual woman is also judged as though she represents and speaks for all women. As Thomas et al. report, an academic woman who was a Chicana was treated 'as though I were directly responsible for all Chicanos,'[16] and Deborah Hay writes that when 'Pollyanna Ph.D.' got a teaching job, she knew that 'if she failed, her failure would not be her own, but it would be generalized to all women ... Pollyanna ... felt some compulsion to prove that she was not an "acceptable" female candidate but an exceptional one.'[17] If a woman claims that she has *not* been judged solely on her individual merits, she may be damned for challenging the myth that academia is a meritocracy. If she feels it is inappropriate for her to speak for a whole group of women by answering such questions as, 'What is native women's position on this?' or 'What do you women plan to do about it?' she is regarded as being a poor sport (uncollegial) and withholding information.

11. Women – especially those who are targets of multiple forms of discrimination – are less likely than others to be hired; but when they *are* hired, they are assumed to be *less* competent than others and pressured to perform in *supercompetent* ways. This may be another catch-33: you lose if you are not hired, you lose if you are hired and people assume you are not as competent as men or as white women or as people without disabilities, and you lose if you are hired because people expect you to be absolutely superb in order to justify holding your job. This no-win set-up is based partly on the myth that affirmative action provides unfair advantages to people who are particularly unqualified. As June

Larkin points out, it used to be likely that 'you wouldn't be hired *because you were a woman*, but now, you are said to be hired *only* because you are a woman.'[18]

12. In academia, there are many unwritten rules; but if you break one, you are condemned for that, and if from time to time you ask what the rules are, you are considered ridiculous, overanxious, or paranoid. The topic of unwritten rules was the subject of chapter 3, but the catch-22 aspect of it is captured by Johnson et al., who quote an assistant professor as saying, 'You keep on trying to figure out what the rules they won't tell you about are, but if you happen to break one of them without knowing, you get called a bitch.'[19] And if you check very much about the rules or expectations, then in keeping with the myth of women as bottomless pits of neediness, you may be thought to be too dependent and demanding.

Thus, women say that they 'never knew when to ask for advice – or when I would be judged for asking or not asking.' Yet when you break the unwritten rules, such as by asking for more (or less) frequent feedback than your thesis supervisor is inclined to give, you are condemned for doing the wrong thing.

13. Young women don't belong in academia; old women don't belong in academia. Theodore writes that, in academia, women are considered either too young or too old.[20] The too-young woman can be classified as immature or as pushing too hard, too fast. The old woman can be devalued for being old and female, as happens throughout our society.[21]

14. Women who socialize with male faculty may be considered loose or predatory; but women who do not socialize with male faculty will be out of the mainstream network and can miss out on information and support. As Delisle writes, 'It is awkward for a female student to have a beer with her advisor, meet in the pub, or go out for lunch as male students do with male professors. This is particularly true in departments with few female students/ faculty.'[22] Yet if you socialize instead with what women are available, you 'may be viewed with suspicion.'[23] This may be a 'catch-

44: damned if you socialize with the men, damned if you keep your distance from them, damned if you socialize with your female colleagues, but isolated if you do not.

15. Women who join the old boys' network thereby help to isolate and exclude other women and members of other marginalized groups (both sexes); but women who don't join are less likely to move up the career ladder. This is discussed in detail in appendix 2, but this catch-22 is especially complex and distressing because it involves a combination of professional and social life and because one of the options means being cut off from other women.

Who wins in these no-win situations?

The catch-22s described above are no-win situations primarily for academic women. By making women's working conditions so difficult, however, they also hurt the academic community as a whole, even though many members (and, often, leaders) of that community fail to recognize that fact. But *someone* wins from academic women's damned-either-way dilemmas, and understanding that is crucial to understanding what is means to be female on a college or university campus.

In most situations in which power is unequally distributed, the people with the most power use scapegoating as a technique for maintaining their unfair share.[24] Scapegoating serves this function in the following way: when anyone has a complaint that might threaten the current power balance, those at the top blame the trouble on the scapegoated group, who expose (but do not create) the problem. Throughout most societies, women are a primary target of such blame. Scapegoating thereby serves the dual purposes of keeping in power the mostly white, mostly male group that now sits at the top of most academic institutions and of keeping members of other groups out of power.

What part do the catch-22s play in this process? The people who wield the power risk losing their control every time one of their scapegoats does something good, because that makes it harder to blame them for every problem. The catch-22s, then, make it possible to demean and dismiss virtually everything good that an academic woman might do. The myths described in chapter 4 support this function by providing the underpinnings, the belief system, that leads inevitably to judgments of women as inferior, bad, wrong, or dangerous. That is why the more familiar we are with the nature of the specific myths and catch-22s, the more quickly we can recognize when we are being scapegoated and disempowered, when we are too readily blaming ourselves as well as accepting blame dished out by others. So, when a problem comes up, or when you start feeling lousy about yourself as an academic, flip through the lists of myths and catch-22s, and ask yourself which ones might be creating the problem or making it worse. Remember that you may need to add some others that you have identified. And remember, too, that chapters 6 and 7 offer some strategies for dealing with these frustrating myths and no-win situations when you encounter them.

6 What You Can Do: Some General Principles

This chapter deals with some general strategies that may help you in coping, surviving, and – one hopes – really enjoying your academic life. Each strategy mentioned in this chapter can be applied to a variety of issues and problems noted in earlier chapters or in the appendices, and each can be useful at various stages in your academic career. In chapter 7, we shall look at strategies more specific to particular issues and stages. Naturally, anything mentioned in either this chapter or the next may apply, in your experience, to situations not mentioned here, and not every suggestion will suit your aims or your personal style; so when you are seeking strategies that might be useful in particular contexts, be sure to scan the suggestions in both chapters 6 and 7, and don't limit yourself to what you read here. Use this material as a jumping-off place for your own creativity and problem-solving or to begin discussions with other people, and do make sure to read from the works listed in the notes and bibliography.

An important word of explanation is in order before you read further. In both this chapter and the next, some recommendations involve women academics organizing, educating others, and taking action to improve the situation for themselves and other women. Naturally, these steps ought to be taken on by the institutions themselves, not left to those who are already overburdened by the mistreatment that needs to be abolished. However, I include these suggestions because we live in a real world, not one in which everything is done as it morally ought to be done, and therefore some changes are simply not implemented by those who should

do so – unless and until the targets of oppression first do some
work to make things happen.

Assume that you are OK

The combination of women's traditionally low self-esteem and the
maleness of the academic environment can make it exceedingly
difficult for a woman in academia to remember that she is basically
intelligent and competent. As political scientist Jennifer Nedelsky
courageously writes, 'In the past, I have frequently been struck
with a sharp sense of almost breathtaking panic upon being sent
a letter or article commenting on my work.'[1] The following suggestions can help keep your intelligence and competence in mind:

**1. Remember that poor self-esteem plagues most academic
women** – and indeed, women in general. Most women find it
easier to recognize intelligence and competence in men and in
other women than in themselves; therefore, it is all the more important to keep clearly in mind that self-esteem among women is
a scarce commodity, and that that scarcity does *not* signify that
they lack real ability. Chances are, then, that if most women's
poor opinions of themselves are not justified, your own isn't either.

**2. Create a savings bank of support for your self-esteem, and
dip into that bank whenever you need to.** This may include any
of the following (and do doubt you'll have your own ideas to add):

– Papers (including from undergraduate and graduate courses) on
  which you received good grades and praise from your instructors
– Positive reviews of articles and presentations you have submitted for publications and conference presentations
– Letters of recommendation that referees may have written for
  you (some institutions encourage referees to provide copies to
  the people about whom they write letters; others do not)
– Good evaluations of your teaching from students in your
  courses

–   Thank-you notes written to you by students at the ends of
     courses or of your work with them on theses and dissertations

Take out any of the above and look them over periodically.

**3. Do not assume that those who have the power to evaluate
your work at any point (hiring, promotion, tenure, review of a
grant application, etc.) are objective or correct.** One of my favourite stories in this regard comes to mind when my work is
unfavourably evaluated. Psychologist Cannie Stark-Adamec, a
veteran of grant-application reviews, reports that, in response to
an application she submitted, she once received comments from
three reviewers. One said she had unjustifiably padded her requested budget, another said she had unrealistically low estimates
of how much her project would cost, and the third complimented
her for producing a budget that was right on target.[2] Even were
it not for the fine thinkers recently calling into question the very
possibility of true objectivity, Stark-Adamec's example shows that
all three reviewers couldn't have been simultaneously correct –
and this was on an issue as relatively concrete as financial cost.

**4. Realize that you will rarely or never feel or be completely
prepared** for whatever task you are about to do. But know that
most of us feel that way. No one ever knows everything – and
although it sounds obvious, many women in their daily functioning operate as though they do not believe it. Academic women
are likely, on account of their self-esteem problems and the maleness of the environments, to spend far more time preparing for
courses and writing for publication than necessary, because we
are always dogged by the certainty that we shall never be able to
do a good enough job.

When my son Jeremy was quite young and had to write short
essays for school, he regularly became so anguished that he could
not begin the work. Knowing Jeremy, I suspected that he thought
he had to have every word of every sentence clearly in mind before
laying pencil to paper. I said as much to him, and he acknowledged
that this was true. When I then suggested that he start writing
without doing any planning, he looked uncomfortable. I reminded

him that he had never written anything truly horrible and that he would have time to revise later on, and I proposed that he give my suggestion a try. He did so and discovered that the writing actually took less work than he had suspected.

Since the experience with Jeremy, I have often suggested to my students that they try going ahead with their work *before* they feel that they know everything they feel they need to know – and many find that it works for them. It works because, if they waited until they had done all they felt they should, they would never get started on the task at hand. Going ahead with the project, they often find that they know more than they had thought. Then, when gaps in their knowledge or thinking appear, they have more time and energy to focus on those.

5. Do not assume that you are supposed to be able to meet the needs and answer the questions of everyone who expects you to do so. One woman I interviewed told me that, during the question period after a colloquium she presented as part of a job interview, a male professor asked her, 'Who is going to teach my courses while I am on sabbatical?' Not being familiar with that department at that institution, and having no power whatsoever to make such decisions, she had no idea what to respond – but what escaped her at the moment was that she should not have been asked, or expected to reply to, such a question. It was totally inappropriate. Having been raised to be an accommodating, polite woman, however, she felt pressured to answer his question. Beware of such tendencies in yourself!

6. Know that you – being human – will make some wrong choices and erroneous judgments, and don't panic about that. Go as easily on yourself as you would on anyone you love who had been in the same position, having to confront the same choices or situations. Related to this is the following suggestion.

7. When you feel you are doing badly, pretend that you are someone else – and ask yourself, 'How would I judge her/him? Would I think that person is a complete fool or totally incompetent for doing that?' Women are usually harder on themselves than on other people.

8. Don't spend a lot of time asking permission to do things. Go ahead and take action, try things out, realizing that having been raised female may make you assume that you are more dangerously powerful and potentially destructive than you really are (see chapter 4).

9. Learn to recognize how much clout you really do have, understanding that this may be much different from official, 'legitimate' power. As will be discussed in the section on 'Getting support' later in this chapter, an extremely productive way to gain this perspective can be working with other people in coalitions or collectives.

10. Learn about physical and verbal ways to keep out of, or help extricate yourself from, a one-down position. I highly recommend Nancy Henley's classic, *Body Politics* (1977), since it has helped me a great deal. Using Henley's description of the physical ways in which less powerful people behave in the presence of more powerful ones, by reducing the amount of space they take up, I have tried quietly but confidently increasing the amount of space I take up when I am in the presence of someone who treats me in demeaning ways. Once, for instance, realizing that I repeatedly pulled my legs and arms close to my torso, leaned forward, and looked up at a man who regularly put me down, I thought of Henley's book, leaned back against the chair, relaxed my legs, and (in what felt like a daring act) clasped my hands behind my head, elbows pointing outward. I don't think the fellow ever understood why, but from that time, he treated me with greater respect. Suzette Haden Elgin's book, *The Gentle Art of Verbal Self-defense* (1980) is recommended also because of its careful detailing of many techniques for verbal coping.

11. Remember that discrimination is illegal (whether or not you choose to do anything about it). As described in chapter 2 and appendix 2, much of women's unhappiness and frustration in academia results from various aspects of the environment's maleness, and therefore much falls under the category of sex discrimination – whether blatant or subtle. Many academic women are also the targets of discrimination on account of their race or ethnic background, age, sexual orientation, disability, or social class. To be a target of discrimination tends to damage our self-esteem, to make us angry – and then, for some, to make us afraid of expressing that anger and to paralyse us. In the face of such treatment, we tend to feel unwarranted shame about ourselves, mistakenly believing that such treatment is evidence of our individual failings. The very naming of such treatment as 'discrimination,' combined with our recalling to mind that it is *illegal*, can be immensely empowering, even if we don't choose to take any action about it. Such naming makes it clear that the perpetrators of the discriminating treatment are the ones who are in the wrong, not us. (The ways of dealing with these illegalities within legal or quasi-legal systems will differ, depending on your institution and the local and larger governments under whose jurisdiction you may fall. More will be said in chapter 7 about such remedies.)

12. Ask yourself whether you really *want* to be like 'them.' In learning to assume that you are OK, it is helpful if you realize that, often, when you feel you are *not* all right, that is because you or others are comparing you unfavourably to a standard you may not wish to match. It may be the standard of the ivory-tower academic whose research is unrelated to real life, or the standards of impersonality and objectivity that tend to be associated with traditional maleness, or the standard of climbing the academic ladder at all costs, no matter who gets trampled in the process. As an interviewee reported, since she had been doing a great deal of teaching and had also been heading a program, she had published very little by the time she was scheduled to come up for tenure. Rather than delay applying for tenure until she had produced more publications, she chose to apply for tenure as she was: 'I felt that, if they don't want me that way, I don't want to go on working there.'

Once you identify the standard in comparison to which you feel inferior, it is relatively easy to figure out whether that is even a standard you want to meet. As Virginia Woolf wrote in *Three Guineas*, 'For we have to ask ourselves, here and now, do we wish to join that procession, or don't we? On what terms shall we join that procession?'[3] Related to this is the next point.

13. Determine to yourself that your goals include retaining your humanity, helping others to retain theirs, and acquiring and maintaining self-esteem and self-confidence. Many of the following suggestions will be helpful in these endeavours:

- Spend time in other universities and non-academic settings, to remind yourself how your work is rooted in the rest of the world.
- Choose your battles carefully,[4] because you will probably get to fight them all eventually, and taking on too many at once, especially since you will probably lose some, is draining and can be demoralizing.

The next suggestions[5] can help you begin and continue to assume that you are OK when people treat you in rude or demeaning ways on the job:

- When you are speaking, 'if you are interrupted, continue talking and continue looking at the person to whom you are addressing your concerns ... or say something like, "Just a minute, please. I haven't finished my point." '
- 'Seek out informal contacts, for example, by arriving early for meetings, and chatting informally with others before business begins.' It's easier to feel good about ourselves when we have found people with whom we can make some human contact on the job.
- Avoid apologizing unduly, baking cookies for meetings, answering the communal phone, cleaning up after meetings, taking notes for the rest of the committee in committee meetings, modifying statements with 'I think' or 'seemingly' when you are conducting business, trying to prove you are 'sweet,' and responding to sexist 'jokes' or mockery of feminists. In regard to the last issue, Vartuli suggests mirroring the objectionable

comment: 'When a male professor at a seminar referred to a female professor as "a lovely lady" with whom he hated to disagree, she countered by referring to him as "a handsome
gentleman," with whom she hated to disagree.'[6]

– Avoid hiding or using non-verbal behaviour; for instance, keep
your hands away from your face, do not cover your mouth
with your hand, and generally avoid behaving in ways that
suggest that you *ought* to be ashamed of yourself.

**14. Remember that if you do decide to play the traditional ac-
ademic game in the traditional ways, there are steps you can
take to be prepared.** Many of these are described in chapter 7,
but here are some general suggestions:[7]

– Be persistent.
– Gain practice in political skills, for example, through volunteer
work.
– Assume you will encounter opposition, so you are not caught
off guard by the sheer shock of being opposed.
– Use your contacts.
– Choose your fights and struggles with care; don't take on
every injustice that you encounter or hear about.

**15. Have an exit path, an idea of what you can do if you leave
your present institution or academia altogether, to help alle-
viate any feeling of being trapped and totally dependent upon
your current setting.** Through networking, make your skills known
to a variety of people throughout your campus and other academic
settings, and also outside of academia. (A woman I interviewed
was a psychologist who chaired an art history department, because
a top university official had become aware of her fine administrative abilities and saw a department that could use them.) Among
the possibilities, consider work you could do with granting agencies or various government bodies or in private consulting. Make
a careful list of the skills you have, and think – and ask others –
about how they might be applied.

Regularly review the potential traps

One of the most frequent replies I received when I asked women what has been most helpful to them in their attempts to survive and thrive in academia was, 'Don't forget that there are all sorts of hidden agendas and myths throughout academe – and don't let yourself be controlled by them.' Over and over, women told stories about heading down dead-end paths because, without realizing it, their steps were being directed by myths, catch-22s, or their conscious and unconscious attempts to cope with the maleness of the environment and follow the unwritten rules.

Chapters 1 through 5 and appendices 1 and 2 are rather detailed, because once the myths, catch-22s, and aspects of the maleness of the environment and unwritten rules are there in black and white, it is easier to recognize when our behaviour, assumptions, and feelings about ourselves are being shaped by them. The primary message of the current section is to take heed: 'Having read through the above materials once will probably *not* be sufficient to make you hear the requisite "click" of recognition each time a myth, catch-22, or other part of the system goes into play. It may be important to reread them periodically and, particularly when you are feeling especially stressed or rather inadequate and ashamed of yourself, to look at each point, asking yourself, "How many of these factors might be contributing to the horrible feelings I am having?" ' It has been truly astonishing, and heartwarming, to see how much of academic women's self-blame and unhappiness can abate as soon as they recognize that the problems do not always come from within.

Periodically, too, look at the information in appendices 1 and 2, or at least at the summaries of them in chapters 1 and 2, to remind yourself of the concrete facts about what it means to be a woman in academia. For the same reason, see if you can obtain hard data on your home program, department, and institution, and compare them with data from other programs, departments, academic institutions, and non-academic workplaces.

Specifically, then, you may want to do the following:

1. On your own, question the truth of the myths and the fairness of the catch-22s, the maleness of the environment, and the unwritten rules.

2. Follow suggestion no. 1 above with others who are in similar situations in your own program or in different programs, departments, academic institutions, or non-academic settings. You can find these other people through such resources as harassment, affirmative-action, and status of women officers within your institution; through official women's network groups and women's centres; through local women's bookstores; through the grapevine; or through posting on key bulletin boards a notice asking people to contact you.

3. Do no. 1 more publicly, in letters to your institution's newsletters and to newspapers, magazines, and local or national newspapers and magazines, or by talking in pairs or groups formed through no. 2. Name the myths, catch-22s, and so on that are in operation when you are feeling oppressed or demeaned by them. You may wish to speak directly to offenders on your own, but you'll feel safer if you have at least one friend with you at the time. For some of the people who perpetrate the harm, your naming of the problem will be either simply irritating, infuriating, or a matter of no interest; but for well-intentioned others who have also been shaped by the traditional belief systems, your naming of the problem can be educational and liberating. At the very least, giving problems labels that do not again implicate women's alleged individual inadequacies tends to promote women's well-being and empowerment.

Above all, as you look at the sheer volume of paper it took to describe these factors fairly succinctly, remember that in many ways you, like so many women throughout the workforce, are attempting a Sisyphean task. The top of the hill will be reached one day, but any upward step we help each other to take is a significant achievement against substantial odds.

Reach out and touch someone[8]

To become truly educated and self-aware, against the current of patriarchal education, a woman must be able to discover and explore her root connection with all women.   ADRIENNE RICH[9]

I feel I made it in academia because of the support of other women.   Senior woman professor in the sciences

Based on my interviews with academic women, my reading of the literature, and my own experiences, I believe that the worst mistake we can make on the job is to remain isolated from other people, especially from other women. We can spend so much time scrambling to meet the traditional standards and demands of academia, learning the methods, and feeling grateful for being the token woman or one of few that we stay isolated or only compete against each other. As one woman told me, 'There's so little power and praise given to academic women that, too often, we fight over it.' *Be aware that, as members of at least one group that is less powerful than others in your institution, women are at risk of turning their frustrations on each other, rather than recognizing that we are often each other's best potential allies.*[10] For instance, one interviewee told me that, when the supposedly progressive women's studies faculty at her university discussed integrating materials about lesbians into the curriculum, two women who described themselves as feminists refused to do so. And Comely et al. have observed that there is anti-lesbianism in the *feminist* academic world.[11] Racialized women have said for decades that whites of either sex who support their struggles in academia are all too rare, and younger women and men often simply fail to notice the needs and troubles of older women.[12]

The isolation and potential for unproductive competitiveness is even worse for any woman who doesn't fit the model of the white,[13] able-bodied, heterosexual woman of 'just the right age': 'Minority women and disabled women often face a lack of collegiality not only from men but from other women as well.'[14]

As Sandler and Hall write, 'Women cannot solve the general

climate issues by their own individual behaviors in specific situations.'[15] Useful support can come from other women on campus, from other professionals in positions similar to one's own on other campuses, or from women's studies or women's rights groups, and we need to look in places from which we have been taught not to expect support; for instance, it is both unfair and inaccurate to accept as true the traditional images of students and faculty in nursing, library science, and home economics programs as being too traditionally feminine and passive to stand up for their rights and align themselves with other women. We can obtain invaluable support and information from such contacts, as well as from those with non-academic staff in our own departments, with other women in our own academic field[16] (such as the women's caucuses, divisions, or sections within the national and international organizations of traditional disciplines), with local women's networks that include members from throughout the non-academic community, with faculty associations, and with individuals of both sexes within and outside our discipline and academia.

I shall here list only a few examples of the various types of support, beginning with groups and then moving to individuals. First, though, some general recommendations:

1. Assume you will find some like-minded people, some supporters, and spend some time watching to identify who are your likely allies, who might be dangerous, and where the power lies. Be aware that, often, the power does *not* lie with the department head or other obvious people. Observe carefully in committee, university-senate, and faculty-association meetings.

2. Remain aware of how you interact with women, and what type of example or role model you are providing to others. Make sure you try to connect, and work cooperatively with other female students, staff, and faculty.

3. Discuss your feelings and reactions to academia with sympathetic colleagues, and support women who tell you about chilly climate experiences by believing them, taking their reactions seriously, and discussing possible solutions with them.[17]

4. Whether in groups or in one-to-one, supportive relationships, make sure there is give and take. Discuss explicitly what you are prepared to do for each other and what your limits are. For instance, agree that when anyone unfairly criticizes one of you, the other(s) will speak up in her defence.[18] Or get together and decide which kinds of requests from department chairs, deans, presidents, or others you want to refuse (for example, sitting on more than one search committee for which you receive no credit or release time per year), and agree that you will 'say *no* collectively.'[19] Also, discuss together the limits of your commitments to each other; for instance, say that you can come to twice-monthly meetings and devote an additional hour a week to whatever the two or the group of you are doing, but that that's all you can do.

IN GROUPS

1. Groups designed to promote talk about how it feels – both the joys and the woes – being a woman in academia can be limited to the women within a department and can include non-academic and academic staff and students as well as faculty, or they can include women from a variety of departments (including non-academic staff and students or confined strictly to one group, depending upon the purpose of the group), a variety of campuses, or even from outside academia. (These alliances help escape the divide-and-conquer technique commonly used by members of dominant groups.) Cummings et al. have pointed out that 'women need a forum in which they can raise and discuss problems that they are experiencing by virtue of the fact that they are women.'[20] The groups can meet formally or more casually, over pizza or muffins.

Groups with more limited membership can be particularly useful for enabling women to understand what is happening in their specific setting, such as the process by which new staff will be hired, whether and how affirmative-action procedures will be implemented, or why the department chair has announced a particular policy. They can also bring women together to combat particular instances of gender-based harassment or mistreatment within the department. For instance, a woman I interviewed described a meeting she convened, of women secretaries and academic staff from the same department, where they learned that the same male professor had been unfairly pressuring his secretary to type papers when she had other departmental obligations to meet and also pressuring two junior faculty women to give several guest lectures each in his courses (thus lessening his workload). Before the meeting, each woman had believed she was the only person upon whom this man was imposing, and each had been trying to be cooperative by agreeing to his demands. But once they got together, they realized that in many ways he was sloughing off his own responsibilities onto other people, mostly women and mostly people in positions junior to himself. As a result of their meeting, each woman felt strengthened in her resolve not to be taken advantage of by this professor.

In a group composed solely of very senior (and, in the eyes of others, extremely successful) women professors and university administrators, I sat for an entire day, listening to virtually every woman describe how insecure and inadequate she had felt for years. At the end of the day, many of the participants said how relieved they felt to have learned that so many other women in similar positions felt that way. Each had been certain that she and only she was unequal to her job, and each was certain that the rest of us had no such self-doubts.

More mixed groups, in contrast, can provide important perspectives as well. Academics, like people in any kind of work, can become so immersed in the written and unwritten rules of our workplaces that we don't realize how unreasonable or strange some of them may seem to people outside of the field. When we are suffering under those rules, it can be helpful to describe what is happening to someone in, say, the business world, and hear their reaction. For instance, a woman professor reported being notified by her department's administrative officer that $1500 in overspending from her research grant had been paid to her research assistant by mistake. Since the administrator was paid to ensure that such things not happen, the professor was surprised when he told her to repay the university out of her own pocket. Not thinking to question the fairness of his demand, she handed over the money, wrongly believing that this was the policy of her institution. Only when a friend in the business world expressed the view that, in his company, no administrator who had fouled up so badly would dare to make such a demand, did she realize she had been duped. Her vulnerable point had been her assumption that, as an academic, she probably wouldn't understand procedures in the realm of finances.

What the various kinds of groups share is the potential to make each woman feel less isolated and, therefore, less weird, inadequate, or crazy – to teach us that, what*ever* we have felt or done, others have too. In each kind of group, going over the lists of myths, catch-22s, features of the maleness of the environment, and unwritten rules can be illuminating, since other women's stories about how they were hurt or misled by one of these factors can help us to understand our own similar experiences.

2. Groups designed primarily for the sharing of information can also be composed in any of the ways described in no. 1. As Cummings et al. write, 'Women need good information about their situation [on campus] and about what resources they can expect the institutional structures of the University to make available to them.'[21]

Even men and women from outside of academia can be important sources of ideas for us: a woman described to one of my interviewees the way that, in her sales company, decisions were made about promotions, leading her to realize that, somewhere in the world, the criteria for promotions were clear-cut. As a result, she says, she felt less like 'an unreasonable, demanding, insecure woman' when she went to her dean to request clarification of the criteria for promotion.

Although many rules and procedures on campuses are unwritten, even the recorded rules can be hard to locate, and many important pieces of information in addition to rules are not systematically presented to those who need them. Groups can help provide these kinds of information. In my own program, some of the first-year graduate students didn't know until late in the spring term – when they had missed the deadlines for applying for financial support for the coming year – that there were student mailboxes in the department's lounge area, and financial-aid notices had been placed there. When some of the more energetic and caring students organized an orientation meeting for new students the following year, they told the latter about a wealth of such details.

Groups can be formed to share information about where and to whom to go when you need particular kinds of help or details about procedures; about the unwritten rules and standards in your

institution or department; about your options when you are unfairly treated, denied a promotion or tenure, and so on; and about
what to avoid saying to whom. There are certain aspects of procedure that women are less likely than men to think of automatically, and people of either sex can inform us about them; for
instance, when I became head of a women's centre, I immediately
went to a store, ordered business cards that I could hand out when
I represented the centre on public occasions, and paid for them
myself. A full year later, I mentioned what I had done to a woman
who worked with the centre's budget, and she said, 'Oh, the centre
would have paid for that!' I had never before been in a situation
in which business cards were important, and it had not occurred
to me that I wouldn't have to pay for them myself.

In order to make their work maximally useful, some informa-
tion-sharing groups have prepared brochures or hand-out sheets.
The students in my program who organized the orientation meeting found that, in preparing a hand-out sheet, they were able to
articulate for the first time some of the fears and uncertainties they
had had. Some had felt overwhelmed, confused, and put off by
the mystifying jargon used by some people in our setting – hence,
they made a tongue-in-cheek list of terms students need to know.
And the new students who saw those words named as 'jargon'
realized that their failure to comprehend those terms was *not their
fault.*

Even if your group does not plan to produce an informational
brochure, it can be helpful to imagine that you are doing so, and
ask yourselves: 'If I were just entering graduate school, or just
being hired, here, what should I be told?' You might wish to
produce a checklist of questions with answers, such as:

> QUESTION: If you are a mid-life woman just beginning gradu-
> ate school, where can you go for help in readjusting to univer-
> sity life?'
> ANSWER: Call your graduate-studies office and ask about re-
> entry assistance of 'transitional year' programs, or ask your
> departmental chair, the Dean of Students, or the Status of
> Women officer.

3. Groups designed to share both information *and* feelings. Although a group may be established initially for the sharing of *either* information *or* feelings, what nearly always happens is that both in fact are shared. For instance, some members of the Canadian Society for Women in Philosophy (SWIP) report that the first SWIP meeting they attended significantly increased their optimism about the very possibility of 'being a female and doing philosophy,' when so many men in their field were telling them such a thing was impossible. They also found SWIP members to be invaluable sources of information about job possibilities, about channels for publication of their work, and about which college and university philosophy departments were most congenial to women.

Similarly, the importance of groups composed of one's peers for sharing both feelings and information is reflected in women's experiences in thesis support groups. In mixed-sex groups, they sometimes learn that the male students are treated differently from the female students by their faculty supervisors. In all-women groups, the female students tend to feel freer to talk about their fears and insecurities in regard to the thesis and the oral examination. But in all groups, they deal with such issues as, 'How often should you show thesis drafts to your supervisor?' and 'Is it all right to ask for help before you have put anything on paper?' In all kinds of groups, when the members are reasonably humane in their treatment of each other, they come to feel less isolated as they hear that other students have dilemmas similar to their own: 'Oh, yeah, my supervisor told me that, too, but I thought it was just *my* failing, not a general thesis problem.'

Another kind of group activity can be brainstorming or practising for difficult situations. The Community Psychology students at my institute decided one year to hold a 'What Do I Do?' workshop. They said they had found their program's course readings and discussions about bias and stereotypes interesting, but they still didn't know what to do when people made sexist, racist, or other biased comments to or in front of them. They prepared a series of sixty-second skits, in each of which one person made an objectionable comment to another. At that point, the target of the comment would turn to the audience and ask, 'What do I do?' and the audience would brainstorm about the variety of ways one might deal with that situation. They came up with such categories of techniques as ignoring the comment, naming it as a form of bias, objecting angrily, asking calmly what led the speaker to say that, asking what evidence the speaker has for the claim, and saying, 'When you make that remark, it makes me feel sad, uncomfortable, scared, ...'

ONE-TO-ONE (FRIENDS, COLLEAGUES, MENTORS, SUPERVISORS)

Many of the functions served by groups can be served by your contacts with individuals from the various sources named above. A topic of particular concern among academic women in recent years has been the importance of finding women to be one's role models, supervisors, and mentors. Women's discussions of that topic are often followed by suggestions about links with non-academic staff and administrators, as well as other recommendations about one-to-one links.

1. **Finding role models, mentors, and supervisors.**[22] This may be easier said than done, because there is a serious scarcity of good role models, mentors, and supervisors for women[23] – and even more so for women from non-dominant groups and for feminists in academia.[24] In fact, 'the ratio of female students to female faculty ... [across] all fields ... is 50:1,' whereas the ratio of male students to male faculty is only 10:1.[25] Furthermore, 'in those areas in which female students are pioneers, where there is not even a critical mass to lend one another support (e.g., Engineering), there are also the least number of female faculty.'[26] This shortage matters so much because scholars' subsequent academic productivity tends to be greater when the candidate and mentor or supervisor are of the same sex.[27] Furthermore, role models and mentors play important functions for students and junior faculty, and these are all the more important for women and other groups who are in the minority in academia. These functions include:

–   Serving as examples of what is possible for women[28]
–   'Learning the real rules of the profession and what really matters in a career'[29]

–   Asking a junior person to co-author work with a senior
      scholar, which is 'a good entry to the world of academic pub-
      lishing and "grantsmanship" [sic]'[30]
–   Providing 'the individualized tutoring and attention ... that oc-
      cur over lunch, drinks, tennis, or other informal social times,'
      including 'time to experiment with ideas and getting feedback
      as they form.'[31]

Since the higher a woman goes on the academic ladder, the
fewer female colleagues she finds (from undergraduate student
through to full professor or top administrator), the problem of
finding mentors and supervisors becomes more severe the more
she advances[32] – all the more so if she is not white.[33] Even those
women who are potential mentors are often ineffective because
they are *insecure* (in fact in terms of their job security, or emotionally, or both) or overworked or because their own positions
are not very powerful ones, so that they are limited in what they
can do for their female students or junior colleagues.[34]

The shortage is even more problematic because so many women
academics do interdisciplinary work, and this makes it even harder
to get good supervision, since faculty who are well versed in more
than one discipline are extremely rare. Thus, for the long and often
arduous process of thesis writing, it is difficult for women to find
adequate support and advice, and it is also hard to find appropriate
people to write letters of recommendation for scholarships, jobs,
or grants.[35]

For feminist students, the field is even more limited. In Canada,
for instance, Eichler reports that the proportion of full-time university professors who are feminists is probably only about 2 per
cent, leading to the following, frustrating scenario for feminist
students:

> [If she works with a non-feminist supervisor,] what about the
> theoretical framework? What about the methods? What about the
> literature review? Which literatures are seen as relevant? Will he
> (or she) feel comfortable with an approach that may be highly
> critical of what he (she) does in his (her) own work? ...
> Here Jane is, just a graduate student, having read some of this

feminist literature, and having come away deeply convinced that the literature which her [non-feminist] professor tells her to utilize in order to construct her framework is fundamentally flawed. What is she to do? Give up? Compromise? Try to find someone else, for instance, at a different university? She goes and finds herself a feminist professor at a different university who agrees to serve as co-chair with her erstwhile thesis supervisor and ... being an enlightened person – agrees to the arrangement ...

[The feminist professor] is well versed in feminist theory and methodology, but of course she cannot possibly be an expert in the various subject areas that are dealt with in theses. So she lets herself be talked into becoming co-chair (or sole chair) of this thesis, but she has the problem of not knowing the literature specific to the subject area with which this thesis deals.[36]

1a. Choosing a mentor. In regard to choosing a mentor, keep the following guidelines in mind:

- Know *why* you want a mentor. Is it to advise you about the unwritten rules in your department? To advise you on topics for publications that are likely to maximize your chances of getting good jobs in your discipline? To talk to you about how she tried to balance family and career responsibilities? You may want to make it clear to a potential or actual mentor that you are not asking her or him for lifelong commitment to meeting all of your needs; thus, being as specific as possible about your request is helpful.
- Consider obtaining more than one mentor, one each for one or more purposes (see above).
- *Never assume* (1) that it was easy for your mentor to get where she or he is today; or (2) that she or he has everything they want, and life is easy for them.

In regard to both mentors and supervisors, here are three more suggestions:

- *Never* feel that you absolutely must take their advice. Being human, they can make mistakes, use poor judgment, or simply be feeling irritable at a particular time.

– Look for people who will offer you information and perspectives but not become angry or punitive if you don't use what they tell you.
– Remember that they have full lives aside from their dealings with you. Graduate students have sometimes asked me angrily why, if they hand in late term papers twenty-four hours before grades are due, that won't give me plenty of time to mark them. I finally realized, to my utter amazement, that they were assuming I have no other work or non-work life besides the portion related directly to them.

Although some men, too, have served women well as mentors and supervisors, some remain frankly unwilling to work with women at all,[37] and others work with them but harbour negative attitudes about the potential of women students to complete programs and to be productive scholars.[38]

1b. Approaching a potential mentor. Remember that choosing a mentor or supervisor is in some ways equivalent to choosing a life partner, with all its complexity. It is usually not a good idea to go up to someone and say, 'Hi. I really want you to be my supervisor.' That is like suggesting you share an apartment with someone you have just met at a cocktail party. You may think she is terrific on the basis of her writing or lecturing, but she may know you very little or not at all, and neither of you can know yet whether or not you can work happily and effectively as a pair.

Some senior women professors told me that women often say, 'I want you to be my mentor' or 'You are my role model.' Most find this disconcerting – 'being a mentor' means serving in a role whose definitions and boundaries are not clear, until and unless the mentor and mentee work out how they should be delineated. And most of us are reluctant to take on yet another potentially unwieldy, boundaryless task. Being told that one is a role model can also be unsettling, because it can mean that people expect you always to match certain templates and 'live up to' the responsibility of being a role model. It can also mean that people choose you as a role model because they think you have everything they want – which may or may not be true. Even insofar as it is true, some will assume that it came to you easily. After a lecture I gave in 1980, a woman I had never met stood up in the audience and said angrily to me, 'Well, it's easy for you! You've got everything – a faculty position, two published books, and a great family life!' I was stunned – at the time, yes, I had had two books published, but one had been absolute hell to write, owing to difficulties with my co-author. Yes, I had an academic position – but it was a one-year job, and I was then being totally ignored by the search committee for the tenure-stream position. Yes, I had a family life, including terrific children, but I was in the throes of an extremely unpleasant divorce and felt daunted and overwhelmed on a daily basis by the responsibilities of being a single mother. Some role model!

In fact, it is probably best *not* to ask someone to be your mentor or supervisor right off the bat – and probably never to ask them to be your role model at all. Instead, ask to discuss a specific piece of work with them, and have specific questions in mind. These could be about some of their work that you want to understand further, or it could be about some of your work, on which you would like to have feedback. *Never* say, 'I'd like to come and pick your brain about possible dissertation [for graduate students] or research [for faculty] topics for me.' The listener will hear that as a code for, 'I haven't bothered to think carefully about it myself and want you to tell me what to do.' Ideally, write your ideas or questions down in a couple of pages and spell out clearly what you would like the other woman – or man – to talk to you about, such as, 'Please help me focus my topic more narrowly' or 'Can you suggest other readings I might look at?' You might consider volunteering – with clear limits – a bit of time to help with their research. In these ways, you can get to know each other and each other's ways of working. That will provide a firmer foundation for both of you in deciding whether or not to work together.

2. Make connections with non-academic staff. I can't say it any better than the woman who gave the following advice in one of my interviews: 'Stop living in isolation from the invisible support staff, cleaners, and cafeteria staff. Many of them hear more useful information than anyone else in the department.' And another woman told the following story: 'When I was under siege from my faculty colleagues, a cleaning woman came to me and said, ''I heard what is happening, and the students love you, so stay in there and keep fighting.'' That meant so much to me, and it gave me the strength to continue the struggle.' Most faculty are implicitly encouraged to minimize their associations with non-academic staff, since that may lower their status in the eyes of some colleagues and administrators. But pioneer engineering professor Ursula Franklin of the University of Toronto has always steadfastly resisted such classist pressure. She reports having been upset when important officials, thinking to praise her, called her 'the first woman in the engineering department,' because the women who cleaned the department offices had been there for years.

3. Link up with administrators, especially female ones. A senior woman administrator from a major Canadian university wished me to advise the readers of this book as follows: 'If all else fails, see if you can find a friendly woman administrator. Women administrators may not know what is going on unless you tell them – and then they *may* be able to help.' And another said, 'Academic women often make the mistake of not relating well to women in administration, thinking they have nothing in common. Go to dinner with them. They know what decisions the president is making, what the budget will be, and so on.'

4. Find a woman or a man, in your department or another one, with whom you can laugh. That was one of the pieces of advice academic women I interviewed gave most frequently. Research and teaching can seem so deadly solemn and cerebral, and many academics take themselves and their institutional culture so seriously, that it is crucial to find someone with whom to laugh. A particularly useful exercise is to talk about mind-games that are played in your settings – you can help each other to see that they *are* games, rather than seeing those who keep them going as the arbiters of truth. They may be powerful, but that doesn't mean they are right or fair, and laughter helps us keep such things in perspective.

5. Use electronic mail to make quick contact with people at other institutions whom you know to be supportive or to have

useful perspectives. Even if you are phobic about computers, it is well worth learning the few simple steps you need to know for using electronic mail, which is a way to write letters and send them instantaneously by computer to people in distant places. This can be especially important for those of you who work in the hinterlands, where you are less likely than those who work in major metropolitan areas to have many women colleagues or even many colleagues in your own field of research, or with your political views, and so forth. For instance, Ann Gibbons has described an electronic-mail mentoring system call Systers, established by women computer scientists.[39]

IN GENERAL

1. Listen to what other women tell you. If you are considering having a baby, really listen when mothers tell you that you may not get a full night's sleep for a year or more. And try to take that into account in making your plans. When women at a university where you are applying for a job tell you that sexual harassment there is rampant and uncontrolled, you ought seriously to consider thinking about whether you want the job there (admittedly a thought that is a luxury in a tight job market), how you would handle it, and so on.

2. Be creative. Two women friends believed the other women who told them that writing a dissertation while being pregnant and then a new mother was absolute hell. So, they did the best they could to become pregnant around the same time, so that each could know that at least one other person in a similar situation would be available with whom she could commiserate. Their plan was so helpful to both of them during and after their respective pregnancies that they did the same thing for their second ones, while preparing to take their qualifying examinations for registration as psychologists.

3. Remember that our society places many barriers between women who are attempting to be supportive to each other. Become aware of these barriers, through reading about them[40] and talking about them. These include women's internalized belief that men's opinions are more valuable than women's and a host of others that can be particularly dangerous to academic women. A two-pronged approach to such barriers is important: one is to work on becoming aware of and overcoming them, and the other is to fight against the feeling that women can *never* work together if a woman or a women's group whose support you yearned for fails to come through for you.

But you do need to be aware that women sometimes let each other down for various reasons,[41] including the need to associate with the more powerful males on one's campus, the fear of getting involved in other people's struggles, and sheer lack of time and energy. Being aware that not all women, or even all feminists, are going to be supportive of you is important. But so, too, is being aware that you may read as rejection something which isn't that at all. If women colleagues don't return your telephone calls, it may be that they don't like you or don't agree with what you are doing, but it may also be that they are desperately busy.

Document everything

For a number of reasons, it can be important to document everything carefully.[42] What does 'everything' mean in this context? It means that you should seriously consider keeping a journal in which you jot down any incidents that make you uncomfortable, even if you feel at the time that they are your own fault. It also means that you may wish to obtain or impel the gathering of data about various aspects of women's status and treatment on your own campus and on others. But *why* is this important?

It is important because any member of a group that is less than fully welcomed in a workplace is likely, at some time, to be treated badly or unfairly. Women's socialization to nurture others and to blame ourselves for whatever goes wrong sets us up to believe that if we feel uncomfortable or are badly treated it must be our own fault. If we venture to object to mistreatment and are told that we were treated perfectly well, we are likely to suspect that we overreacted, distorted what happened, or simply forgot the real specifics of the event. At a different level, if we suspect that we were given less comfortable office space, less access to secretarial assistance, heavier workloads, or lower salaries than others, it is essential to be able to compare our own situation with those of others of both sexes, both in our home institution and in similar ones. Hence, the following suggestions are made.

1. **Keep a journal.** You may wish to include both good and bad events, thoughts as well as incidents, and comments from other people in addition to your own experiences, depending upon how much time you have to do this. But the sine qua non for this exercise is to record anything that makes you feel at all uncomfortable, inadequate, or ashamed. And as Sandler and Hall advise, 'When instances of differential treatment occur, write down what has happened.'43

Many interviewees told me that keeping such records had more than once helped them avoid the feeling that they were crazy or forgetful, and that has certainly been my own experience. Even if I don't know at the moment *why* I feel uncomfortable, if I record the event that gave rise to that feeling, I find almost invariably that, when I come back to look at what I wrote, one of my notes brings to mind something helpful that I had forgotten. For instance, a male in a position of power over me at work told me he would check with another administration official about a request I was making. I told him that the other fellow had been singularly unhelpful to me in the past, and the man to whom I was speaking replied, 'I guess that's because you haven't charmed him as you have charmed me.' That made me feel uncomfortable and, somehow, ashamed. I made notes immediately after the conversation, even though I couldn't figure out why I felt so bad. Two weeks later, I realized that it was because he had ignored the fact that my request had merit in and of itself; he had acted as though the important issue was whether or not I had been 'charming.' It struck me that it would be hard to imagine him making a similar comment to a male professor. Looking back at my notes, I realized that the man to whom I had spoken had not made any acknowledgment of the legitimacy of my request, and that reinforced my feeling that my discomfort had not been a 'typical, female overreaction.'

Keeping a journal can also be invaluable for letting others know how events actually took place. This may mean pointing out, based on your journal entries, that a particular decision had been made in a planning meeting for your program but never implemented, or it may mean using your entries as support in formal proceedings such as grievances or lawsuits.

Your journal entries can also help other people who have been treated in similar ways, by showing them that there is a systemic atmosphere that encourages such treatment of people. Simply seeing your written record of what has happened to you can help to legitimize the feelings of others who have been treated in like manner. Finally, if enough women and members of other mis-treated groups in academia kept such notes and put them together into a formal document, it could be an invaluable tool in bringing about change.

2. Find, or help promote the gathering of, data relevant to the position of women on your campus and throughout academia.[44] As Haley has pointed out, 'A major problem in examining women's problems in graduate school is the lack of accessible data to investigate gender differences in completion rates, funding, and in professional training opportunities (research assistantships, teaching assistantships). Some ... universities may query students on their reasons for withdrawal, but this information is not gathered in a form that would allow comparison between universities.'[45] Many of the kinds of data that might be or become relevant to you are noted in the check-list at the end of this book. However, a few examples of types of useful data are given here to get you started:

–   Those that help to reveal whether 'there are differences in the stringency of the standards applied to evaluate women and men'[46]
–   Comparisons by sex of drop-out rates from various graduate programs at both the master's and doctoral level (thus indicat-

ing where interventions might need to be made to keep
women in those programs)[47]

− Data on such questions as: 'Are women students less likely to
be called upon directly than men students? ... Are women interrupted more often than men during class discussion? ... Are
graduate advisors more likely to contact men students when
publication, research, and other professional opportunities
arise? ... Do some professors use sexist humor to "spice up a
dull subject" or make disparaging comments about women as a
group?'[48]

− Data about *whether* student evaluation forms include questions
about classroom 'climate' and, if so, *what* students are telling
us about the relative warmth of that climate for people of each
sex, race, and other group

− Data that reflect not only how many new women your administration is hiring but also how many current women faculty
they are retaining, promoting, and moving from part-time to
full-time and from insecure to tenured positions

This last example illustrates how crucial data collection can be:
many administrators boldly announce new initiatives aimed at
hiring more women but then fail to reveal that either these newly
hired women are hired only for temporary positions or that, even
if *they* remain, the contracts of so many previously hired women
are not renewed that the latter outnumber the former, and there
is actually a net loss of women faculty.

Educate and act

You may or may not think right away that education and action
about women's problems in academia are for you, but I urge you
to consider either getting involved now or being open to doing so
at some later date.

Why? Because, insofar as you are treated ill because of your sex,
taking action of *some* sort related to some aspect of women's issues
can switch you from the role of 'done to' to 'doer,' and that usually
makes one feel better. It can reduce the isolation you might be
feeling. Then, too, working to reduce oppression can help others.

What to do? Any issue mentioned up to now in this book could be a place to begin, and no doubt you will find other issues in your own and your friends' experiences. Since so much needs to be done, it can be tempting to choose to work on the most fundamental and sweeping changes that are needed, but I would urge you instead to choose something that grabs you at a gut level, that really inspires your emotions. You might begin by simply writing down any sexist behaviour or remarks you observe and then, one step at a time, expressing disapproval of these (perhaps first ensuring that someone supportive will also be present). When feminists pointed out two decades ago that 'the personal is political,' it began to dawn on me that the reverse is also true, that the political is also very personal, that the kind of political work that attracts us is a function of our personality and personal history – and that there is nothing wrong with that: what interests us is most likely to be what we do well.

Again, one purpose of the chapter 8 check-list is to document many of the areas that could use a little or a lot of your help. Even that check-list is incomplete, however, and I shall certainly not attempt in this chapter to describe the full range of possibilities for action. However, a few examples will be mentioned later in this section.

How to educate others and work for change? You can do it on your own, paired with someone else, or in groups (see earlier sections in this chapter). Sandler and Hall suggest setting a limit of dealing with one issue per week,[49] but for some people, that is far too much. You might want to set your limit in terms of hours each week that you can set aside for this task. But as you set limits, do *not* feel guilty for not taking on every issue, because in the first place no one can do everything, and in the second place many of the same issues arise in dealing with nearly any topic related to women.

Another aspect of the *how* of education and action was suggested by a woman I interviewed, who said, 'Form committees, *don't ask anyone's permission to do so*, do projects, announce your findings and recommendations, and see if the shit hits the fan – and if it does, there is more political mileage you can get from that reaction.'

Still another part of the *how* is to *be creative*. Sandler and Hall

propose that women offer awards for people who come up with
innovative ideas for improving the climate for women on campus.[50] You could make up your own categories, run the contest,
choose the winners, and announce them in your university newspaper and other media.

Now let us look at a sampling of possibilities for action. A few
can be mentioned briefly:

–   Set up peer counselling programs – for graduate students, for
    new faculty, for faculty at the stages of applying for tenure or
    promotions.
–   Request that the president of your institution issue a public
    statement to the effect that sexism, racism, ageism, homopho-
    bia, and anti-disability behaviour are not acceptable or consis-
    tent with the aims of that institution.
–   Plan a campus program or workshop on the professional cli-
    mate for women (see Sandler with Hall, 1986, for a wonder-
    fully detailed description of how to go about doing this).
–   Set up a free-to-the-public series of lectures by women about
    how the women's movement has affected their work (we did
    this at the Centre for Women's Studies in Education at the
    Ontario Institute for Studies in Education and found it to be a
    terrific way to bring academic women and women from the
    wider community together).
–   Set up workshops for teachers illustrating what behaviour is
    unacceptable to many women, since some professors have
    no idea what sexism is or how it concerns them or their stu-
    dents.[51] Briskin goes even further, urging that university
    administrations collaborate with faculty associations in provid-
    ing 'extensive, and perhaps mandatory, consciousness-raising
    on issues of sexism and anti-feminism.' Briskin believes this is
    important because 'women are not solely responsible for deal-
    ing with these issues.'[52] Johnson et al. make similar proposals,
    adding that such training could be a supplement to existing
    training for department chairs on affirmative-action recruitment
    and be mandatory for search-committee chairs as well; they
    say that these sessions ought to include 'training modules on
    the "chilly climate," gender harassment, and racial harassment'
    as well.[53]

–   Write out and circulate to students information about 'the various forms of protection and redress available to them to avoid abuses of power between the student and her adviser.'[54]

–   Following the example of a group at Yale, encourage male colleagues to send a memo to all faculty urging them to be aware of the fact that women do far less talking than men in class, and asking them to do all they can to make it possible for women to speak more often.[55]

Another suggestion about what to do in the realm of education, which often overlaps extensively with action, is to make a personal decision to talk continually – or at least once a week – about how one's gender affects one's treatment and opportunities in academia. Don't allow people to *assume* that being a woman feels no different from being a man on campus.

Still another possibility, which would be relevant at some point to every woman in a faculty position, is to make sure that a list of recommendations for search, promotion, and tenure committees such as the one in appendix 3 is given to every member of the administration and of every search, tenure, or promotion committee at your institution. Also, ensure that this list is published in the faculty handbook and the relevant newspapers, as well as in more wide-ranging media, such as publications of associations in your academic field or associations of personnel from various colleges and universities.

And finally, *a word of caution*: know that, often, the way institutions 'respond' to sincere and justified objections, complaints, and requests for action is with silence, with victim-blaming replies, or with what feminists have called 'crazy-making' behaviour, which makes the protesters feel crazy and does not constitute a real response to the request or protest. As an example of the latter, an interviewee who had immigrated to the United States from an Asian country told me that when she was doing a residency in a medical specialty, she asked her supervisor for suggestions about how to prepare for a major presentation she had to make. She specifically asked if he had recommendations about what she should read, how to organize her talk, and so on. His reply was, 'Wear lipstick and a suit,' followed by poking her in the stomach and saying, '[You are] too zaftig but you have nice legs.' She filed a complaint about this treatment, and the complaints officer said that because the offender was gay, no action would be taken because 'he couldn't have meant anything by it.' She appealed this decision to the equal-opportunity counsellor, a Black woman, who took no action but told the resident she had learned in a night class that third-world women bring harassment on themselves.

If anything like this should happen to you, remember that you are *not* to blame.

Although the suggestions in this chapter often apply across a broad range of specific dilemmas or issues, it can also be important to have some ideas that are tailored to those specifics. In the next chapter, you will find some suggestions that are specific to particular stages and situations in your academic career.

7 What You Can Do: Suggestions for Specific Situations

No single book could include all the suggestions a woman in academia might need between her entry into graduate school and her retirement from academic life, but those included in this chapter were chosen to illustrate a variety of strategies and steps, each of which has been found useful by at least some women. As noted in chapter 6, however, before taking action in any situation, I strongly recommend that you check the bibliography in the back of this book and carefully read the references listed under the category relevant to the situation you are confronting. Women and men have already written a fair bit about many of these issues, and you will find much of it useful.

We shall begin with some of the issues that arise in graduate school, move to preparing your curriculum vitae as you begin your job search, and then address the job interview, issues at the time of hiring, and on-the-job, promotion, and tenure issues, and issues for women at the top of the academic ladder. Although some of the specific points apply to every academic, those included here were chosen because, on account of their socialization, women are often likely to find them problematic. As the issues at each stage of the academic career ladder are discussed, other references that give more information and advice are cited in the endnotes, and the reader is encouraged to look at those as well.

As in the previous chapter, when you read recommendations for women to organize, educate, and act about ways they are oppressed on campus, it is important to be aware that this ought to be taken on by the institution, but in reality it often is not.

Graduate school[1]

1. Explore ahead of time the implications of your chosen degree.
Some of us apply to a particular graduate program because we
feel that we know exactly how we want to spend our working
lives, and we believe that that program is the best way to begin.
But some of us apply for less well-defined reasons, such as 'My
history courses were my favourite ones during my undergraduate
years, and I jumped at the chance to spend several more years
doing work in that field.' Some women are reluctant to choose a
graduate program with plans for the future well in mind, because
even in today's world we have been taught that it is unwomanly
to take our career – or, indeed, any intellectual activities – too
seriously. In order to make optimal use of graduate school, from
choosing your first courses to selecting a thesis topic to knowing
which professional meetings to attend, it is best to know as much
as possible what you want to do when you complete your degree.
*But do not worry if you do not have a thesis topic or specific career
goal in mind during orientation week.* Whatever uncertainty you may
feel, you will have plenty of company in some of the other students, whether or not they tell you so.

Seek out and talk to people who some years ago received the
degree toward which you will be working, and ask them what
you can do in graduate school that is most likely to be helpful
after you graduate, as well as about the range of work possibilities
– both in and out of academia – available to people with that
degree. For instance, whereas in some academic departments the
people who have practical experience are the most highly regarded, in others the opposite is the case; so, if you want to teach
at a college or university, you may want to know ahead of time
what kinds of experience will help you get where you want to be.
Also ask more advanced students in your own program the same
kinds of questions, as well as which professors and courses are
the most informative and helpful and which ones should be
avoided.

2. Be aware of the financial ins and outs of graduate school.

When you were notified of your acceptance into your graduate program, you were probably given information about how to apply for teaching or research assistantships. Institutions vary in the degree to which they inform students how assistantship applications or other financial-aid forms should be filled out. In my own institution, the graduate students have a very strong union that specifies in great detail the criteria by which faculty are to rate the applicants. Thus, it does not matter whether one of us knows that a particular applicant has more teaching or work experience than she recorded on the form; if *she* failed to record it, then we are not allowed to count it. Be sure to check with a program administrator or students' union before you fill out those forms.

Even if you are a full-time student and have an assistantship, you may be forbidden from working more than a few hours a week at paid employment other than the assistantship. Thus, if you enrol full-time, you may get an assistantship but will therefore be limited in how much other money you can earn; but if you enrol only part-time, you will never get an assistantship, and your life may be more fragmented.

3. If you do have a research or teaching assistantship, ask for a job description before you begin your work, and keep careful track of both the work you do and the hours you spend. Such steps can protect you from overly demanding supervisors as well as from those who are so vague and non-directive that it takes you a while to find out what they want you to do. Ask to have the expectations for work, time, and frequency of meetings with the supervisor carefully spelled out. Furthermore, you may want to ask an assistantship supervisor to write you a letter of recommendation for a job at some point, and if you have documented your work – and given a copy to the supervisor – it will make the letter easier for her or him to write. In some assistantship programs, your supervisor's evaluation of your work this year is used to help place you in the priority list for getting an assistantship in the coming year. If that is true for yours, make sure that your supervisor fills out your evaluation form by the deadline.

4. Consider bringing many women graduate students together to ask them how money can best be spent to help them. This suggestion from Anne Innis Dagg[2] becomes increasingly important now that some universities are becoming willing, or are under pressure, to ensure that women graduate students are given fair and reasonable access to financial aid.

5. Make sure you take up a reasonable amount of space and get your share of other resources. Some women feel so lucky to get into graduate school at all that it doesn't occur to them, or they are reluctant, to demand office space, laboratory space and equipment, and a locker. As McCurdy-Myers writes, part-time students are even more likely to be marginalized in those ways than full-time students, who are less likely to be women.[3] Women, too, often report that it never occurred to them that professors' secretaries might type term papers for students – until they learned that professors were asking them to do so for some of their *male* students. This does not mean that it is right to ask a secretary to do students' work, and certainly not if it is not in their job descriptions, but it is another indication of a pervasive sex difference in expectations of assistance. A secretary may be required to type papers that are co-authored by a graduate student and a professor, but women students may assume that they themselves should do that typing, whereas men students will assume that is the secretary's work.[4] Most important, remember that if you do not ask what the department can provide, you may not find out until it is too late. So, when you begin graduate school, go straight to the administrator or faculty member who is in charge of your program, and ask what resources are available to students. If you suspect unfair distribution of these resources, enlist the help of other students or supportive faculty in documenting and reporting that unfairness, and ask that fair procedures and explicit guidelines be implemented.

6. Find out if there is space for the students in your program or the women students in your department to meet. If no such space is available, form a committee or write a petition to request that such space be set aside. This may be done within your department or through a women's centre or a women's studies program. Such space is invaluable for coming together to study, to discuss issues of common concern, to work on collaborative projects, to relax, and to trade all kinds of information about how to survive and thrive in your program.

7. As you enter graduate school, give yourself permission to feel confused and unsettled for a while. Don't fall for the mistaken belief that most people feel relaxed and at home at this point. Too many students waste a lot of energy worrying that they shouldn't be worrying. It is normal and healthy to feel uncertain and apprehensive in a new environment. Just before starting graduate school, you may have moved to a new geographical area or a new residence.[5] If you came straight from undergraduate school, you have probably been abruptly separated from many of your closest friends, and if you have been working or raising a family in between undergraduate school and now, you are likely to be concerned about your ability to meet the intellectual and social demands of academia. The switch from undergraduate courses, which are likely to be highly structured and come with clear expectations, to the less clear-cut demands of graduate education can be especially disturbing for those who already tend to feel inadequate and to blame themselves for whatever goes wrong (especially, therefore, for women).

8. Pretend that your dissertation is just an extremely time-consuming, lengthy paper that you have to write for a course. I have seen so many students drained of time and emotional energy by their fears and fantasies about what The Dissertation is supposed to involve. True, some professors feed such fears, making students feel that The Dissertation has to contain monumental discoveries or The Last Word in theoretical explorations. Your fears about not measuring up to the task of writing The Dissertation can make you assume that far more is required than actually is. Therefore, ask your reference librarian to take out about twenty of the mostly recently completed dissertations from your program. Look through them, and you will probably discover among them a wide range in length, ambitiousness of project, and competence of production. Remember, as you do this, that because you are not an expert in all of those subfields, some dissertations may seem more impressive to you than they really are. And remember that, because you will be spending at least a year and probably more on your specific topic, by the end of that time you will certainly be one of the world's experts on it.

A similar attitude can be helpful in regard to term papers and seminar presentations.

9. Check out your situation carefully in choosing paper or dissertation topics. Depending on the attitudes of the powerful people in your department, on your committee, or on the faculties where you eventually want to work, you may decide to do research in the area that interests you the most, or you may decide that that area is so controversial that you would thereby risk getting a low grade, having trouble with your committee, or not obtaining the job you want. A woman who moved to Canada from Pakistan told me, 'I wanted to write about women in situations similar to mine, but that kind of population is not considered a glamorous topic for research. Even more than wanting to stick to that topic, I wanted to get my degree, so I chose to write about something more mainstream. Now that I have my Ph.D., I do write and give workshops about racialized women.'

10. When you receive negative feedback on papers or drafts of your thesis or dissertation, do not assume automatically that they are right and you are wrong. Even world-famous full professors often receive negative feedback, some legitimate and some not, on papers and books they submit for publication. Try to evaluate honestly the worth of each comment, and do keep in mind that 'women are more likely than men to believe negative feedback on their dissertations or other work is justified, not the reviewer's error'[6] and not open to discussion or debate. Women are also more likely to believe that they can never hope to do better. Try to think of such feedback as material you can use in 'debugging' your work or honing your arguments rather than as proof that you are inadequate.

11. If there is any chance this could affect you, or if you want

to help other women whom it could affect, find out whether your university has a good maternity-leave policy for students. If it doesn't, work to get one implemented. Some academic institutions have no maternity-leave policy for graduate students whatsoever, and even where they are in place, some have provisions that are punitive.[7] The punitive aspects can be academic or financial. An example of the latter: 'A student wanted to take a maternity leave but had to give up full-time student status to do that and therefore had to turn down [a large and prestigious scholarship].[8] Still worse, this was one of those scholarships that may not be awarded to someone who has had to turn it down before.

An example of an academic problem that results from taking maternity leave is the difficulty a returning graduate student may have rejoining her previous research team (especially in the sciences) or simply catching up with the developments that appeared while she was on her leave.[9] For that reason, the proposals by the Canadian National Science and Engineering Research Council to institute one-year reorientation scholarships and three-year postdoctoral fellowship reorientation grants are particularly exciting.[10] You might wish to form a lobby group to have similar programs implemented in your area.

12. As described in chapter 6, make supportive connections with other individuals, and seriously consider forming groups for various kinds of support.[11] In a study of various kinds of graduate-school environments, Haley found that departments that actively fostered community feeling among students and faculty had more students who finished their programs quickly, published and presented papers, and won scholarships.[12] If you are in a program where female students and faculty are few, consider forming support groups that also include men who are supportive and helpful. Also consider setting up a group to review the situation in your department in order to identify areas of clear discrimination or 'chilly climate' factors.[13]

Hall and Sandler make a number of excellent recommendations aimed at warming the chilly climate for graduate-student women: 'Include classroom climate issues in student evaluations ... Hold informal meetings to discuss classroom climate and to stimulate awareness of the issues ... Set up a committee of women and men students to develop a questionnaire or survey geared to those climate issues of greatest concern on your campus.'[14] Sandler et al. also warn that these issues are especially important in fields that traditionally have included few women, because women consequently are less likely to have opportunities to work and socialize with other women there; because they are less likely to find female teachers as role models, supervisors, or mentors; because faculty are less likely to have set up support systems to help women students negotiate the bureaucratic mazes; and because there are more likely to be some professors who are simply not accustomed to having women students in their classes. But in many programs, even those that have traditionally included many women, 'women may be passed over for interesting research projects, or not invited to recreational poker games or beer drinking sessions.'[15]

13. Make sure that you write and submit papers for publication or for presentation at conferences and apply for scholarships and for research grants. If, in order to get started doing this, you have to pretend to have more self-confidence than you really have, that is perfectly fine. In regard to papers, consider using ones you have written for courses. Consult with other graduate students and with faculty in your field about which journals are most likely to accept papers on which topics. Do not be shy about asking faculty to look at and give you feedback on drafts of papers for publication before you submit them. In regard to conferences, you may have a better chance of having a presentation accepted at a large conference sponsored by your discipline's national association if you submit it through the division or section of that association under which your topic falls. For instance, many associations have divisions dealing with research on women, and the national psychological associations in North America have divisions in such areas as school psychology, community psychology, psychoanalysis, and industrial psychology, to name but a few.

In regard to applying for scholarships, your department or institution will likely have one or more officers who provide information to students about various sources of support and the procedures and guidelines for applying for them. For advice on writing research-grant applications, the same officers may be helpful; so, too, can professors in your area who have good records of obtaining such grants. Part of their job is supposed to be training students in grant-writing skills.

14. As part of your work toward obtaining a faculty position after you graduate, try to obtain some teaching experience, whether as a teaching assistant or as a lecturer or seminar leader in an undergraduate course.

15. In acquiring credentials that will help you get a faculty job, you may want to obtain work experience that is outside of academia but could be useful in your application.[16] For example, if you want to teach in an M.B.A. program, get experience in the business world, and if you want a faculty position in the sciences, consider doing some research for an independent company or a government agency.

16. Keep careful records of the work you do and the time you spend when collaborating with others. Sad to say, it is not uncommon for students to discover that other students whom they had trusted to do their share of joint projects have not carried out their commitments. It is also shockingly common for students to find that their work is used by a professor who claims it as her or his own. Some professors do this purposefully; but some men do not recognize that they are stealing work when the person who produced the work is female, because they are so accustomed to thinking of women in the helping, serving roles. And women are often inclined to minimize how unethical the professor's behaviour is, because they may minimize the importance of their own contribution to the work. Any student in such a situation with a professor is likely to feel stunned and also to feel intimidated about voicing objections or taking more formal action, since the professor clearly has more power. Furthermore, in an example given by Aisenberg and Harrington, a woman whose work was published by a senior professor without her name on it kept silent because she didn't know what her rights were and thought no one would believe her, since he had so many publications.[17]

A woman science researcher was taken out by her boss for a fancy lunch, during which he asked how she would describe her work, which was in fact ground-breaking research. She did so, and the next day she heard him present that work at a conference as though it were his own. And when I was a graduate student, a senior professor once asked me to read a set of papers on which he was to comment at an international colloquium. He claimed that he had read them but could not think of anything to say. Flattered, but nervous, I spent hours reading the papers, making careful notes, and pulling out common themes. When I told the professor, he smiled and said, 'That is what I had planned to say.' I said, 'But I thought you said you couldn't think of anything.' He said, 'Well, I had. But I wanted your unbiased opinion about the papers, and I didn't want you to be influenced by my ideas.' After the colloquium, as I typed for him the paper based on the presentation, which was going to be published in a refereed journal, I asked in a joking tone of voice, 'Why isn't my name on the title page as co-author?' Had he not looked uncomfortable and replied, 'Well, *I* thought of the ideas first,' I probably would never have had the courage to say, 'But I didn't know your ideas when I had the same ones a few hours later.' He then listed me as second author.

In such cases, having documented the work you did can be enormously helpful. Confronting people who shirk their responsibility or falsely claim your work as their own can sometimes be effective. In such a confrontation, your documentation may alarm the offender into giving you the proper credit. If you go through formal channels, such as approaching the department chairperson or a dean, your documentation will enhance your credibility.

17. As you approach the end of your dissertation, if you are interested in an academic career, consider delaying applying for teaching jobs for a while and applying for postdoctoral fellowships instead. There are several reasons to do this. First of all, in areas where jobs are few and applicants are numerous, the more publications you have, the better your chances are likely to be for getting the position you want. Time spent in postdoctoral work can give you time to publish, often beginning with the publication of your dissertation as a book or of several articles based on the dissertation. Furthermore, a postdoc can give you time to rest from the drain entailed by writing and defending a dissertation, as well as to check out possible longer-term jobs carefully and get more information about who is doing good work in your field.

18. At any point in your graduate work, consider organizing a group of students to request that seminars be held for professors about the effects of the chilly climate on the learning and achievement of women and on members of racialized groups, students who are not able-bodied, older students, and lesbian and gay students.

19. Urge your graduate-student association to push for day care and for non-punitive maternity and paternity leave for students.

20. Ensure, either on your own through inquiries to individuals or through organizing a group, that students are informed of the various forms of protection and redress available to them when faculty abuse their power over the student.[18]

21. In preparing for your defence of your dissertation, remember some helpful guidelines:

– Ask your supervisor and, depending on your relationships with them, other members of your committee, what kinds of questions one tends to be asked in the defence.
– Ask your supervisor such questions as, 'What is the purpose of the defence? What is expected of me? What will *they* (the committee) be trying to do? What exactly will be the procedure from the moment I arrive in the room?
– Consider having a friend or relative come with you and wait outside the room, for the time or times when you will be waiting for the committee to conduct its business and then vote on whether or not you passed.

- Go to the room a few days ahead of time, practise your introductory remarks there (if your institution's practice is for the student to make an opening statement).
- Ask other students to read your thesis and do a practice defence with you, asking you the toughest questions they can imagine.
- Write down the questions you are most afraid of being asked, then think carefully about what you could say, and if you still feel uncertain, discuss those issues with your supervisor and with colleagues.
- During the defence, remember that every member of your committee probably went through a defence too, and although some professors do act very nasty, most have at least some understanding of how nerve-wracking the experience is and will make some allowances if you are so nervous that you forget the question you have just been asked.
- Do not be afraid to ask for rephrasing, repetition, or clarification of any question you are asked.
- If a vague question is asked, feel free to define or focus it and answer as you wish.
- Expect at some point to feel certain that you are failing, but remember that, if that feeling comes, it is proof of your nervousness but is not by any means proof that you really are failing.
- Remember that rare is the committee that fails a student for being unable to answer one or two questions during a defence; what most committees are looking for is a reasonable degree of knowledge of the issues and material in the dissertation, a professional and undefensive attitude about the work, and a willingness to acknowledge its limitations as well as the validity of other people's interpretations of your findings or claims.

22. Be sure to read the references cited in the notes for this section of this chapter as well as others in the bibliography.

Beginning to look for jobs[19]

1. Consider applying for jobs not only in your own field but

in others as well.[20] For instance, if you are a social psychologist, depending on your research area, you might consider applying for jobs not only in psychology departments but also in sociology, criminology, or women's studies; a biologist might consider applying to a life sciences or human development program; and so on.

2. **Read the advertisements in regular publications – newspapers, newsletters, and scholarly journals – for your discipline and related ones.** Check with reference librarians, people in the relevant departments at your institution, and people in your field about which resources will list ads that might be of interest to you. Be sure to read the *Chronicle of Higher Education* and, in Canada, *University Affairs* and the *Canadian Association of University Teachers Bulletin*. For jobs advertised by 'equal opportunity employers' or for jobs specifically related to women, don't miss the *Women's Review of Books*.

3. **Tell everyone you know that you are looking for a job and, insofar as possible, what kinds of jobs interest you.**

4. **Attend large conferences that have job placement services, and enrol as early as possible with those services.** At conferences, interviews between those wanting to hire and those wanting to be hired are often set up. Even when such interviews do not lead directly to a job, some interviewers are funds of information and can give you names of other people to contact.

5. **Read advertisements or make personal contacts even in the late spring and the summer, since last-minute positions sometimes become available.**

6. **When you ask people to write letters of recommendation for you, give them your c.v.; a copy of the job advertisement, and a note about which of your qualifications you think would be especially important for them to mention.**

7. **You may wish to try to arrange to see the letters people are sending out about you, either by asking outright if you can see them or by asking them to send a copy to your department's file or to your institution's placement office.**[21] Legally, you have access to both of the latter kinds of files.

8. **Plan to send out far more applications than you ever dreamed possible.** The job market in your field may be very tight,

and even if it is not, the more applications you send, the better your chances of finding work.

9. Expect that it may take several years before you find the job you want. Bronstein suggests aiming for four years and, in the meantime, doing postdoctoral training and research, taking soft-money research positions, or filling in for faculty on leave in one-year, temporary jobs.[22] She advises that you consider these kinds of work not as setbacks but rather as opportunities to make contacts and to produce work that will help you get the job you really want.

10. Be sure to read the references cited in the notes for this section of this chapter as well as others in the bibliography.

11. If you are a member of a non-dominant group, consider registering with the Minority Faculty Registry (address given in the bibliography's 'Non-dominant groups' section). The Registry collects one-page c.v.'s from 'minority candidates who wish to be considered for faculty teaching positions,' as well as a list of colleges and universities that participate in that registry.

Preparing your curriculum vitae[23]

As you prepare to apply for an academic job, a promotion, or tenure, you need to have a detailed, professional-looking résumé, which is usually called by the Latin term curriculum vitae, in which you give the details of your work history. Your home institution probably has a format that it prefers or recommends for your curriculum vitae, or c.v., as it is informally called.

1. Make sure you include all the relevant information for the job for which you are currently applying. This may entail thinking analytically about the skills and activities that have been involved in each thing you have done. For instance, your current c.v. may include primarily your history as a scholar and writer; if, then, you want to apply for a job that includes some administrative responsibilities, you should add to your c.v. a section that details administrative responsibilities you have previously carried out. For instance, you may already have listed an item such as 'Director, Community Psychology Program, 1986–1987.' When you apply for a position that may include membership, say, on an admissions committee or an ethical approval committee for research projects, it would be a good idea either to add a succinct listing of the administrative duties you carried out as Director of the Community Psychology Program or to include such a listing in the letter of application that you send when you first apply for the new job.

If you are a graduate student applying for your first faculty position, it is probably safe to use the c.v. format of your home institution. However, soon after you get your first job, you should revise your c.v. in accordance with the format of your current institution. This is because contract renewal, promotion, tenure, and merit-raise decisions are based heavily on your record, and your institution's preferred c.v. format is probably designed to make it as easy as possible for the committees that make these decisions to spot those accomplishments of yours that are relevant to the decision in question.

At my institution, just as an example, we are requested to use the following format:

Date _____

Name _____

Current rank _____

Address _____

Degrees (institution, year granted, field of study) _____

_____

Employment history _____

Honours _____

_____

Scholarly and professional activities

(a)   Executive and editorial positions _____

(b)   Memberships _____

(c)   Other _____

Career number of theses and dissertations supervised (divided according to degree program of student and according to those completed and those in progress) _____

_____

Completed theses and dissertations supervised (by degree program, student's name, title of dissertation, and year completed) _____

_____

Career number of thesis and doctoral-committee memberships (divided according to degree program of student and according to those completed and those in progress) _____

_____

Courses taught (by course number, title, and level: graduate or undergraduate) _____

_____

Funded research and field development activities _____

_____

Unfunded research and field development activities _____

_____

Invited addresses and workshops _____

_____

Publications

(a)   Doctoral dissertation _____

(b)   Books _____

(c)   Monographs _____

(d)   Special issues of journals edited _____

(e)   Curriculum units written _____

(f)   Chapters written _____

(g)   Papers (in refereed journals) _____

(h)   Papers (unrefereed journals) _____

(i)   Papers (published in conference proceedings) _____

(j)   Papers (presented at conferences, not published) _____

(k)   Other publications (include book-review, newspaper, and magazine articles) _____

Additional teaching experience _____

Additional clinical experience _____

Other _____

You may also want to include time and experience spent in counselling and advising students and work on committees in your institution or professional association.

2. Remember that, because of human variability, you cannot predict for certain exactly what a search committee will want to see and not see on your c.v. Even the experts disagree on such points as whether or not you should include summer-school courses you have taught (some imply they are not significant enough, but I do not agree[24]), so read and consider what the authors listed in the notes and in the bibliography under 'Job searches' have to say. Then, if possible, talk to some from the settings where you are applying, to find out what their preferences and conventions seem to be.

Women who have done research about lesbian issues or who are openly lesbian, as well as women of colour who have done research on ethnic and racial issues and anyone who has done work in women's studies, face the dilemma of whether or not to list such work. An interviewee who described herself as a 'quietly out' lesbian told me she did not list her papers about lesbians on her c.v. when she was applying for tenure, because she felt that the committee was likely to include some people who were homophobic, and she felt quite vulnerable. Now, however, as she applies for a promotion and feels she has a strong reputation as a good teacher and researcher, she plans to include such work.

3. Be aware that a particular danger for women is their learned tendency to minimize or even fail to mention their experiences and achievements. In particular, women are likely not to think of mentioning service work they have done, whereas such activities as having served on departmental program committees or done work with your graduate student organization can be good items for your c.v. To counteract this tendency to minimize what you have done, when preparing your c.v., pretend you are a press agent preparing someone else's c.v. Throw modesty right out the window. Be as straightforward and accurately descriptive as you possibly can.

4. **Be sure to read the references cited in the notes for this section of this chapter as well as others in the bibliography.**

Interviews[25]

1. **As with your c.v., when you prepare for a job interview and when you are actually in the interview, try to compensate for what is likely to be your lack of self-confidence and undue modesty by pretending you are your own press agent.** Remember that a good press agent does not make false claims but does take care to let others know what is skilled, exciting, and interesting about the client.

2. **Consider the fact that, unlike you, most or all of the members of the search committee who will interview you are likely to be white males.** Think about how you feel about that, such as whether you are particularly apprehensive about coming across as 'too feminine' to be intellectually disciplined or whether, as a Black woman, you will not only be trying to demonstrate your competence but will also probably be dealing with their overt or covert racism. Talk with as many different kinds of people as possible about the ways in which you might handle such problems. And keep in mind, during the interview, that if you feel inadequate, it just might be because the interviewers are in some ways different from yourself or are intractably biased against people like you.

3. **Keep in mind that some interviewers will use the interview as an opportunity to demonstrate their own knowledge or achievements, to make themselves look good, possibly at your expense.** Women in particular are likely to feel that such an interviewer is not so much obnoxious as aware of the interviewee's inadequacies. Remember that such feelings are probably not justified. Operate on the assumption that you *are* reasonably competent, even if someone is trying to cast you in a bad light.

4. When someone from a search committee calls to ask you to come for an interview, ask what it is about your qualifications that interests the committee, what questions or reservations they have, and what in particular they are looking for.[26] You could say that you feel it is important that both sides try to determine whether or not it would be a good match. What is said about their interest in you and their reservations may help guide you as you prepare for the visit, and there may turn out to be reasons you would choose not to take the job even if it were offered to you; for instance, they may say, 'We don't want someone who is going to focus on research in such-and-such an area.'

5. Don't worry about dressing the way you think they want you to dress, but do dress in a way that feels comfortable for you – keeping in mind that some people would interpret sloppy jeans and sneakers as a lack of respect for them. Even if you think the latter attitude is unjustified, it makes sense not to dress so aberrantly that you alienate just enough people unlike yourself to make it impossible for you to join a department that includes some people with whom you want to work.

6. If you are asked to give a lecture, prepare very carefully, but try your best not to read it word for word. Though aware of how important it is to make human contact with one's audience, women often feel so unsure about their ability to present a good talk that they stick closely to a prepared text. This is likely to alienate your audience, however. Furthermore, one aim of your presentation ought to be to let you and the audience get an accurate feeling for whether you like each other's styles – and reading a paper can seriously interfere with this aim. If you choose a topic with which you are very familiar and which you find exciting, rather than tackling a new subject or one on which your ideas are still pretty vague, you are more likely to be able to relax, be yourself, and, most important, interest and excite your listeners.

7. Before your visit and interview, think carefully about how your daily life at that institution might go, and on that basis prepare a list of questions you genuinely want answered. Picture yourself teaching courses, advising students, attending faculty meetings, doing your own or collaborative research, and going to departmental parties – and ask yourself what factors would probably enhance and what factors would probably reduce your sense of joy and freedom in doing those things. Then construct questions designed to find out about those factors, such as the frequency and nature of faculty-administration contact, expectations about teaching and student advising loads, the friendliness of colleagues outside working hours, the ease and support for doing collaborative research, and the institution's readiness to provide seed money for beginning new research.

Also ask friends, colleagues, and more senior people about the range of questions you might ask about the whole spectrum of possible issues. Consider asking where the department feels their current needs lie, since ideally you and they want to know in advance if you and they will be a good fit. What salary range are they considering for this appointment? When would you be allowed to apply for tenure? (See the section on hiring for a more detailed list of items to consider.) If the institution has graduate students and you are interested in being appointed to the graduate faculty so that you can teach and supervise advanced students, find out beforehand whether you would qualify for such an appointment. You also might want to ask about the criteria for admission of graduate students, information that might help you determine whether or not you want to work with them. Bronstein urges that you ask questions about the program, the students, the teaching load, research assistance, secretarial help, computer facilities, research space, and available funds for equipment, travel, and library books. She also notes that it is useful to ask about the cost of housing, the climate, and the quality of life for someone in your situation (single, lesbian, married, widowed, and so on), although she recommends not mentioning whether or not you have a husband, lover, or children. Bronstein also suggests asking about the department's and the university's hiring and retention practices: 'How often does a junior faculty member get reviewed for reappointment, and when does she or he come up for tenure? Have the junior faculty most recently hired been reappointed, and what percentage of eligible faculty has in fact gotten tenure? What are the bases for raises, reappointment, and tenure decisions – for example, how much emphasis is put on research, how much on teaching, and how much on service? How many women are in the department, and are they tenured or on tenure track?'[27]

If you meet an administrator, says Bronstein, it's a good idea to show your interest in larger academic issues: 'Ask about faculty–administration relations – who sets academic policies, how are standards for raises, promotion, and tenure determined, what is the university record for tenuring faculty, and are there any special affirmative-action efforts underway?'[28]

8. Ask other students or friendly faculty members at your current institution to rehearse your interview with you before you go. Ask faculty what kinds of things search-committee members are likely to ask, say how you would respond, and ask them for feedback on your answers.[29] Consider carefully what strategy is best for you: Do you want to lay on the line exactly who you are and what you most want to do, on the theory that you and they need to find out right away whether you will be a good match for them, or do you want to take the less risky route of concealing your fondest career dreams until after you are hired, promoted, or given tenure? For instance, if you long to do applied research rather than 'basic,' but the department prefers the latter (or if you are a feminist but the department is known for not hiring feminists, or if you want to do research with disabled women but the department considers that to be 'fringe' work), are you willing to do what they want until your position is secure?

Think carefully ahead of time about what you might say in reply to the often-dreaded question, 'What is your research plan for the next, say, five to ten years?' If they ask you that question, do not be alarmed, and do not assume that you are supposed to know right now what you will actually have accomplished five years down the road. Do not assume that the other candidates for the job will know the answer to that question or that you will be obliged to implement your answer if you do get the job. Keep in mind that search-committee members who ask such a question are likely to be looking for signs that (a) you can think in terms of more than the 'one-small-study, one tiny variation on a previous study' approach to research, and (b) you have a grasp of a number of fundamental issues, debates, and questions in the field. So, plan a response that speaks to those concerns, such as, 'I've been doing some interviews with nurses about what they have found most and least useful in their training, and I plan to use that as part of a wider investigation of manifestations of the distribution of power in the patient–nurse–physician–hospital relationships' or 'I'm investigating differences between people who do and those who do not have cirrhosis of the liver after drinking equal amounts of alcohol for equally long periods of time, and I hope ultimately in this way to learn something about genetic bases for individual differences in susceptibility to organ breakdown.' Such statements should be followed by a sentence that begins with the words, 'My next step after doing those investigations ...'

9. Try to talk with graduate and undergraduate students in the department alone. Ask them about their experiences, both good and bad, about factionalism and supportiveness in the department, about how it feels to be there.

10. Remember that a generally good university can have a bad department, and a great department can be found at a generally poor-quality university.

11. Remember that, if they ask you questions about your personal life, that is an infringement of your legal rights. You do not have to answer such questions. Plan a simple statement that you can use if inappropriate questions are asked; for example, 'Perhaps we could use our limited time here to focus some more on the work.' If they persist in asking you personal questions, you will probably want to point out that it is not considered to be a legitimate part of a job interview – and be sure to document those events the minute you have a chance. If you are turned down for the job, you might want to have a record of the irregularities that were part of the interview process.

12. Consider the principle that, if you cannot 'be yourself' as

much as possible during a visit and interview, then neither you nor they will be able to judge how compatible you will be if you actually go to work there.

13. Try to enjoy yourself as much as you can. This is a chance for you to learn a great deal – about the program and department you are visiting, about the work of the people with whom you spend time on your visit, and about how to do better at your next interview. And as Bronstein points out, even if you are not hired there, you may make contacts that will be helpful in finding other jobs or in developing other aspects of your career later on.

14. Be sure to read the references cited in the notes for this section of this chapter as well as others in the bibliography.

At the time of hiring[30]

Everyone wanted to hire a woman. Of course, they didn't want just any woman. They wanted a woman who had strong teaching and research credentials, a solid list of publications or publication potential, expertise in a specific area of psychology, who was registered or eligible for registration, who would be active in clinical work and supervision as well as research, who could provide a supportive and positive role model for female students, and whose feminine perspective would contribute to the growth of the discipline, department, and university. The first time Pollyanna Ph.D. heard this list of requirements, she thought the interviewer was teasing her (which may be why she was not offered the job).

DEBORAH HAY[31]

1. Ask in detail about your contract. You should never accept a job without having a written contract. It may be an individual contract, or it may be a collective agreement if you will be part of a faculty association or union. What does it say? Does it specify your duties concretely? Are the criteria for renewal of contract, promotion, tenure, merit increases, and firing clearly spelled out? Are the relevant weightings that will be given to each of those criteria specified? What items are covered in the contract – moving expenses to get you to your new job (if you have to relocate), salary, insurance of various kinds, pensions, retirement options and restrictions, office and laboratory space and equipment, travel and professional-development funds, secretarial assistance, research and teaching assistance? Who decides how many and which courses you will teach, and how is that decided? In our youth-obsessed culture, too few women consider pension and retirement issues, but these are of tremendous importance for all women, especially for those who begin careers relatively late in life.

2. For any items in the above list that are not spelled out in your contract, talk with the chair of your department, the dean, or whoever is in charge of such decisions. Make sure that the details are clear and acceptable to you, and then send that person a memorandum in which you document what you two have agreed on. Be aware that it is not unusual to find that little information is offered you, and that you have to ask for it. In one study, 44 per cent of the women faculty 'said that the chair of their department had not been helpful to them in clarifying job performance expectations.'[32] In your discussion, ask such questions as, 'If I am to share a secretary with Professor Y, then when each of us needs work done, who decides what takes priority, and how is that decision made?' In your memo, say that your understanding from your discussion was that you will receive X amount of secretarial assistance, etc., and ask the administrator to write back to you to confirm these details. Word that request so that the administrator's failure to send a confirmation will clearly indicate that she or he agrees with you.

3. If you deviate from the norm in your department, get it in your contract or in a memo that your unusual work will count for tenure. This should be discussed in the kind of conversation outlined above. If possible, make sure that the weight given to that work is specified in advance – for instance, 'Although she will be doing more teaching and less research during her first two

years, this is because of the department's intensified teaching needs
at this time, and in the deliberations about renewing her contract,
her teaching will be given the same weight that the combination
of teaching and research are ordinarily given.'

**4. When you are offered a particular salary, job category, and
resources (see above), be sure to negotiate for more and better.**
Some unions will help you with this process if you ask. For anyone,
the jump in income from a graduate student's or part-time lecturer's pittance to nearly *any* full-time faculty salary can sound so
tremendous that it might seem greedy to ask for more. However,
many people – and women in particular – feel either too unworthy
to negotiate or simply uncomfortable because they have never
done it before and don't know what is reasonable. You can remedy
the latter by checking with the dean's office and with friendly
faculty members about the range of salaries and other relevant
information. You can remedy the former by role-playing ahead of
time and by pretending, when you begin the negotiations, that
you are someone who is supremely self-confident and has a certain
amount of chutzpah. Remember that, if you start with a relatively
low salary, since salary increases usually proceed one prescribed
step at a time, one year at a time, it is nearly impossible to catch
up to where you should be.

Remember that you *do not need to feel grateful* for whatever
money, job level, and resources they offer you at first, because
administrators are paid not only to hire good people but also to
save money for their institution.

If you do *not* negotiate, you will probably regret it later. Many
new faculty members simply do not realize how many issues at
the time of hiring are not dealt with according to hard-and-fast
rules. Women faculty have often been assigned heavier course-
loads of introductory classes than men at the same rank.[33] And
in most institutions, an assistant professor can be hired at any one
of a number of salary levels, and 'the initial salary is usually determined in discussion or negotiation with the Chair of the unit
doing the hiring.'[34] Backhouse et al. were told the following, not
atypical story by a woman about her first job: when she was being
hired, she said, she did negotiate and felt good about it initially,

because 'I ended up with $3000 over his original offer. I signed the contract.' The next day, however, 'I found out that a male had been hired with eleven years' teaching experience and one publication. I had sixteen years' teaching experience and two publications. He got a salary of $18,000 more than I did.'[35]

According to Bronstein, it is a good idea to find out what your recently hired peers are receiving and aim for the upper end of that range, because '(1) you will have more money for yourself, which can be especially helpful when you are relocating; (2) perceptions of a person's worth are affected by the amount of money she or he is paid ... (3) the annual raise at your institution [is very likely to be calculated] as a percentage of your current salary ...; and (4) you will be recognized as someone to be reckoned with, rather than ignored or overlooked, when it comes to distributing departmental resources in the future.'[36] Bronstein also suggests that you say you had a higher figure in mind than the one the administrator names, and give some reasons you think that is warranted, such as your postdoctoral training, publications, teaching experience, or general life experience that can be brought to bear on your work. She recommends that, if you have received two offers, you say you are trying to choose between this and another that would be hard to turn down, and name the figure they have offered you, if it is higher.

When salary has been agreed on, negotiate for other things, like moving expenses, a computer, laboratory equipment, seed money for research, and release from teaching time the first year so you can get your research started or, if necessary, your dissertation finished.[37]

In fact, *some* administrators will try to get away with anything. Some women have been hired to work full-time but on part-time salaries, have been given no benefits that full-timers are supposed to receive, have not been allowed to accumulate sabbatical leave time, and have not been allowed to vote in departmental meetings. One woman told me that a dean informed her calmly that they would not give her any benefits such as health insurance, since she could surely get those from her husband. Heed the warning of a female associate professor who told Johnson et al. that 'access to departmental resources are only available to those who deliberately and relentlessly ask for it ... and one must know that it is necessary to ask![38] Johnson et al. further report, based on their data, that 'women in the social sciences and humanities complained of inadequate clerical and technical help. In contrast with male colleagues, many women said they did most of their own clerical work. One faculty member even paid for a research assistant out of her own salary.'[39] And Larkin reports the experience of one woman who said the administration was disappointed after hiring her, upon learning that she could not type.[40] They had assumed that she could and that, therefore, they could save money on secretarial services for her. They had not expected this 'qualification' from the men. These women should have negotiated better working conditions for themselves at the time of hiring.

5. Ask the dean or other top administrator if the institution provides any assistance in handling the debt that you are bringing with you from graduate school.

6. If you are considering accepting a part-time faculty job, be aware of the risks involved (see appendix 1). None of the risks described below is meant to frighten you away from accepting a part-time job, since you may have reasons for preferring to work part-time in academia, or that may be all that is currently available. But it is important for you to know ahead of time what some of the danger areas might be.[41]

You may have few or no benefits such as health insurance, a pension plan, or leave time. You will probably have no time built into your contract to do research, and getting the next job or a full-time one may depend substantially on your producing research-based publications. You may be told at the last minute what you will have to teach, thus giving you inadequate time to prepare[42] and perhaps resulting in poor teaching evaluations from your students, which would make it more difficult to get the next job. Your salary will likely be decided using a lower pay scale than for full-timers. Some search committees find it hard to take seriously the candidacy of a part-timer who is applying for a full-time position.[43] You may even be vulnerable in ways you had not suspected, as illustrated by the interviewee who told me, 'My husband had a full-time, tenure-stream job, and I had a part-time one at the same university. He got into political fights, and they fired me because they couldn't touch him. This left me particularly vulnerable financially when my husband left me shortly thereafter.'

As Gordon and Breslauer note, 'Both Lundy and Warme [1986, 1988] in Canada and Aisenberg and Harrington [1988] in the United States have shown that women consider part-time work a foot in the academic door, an opening prior to the procurement of a full-time position. It then comes as a shock to them to learn that teaching experience as a part-timer is not highly valued in the competition for academic jobs.'[44]

7. Do not assume you have to prove you know everything and can be all things to all people in the department. In other words, beware of what Symons calls the 'Hercules game' in job searches: 'This game is played by departments who want their applicants to know everything about anything. This includes text books they would use in second year courses they could be asked to teach and how to solve some of the roadblocks in the research programs of some of the interviewing faculty.'[45]

8. If you are offered a job, be aware that you do not have to give them an answer immediately.[46] You may ask for a few weeks to decide, saying you are interested but have other possibilities in the works.

9. Ask that they send you an offer in writing,[47] since a spoken offer alone carries little or no legal weight.

10. If you receive one offer and have not heard from other places where you have applied, let the search committee chairs or department heads at the other places know that you have had a firm offer and that you want to know what stage they have reached in their searches.[48] You need not tell them the name of the place from which you have an offer.

11. If you are not hired, ask for feedback from some of the places where you applied.[49] Tell them you are interested in the reasons your application was rejected because you may want to strengthen those areas.

12. Be sure to read the references cited in the notes for this section of this chapter as well as others in the bibliography.

On the job[50]

1. Remember that during the first months – or even the first year – of any new job, virtually everyone feels insecure. Do not confuse your lack of self-confidence with a lack of ability. For the first months, you will be unsure what to do about many issues (for instance, when students complain that you don't give them enough time to discuss the readings you have assigned; when a student you barely know asks that you write a letter of recommendation for her application to graduate school). When you begin each class you are teaching, remind yourself that your task is not to pronounce the definitive word on a particular topic but simply to present some information or some ideas from one or more perspectives and encourage the students to think and to question. Do not assume that as a professor you ought to know all the answers to questions students might ask. Most of us recall that our own best teachers were those who were excited by thinking and exploring and who weren't afraid to admit that they didn't know an answer.

You can also expect to discover that there are important answers to questions you had not even thought to ask (such as, Is the decision about giving a deferred grade to a student who claims to have had an emotional crisis the day of the final examination completely at your discretion, and do you need documentation from the student's physician in order to do so?). That is all part of growing into any new job, so do not think of yourself as abnormally clueless. Don't be afraid to ask for information and for consultations with colleagues, department and program heads, and deans about matters of principle or style.

As a junior faculty member, you are even less likely than others to have much choice or flexibility, which can make you feel even more insecure because you feel so overwhelmed and trapped. This situation is all the more problematic if you have taken a faculty position while still trying to finish your dissertation and if your contract was contingent on your completing the dissertation by a certain deadline. If this applies to you, be sure to find out to what extent your keeping or losing the job *really* depends on getting your doctorate by a certain deadline, since in some settings such requirements are hard and fast, whereas in others they are far more flexible.

2. Recognize that there is a wide range of ways to cope with the pressures of the job, and within reason most of those are normal and even healthy. Psychology professor Cannie Stark-Adamec reports, 'You see, one of the ways I cope with the work overload is to take on more work. My favourite stress-reducer is to get my teeth into more research'[51] – perhaps not everyone's favourite coping strategy but nevertheless sometimes a healthy one. Others try physical exercise, meditation, persistent movie-going, or political action.

3. Seek all the advice you can about how to juggle the various demands of your job, as well as how to balance those with your personal life. Do not lose sight of the fact that, as a junior faculty member and also as a woman, you are likely to have a disproportionately heavy workload imposed on you in terms of teaching, advising, supervising, and committee work. The overload is likely to be even worse if you are involved in women's studies,[52] partly because of the rapidly increasing demand for courses, advisers, supervisors, role models, and speakers by students who are interested in the field; partly because administrators are under pressure to implement affirmative-action or employment-equity and sexual-harassment programs and to create and run status-of-women offices; and partly because of requests for you to review manuscripts and grant proposals, to represent your group(s) in professional associations, to speak out publicly about women's issues, and to deal with the media.[53] These demands tend repeatedly to draw from the same, relatively small pool of interested faculty. The situation can be even more demanding for women from non-dominant groups, who may be asked to represent not only their sex but also their race in such positions: 'The very few women of colour on faculty encounter escalating pressure as the universities attempt to address institutionalized racism.'[54]

Ask more senior colleagues what they found to be the most time-consuming and least-productive drains on their energy. What pitfalls would they warn you to avoid? What are their techniques for avoiding burn-out? What do they think is a reasonable amount of time to spend preparing for a course lecture? Be sure to check with a range of people about such questions. What general principles and detailed, practical tips have they found most helpful in balancing work-life and personal life? Finding out as much as you can about not only the written rules but also the unwritten guidelines for merit increases, promotions, and tenure at your institution (see chapter 3) will help you decide how to set your priorities.

4. Spend substantial time making connections with other people. See the suggestions in chapter 6 under the heading, 'Reach out and touch someone,' and apply them to your current situation. Also, read Rose's chapter in *Career Guide for Women Scholars* (1986) about building a professional network. Perhaps you can ask congenial senior faculty members to advise you about the issues listed in no. 1 above or to help you prepare, beginning immediately, for your eventual application for tenure. Explore ways, such as attending conferences or serving on committees of your professional organization, of making contact with colleagues working in your field with whom you can exchange ideas and support and who can advise you on ways of making your work known, attracting research funding, and so on. Ask colleagues to look at drafts of papers before you present them at conferences or submit them for publication in scholarly journals.

Before oral presentations, arrange to rehearse in front of at least one honest friend who will give you suggestions about your ideas and your delivery. As noted in chapter 6, if you work in the hinterlands, establish and maintain a network with people in other universities for purposes of providing mutual support, both from a distance and when you are together at conferences, and so that you can write letters for each other for tenure, promotion, and grants.

Consider getting more involved in your faculty union or association, which might already be doing or could be convinced to do work such as the following that would benefit you:[55]

– Conduct educational programs for administrators and administrative committees promoting equity.
– Negotiate new criteria for pay and career advancement.
– Make information about university personnel practices available to faculty women.
– Support status-of-women committees, and give them a mandate to affect policy.
– Push for pay and employment equity, daycare, and nonpunitive maternity and paternity leaves for faculty.
– Lobby the administration to set out a formal policy involving the assignment of credit and a certain amount of weight to committee work done when deciding on merit awards and promotions.

Ask that your institution, department, or program organize discussion groups to deal with such issues as some students' discomfort and uncertainty about relating to women faculty or some students' expectations that women faculty more than men ought to honour requests for special treatment, such as extending a deadline, taking a test late, or giving help outside of class.

5. Seek help from colleagues in planning your research program for the near and perhaps the more distant future. Think carefully about how you would *want* to spend your research time during the coming years, if you could do anything you liked. Choose your research area with care. You may wish to discuss your research interests with your department chair and senior colleagues, to get a feeling for whether or not they believe such research is important, since they or people like them will be making decisions later on about how far you can progress on the academic ladder.[56] Depending on their reactions, you will at least be aware of the nature of their concerns or prejudices, and you may wish to change your focus or, if not, attempt to educate them about the signifi-

cance of such work.[57] Some faculty choose to do research in two
areas, one mainstream and the other not, in order to reduce the
knee-jerk prejudices directed their way.[58] You may wish, for instance, to alternate presenting research at feminist and mainstream
conferences and publishing in feminist and mainstream journals.

Then ask advice from colleagues, from the research office on
your campus, and from officers of granting agencies about the best
way to do your desired research, in view of agencies' current funding guidelines. In any field, some topics and research questions
are likely to be more respected and to be awarded more grant
money than others, and ways can sometimes be found to connect
the work you most want to do with those topics and questions.
Especially if your work is in the sciences, your whole career could
be shaped by the first research grant you receive, so ideally your
topic will be an important one, with great potential for future
research – part of a research *program*, not just a one-time project.

Think about whether you are happiest doing library or basic
research or working on research that requires direct contact with
people in some community or other.

Remember that it can be harder for women than men to obtain
research funding for a number of reasons:

–   Women are often more reluctant even to apply for funding, because they suspect their work isn't good enough.
–   Women often feel daunted by a grant-application process that
seems too mystifying or demanding.
–   Women are less likely to belong to the networks through
which they learn of the most likely sources of funding for their
kind of work, the particular people to contact about funding,
and such details of procedure as whether an applicant to a particular source is expected to recommend reviewers for her proposal.[59]
–   Projects dealing with women are less likely than projects dealing with men to be funded by many foundations and agencies.
(Dagg and Thompson report, for example, that in 1985–6, the
Social Sciences and Humanities Research Council of Canada
funded 797 research projects with over $24 million, but only 8

per cent primarily involved women as individuals or as a class.)[60]
- Most professors who decide what research to fund are white men, and so are most of the people who write letters of support.[61]

For advice about and assistance with all of the above, as well as on the many ins and outs of writing a grant proposal, go to the research office on your campus, and also talk to people who have been successful in attracting grant money. They ought to be able to tell you which funding sources are most likely to be interested in your work. Also, see such useful sources of information as Daniels' chapter on 'Acquiring skills for the funding search.'[62]

6. Remember that, as a teacher, your words can pack more of a wallop with students than you may suspect. Especially if you feel at all unsure of yourself, it may not occur to you that your flippant remark the first day of class about what a tough grader you are may strike terror in the hearts of your students. Some new faculty write mostly negative comments on students' papers, assuming that students will know that anything not criticized is OK; but students with such teachers usually believe either that their own work is no good, that the teacher is ruthless, or both. Some women faculty in particular fear that handing out praise as well as criticism, whether in class or on papers, will get them branded as intellectually soft (see chapter 4).

7. Part way through each course (at least for your first couple of years of teaching), ask students to fill out evaluation forms. Keep in mind as you read them that students can be tough in their evaluations, and do not assume that every criticism is warranted or accurate. But do read them with an open mind, look for patterns, and consider making changes in keeping with the evaluations. As a teacher, you can model ideal learning by showing an openness to constructive criticism. Be careful, however, because if they tell you the workload or assignments ought to be changed, you can get yourself tangled in legal issues, since the handing out of the course outline and assignment sheets at the beginning of the semester is considered a legal contract between you and the students. If, part way through a course, you want to make changes that go much beyond your own lecturing style, check with your program or department head about any restrictions or procedural technicalities you ought to know before making those changes. For instance, in some institutions, a professor may change an assignment if the majority of the class votes to agree to it.

8. If your students are complaining about your teaching or if they are falling asleep in class, or if you are not sure what aspects of your teaching need improvement, ask a colleague who is known to be a good teacher to observe you and give you feedback. Or, see if your institution provides the service of videotaping you as you teach, then assigning someone to give you suggestions for improvement. Ask specific questions about how to cope with difficulties in the classroom or laboratory and how you might revise your course outline and assignments.[63] Do not, however, feel that you have to follow whatever suggestions are forthcoming; a woman who began her teaching career in a prestigious dental school told me that the woman her institution employed to give feedback on teaching focused almost totally on the lecturer's clothing, even offering to show her a secondhand store where she could find colour-coordinated purses and high-heeled shoes at low prices.

9. Don't put off submitting papers for journals and conference presentations until you are certain that the work is perfect. That day will never come, and little or no work ever reaches that standard. For helpful advice on publishing your work, read Stake's chapter in Suzanna Rose's book, *Career Guide for Women Scholars*.[64] Also, trade papers with a colleague, and give each other feedback. Find out where the best and most highly regarded journals are in your field, and seriously consider aiming for those,[65] keeping in mind that you are likely to underestimate your chances of producing work that is good enough to be published there. (Remember that the editors of some journals more than others tend to ensure that work is accepted or rejected on the basis of its merits, rather than because of who the author is, or who the reviewers suspect the author might be, for journals that use 'blind' review.)

10. Log your achievements as you go, entering them in the appropriate places on your c.v. Women often neglect to do this, out of their learned 'feminine' modesty or simply because they are too busy to stop to think about what might be helpful when the time comes for contract renewal, merit increase, promotion, or tenure. Be sure to include the committee work that you do, probably under the heading of 'Service to the university or the discipline.' This category can include anything from work on developing course-evaluation forms to organizing departmental colloquia to working in a professional association of your discipline.

11. If your department regularly does a review of faculty members' work, make certain that this is done for you and that you receive a copy of the evaluation. If such a review is not part of the routine, request that it be done for you, so that you will know in which areas you need to improve. Such documents may also make it more difficult for you to be penalized later on (when you apply for renewal, a promotion, or tenure) for something about which you were not informed earlier. If there are errors or biased comments in the evaluation, write a reply, documenting the errors and bias wherever possible.

12. When you are criticized, ask for clarification. For instance, if you are told you are uncooperative and uncollegial, ask the person who makes the remark to give a specific example, so that you can then decide whether or not there is merit in the criticism and, if there is, you can know what you need to change and decide whether or not you wish to do so.[66]

13. Just say 'no.' As Sandler and Hall put it, when demands are made on you, 'recognize that refusing the request is one of your options. Offer to work with others to explore ways to get the task done, such as rotating it,'[67] for instance, but do not feel that you have to agree to whatever anyone asks you to do.

When you are asked to do extra work, do not assume that if you show what a nice person you are by agreeing to do it, you will be rewarded for that. Don't take chances: say that you will do the extra work *if* you can be released from some other task *or* if someone in authority will put it in writing that you should receive extra credit for this when you apply for contract renewal, merit increase, promotion, or tenure.

Women have actually been penalized for agreeing to do extra work: 'the department did not give them recognition for their willingness to be more flexible by taking on new courses in order to accommodate departmental needs. Instead, they were penalized if their inexperience resulted in lower student evaluations.'[68] Even if you are not penalized like that, taking on extra work for no credit can be harmful. A professor told me that, when a man in her department became physically quite debilitated, she agreed to help teach his course. This left her with less time to do her regular work, and she got nothing for it beyond feeling like 'a good girl' for helping out, she said. Now, she wishes she had asked for extra money or absolution from some of her other responsibilities. Particularly if you are a woman, say many of the women I interviewed, taking on additional burdens in the workplace does not tend to increase most people's appreciation of you (after all, each person probably only knows about some of the things you do), whereas asking for more pay or to be excused from committee work in exchange for taking on other tasks makes it clear that your time is worth something. Remember, though, that if your department chair or dean agrees to such compensation or trading, get that agreement on paper.

The Committee on Women in Psychology of the American Psychological Association cautions women not to take on too many departmental and university service activities, but warns further that 'turning down a committee appointment may incur greater costs for women and ethnic minorities. This may be perceived as irresponsible, unappreciative, or lazy. The same behavior by a white male is often accepted and may even be praised.'[69]

As you mull over the question of whether to say 'no' to a particular request, consider as one factor in your decision the possibility that you may turn down an opportunity you won't be offered again. Ask yourself whether that would feel like a relief or an unfortunate loss.

14. Put some effort into trying to be collegial in your depart-

ment, but realize that in some settings it will be 'very difficult, if not impossible, to establish collegiality no matter how hard you try.'[70] 'If you find yourself in such a dysfunctional situation,' advises the Committee on Women in Psychology, 'it is important to recognize the antifemale or antiminority stance and not blame yourself for being unable to achieve the unattainable.'[71] In fact, they point out, it is poignant that women and members of non-dominant groups are expected to try to be collegial even while they are being excluded.

15. Develop techniques for dealing with sexist comments, sexist 'humour,' and sexual harassment on the job. At all times, remember that sexual harassment is illegal. In the United States, it is a violation of Title VII of the Civil Rights Act of 1964. In Canada, it is covered by the Canadian Human Rights Code, subsections 6(2), 6(3)a, and 6(3)b. Some smaller units of government also have antiharassment provisions, so obtain copies of your institution's, city's, province's, or state's information pamphlets or harassment, which will list your rights and responsibilities. It is important, however, to be aware that the coverage provided by such legislation can sometimes be maddeningly limited or slow in implementation if you do appeal to it for help.

Some techniques that women have found useful include:

–   Call sexist reasoning and sexist humour what they are and what they are not (not reasonable and not funny); let your male colleagues know that neither becomes them.[72]

–   Define clear boundaries about sexual behaviour – a clear statement such as 'I don't have sex with colleagues' or 'I am committed to another relationship' works best.[73]

–   Find out whether the course-evaluation forms include questions about sexist and other biased comments, and if they do not, lobby to have them included.

–   Post a copy of your institution's guidelines on your office door (and if your institution still doesn't have any, use the guidelines from another setting in academia).

–   Write the names of sexual harassers on the walls in the women's bathroom, so that other women in your institution will know that, if those men seem to be 'flirting' with them, it may instead be harassment.

– Be aware of the insult involved in asserting that recruiting women compromises the standards of excellence of your institution, and question colleagues who make this assertion.

16. If you have a part-time position, know that there are two ways your future can go. Although part-timers are often treated with disdain, and although part-time work may give other faculty a chance to learn about your weaknesses, it can also happen that you will form an alliance with a member of the department who thinks highly of your work and has enough clout to fight for a full-time position for you. Some part-timers have been known to make themselves so valuable to the department that the chairperson works hard to find ways to keep them by moving them into a full-time or more secure position.

You might also wish to work to improve conditions for all part-timers at your institution, since anything you could achieve in that respect could be helpful to you as well. Smith et al. suggest that 'guidelines should be established to ensure that those occupying contractually-limited positions are treated as full-fledged members of the department, including access to travel funds for conferences and small-scale research or study funds available in the department and function as regular voting members of the department.'[74] On some campuses, part-timers are assigned heavier teaching loads than they had been promised initially and may be paid less than the teaching assistants they supervise.[75] This area, too, needs work. Less obviously political steps you can take include ensuring, for instance, that part-timers are on the list of faculty to whom notices about faculty meetings and invitations to parties are regularly sent.

17. If you are interested in serving as an advocate for others, whether for students, colleagues, or some other group, in trying to change the academy, think carefully about your priorities. One frustrating fact is that time spent in advocacy work will be time you cannot spend publishing, so you are increasing the risk you won't get tenure and be able to stay in academia and go on being an advocate. Some women choose to delay most such activities until after they have some real job security. Others go ahead with such work, knowing the chances they are taking. An added risk is that, in some settings, the knowledge that you are doing advocacy work can directly prevent you from having your contract renewed or from receiving a promotion or tenure, if the powers-that-be disapprove of your activities.

A senior woman administrator told me, 'You're damned either way – if you speak up, you're a loud bitch, and if you're silent you are invisible, or they think you are passive, spineless, and unimaginative.' She advised new faculty women to 'choose your issues so it will be harder for them to say that you're *always* interfering.' and she further points out that it is risky to speak out on political issues before you have tenure: 'Try to get someone else to do it for you until you have that job security,' adding 'I *hate* having to give that advice!'

18. Learn to handle rejection productively. If a paper or grant proposal you have submitted is turned down, read the reviewers' comments carefully. It is natural to panic if you see a long list of criticisms, and that panic can get in the way of your making a reasonable judgment about the validity of each one. Women's generally poor self-esteem usually feeds that panic; we assume that every criticism of our work is valid.

When you read reviews, though, remember that many brilliant papers, proposals, and books have been repeatedly rejected with scathing comments. Remember, too, that reviewers are human beings, so they are sometimes right and sometimes wrong; some have prejudices about your ideas or about you as a person that will make it impossible for them to make valid comments. As you begin to read a review, keep all of that in mind, and try to adopt the attitude that you are going to find out whether you can learn something useful from it. In order to avoid feeling overwhelmed, I read only one comment at a time, think about it carefully, and decide whether or not I think that acting on it could improve what I have written. If I read through the whole list at once, each criticism grabs some of my attention, and I can't deal effectively with *any* comment. I make notes as I read, commenting both on what

I can do better and what signs of undue bias and blindness I see in the reviewer's remarks. Then, as one group advised, 'If you perceive the reviews ... to contain sexist or racist assumptions or in other ways to be systematically biased against your work, it is appropriate to tell the journal editor of your concerns. Often, if your concerns sound legitimate, the editor will secure another review.'[76]

19. When you encounter obstacles and problems, consider going straight to the top (the president of the university, the dean, and so on), contacting your faculty association or union about the possibility of filing a grievance or doing something less formal, calling a meeting of potentially interested parties, forming a discussion and/or action group, putting together a petition, or attracting media attention. If you are a part-time or sessional instructor, group efforts are likely to be particularly necessary, since alone, one person has little power and prestige; be sure to find out whether the faculty association or union will assist you, since some are terrifically supportive and some quite passive.

20. Consider taking action to overcome some of the problems that you and others encounter. Inspect the chapter 8 check-list to get a sense of the range of issues and goals you might want to choose. Here are a few examples:

(a) Take action to help equalize the workload. For instance, 'Recommend that department chairs, in collaboration with their deans, develop guidelines for office space and laboratory allotments, and suggest that actual space and facilities allocations be a matter of public record.'[77] Or consider proposing in a faculty meeting that responsibility for undesirable courses and class meeting times be rotated among all the faculty.[78] Before taking such a step, however, make some preliminary explorations into how the more senior faculty are likely to respond, because if they are particularly punitive, they may become angry at you for proposing that they given up some of the privileges that go with tenure.

(b) If you have family responsibilities, make sure you know whether your institution has formal rules about when and how you can take time off to meet those responsibilities. This can include taking maternity leave, cancelling a lecture because you have a sick child, and obtaining leave to take care of a parent or other elder. If there are no such rules, and if you find that there is little or no support on the job for people who have such responsibilities, form a discussion group at least to provide support for those people and at most to lobby for changes. If you form a group to work for change, Richardson suggests requesting that the institution 'develop better parental leave policies and policies that recognize the demands of raising children' and 'allowing variations in career path for family responsibilities.'[79] One important variation in career path that has been implemented on at least one campus is the 'stop-the-tenure-clock' policy; this allows primary care-givers up to a one-year extension of their tenure decision, so that they have an extra year in which to produce the requisite work.[80]

(c) If day care for children is important to you, follow the same steps as in (b).

(d) Help develop an information campaign and workshops for faculty and teaching assistants to sensitize them to issues of sexism, racism, and other forms of bias in the classroom.[81]

(e) Lobby to ensure that faculty time spent in counseling and advising students will be considered important when decisions about promotions, raises, and tenure are made.[82]

(f) Since women and other non-dominant groups are underrepresented on most promotion and tenure committees, start a campaign to ensure that this situation is changed.

21. Be sure to read the references cited in the notes for this section of this chapter as well as others in the bibliography.

Applying for contract renewal, promotions, and tenure[83]

In addition to the suggestions given here, be sure to read Quina's excellent chapter, 'Helping yourself to tenure,' a step-by-step account of what to do, how to prepare your case, what to include, and more.[84]

1. Be aware that, although white women and ethnic minority women and men are being hired in academia more frequently than in previous eras, white men are still the most likely to receive tenure.[85]

2. Assemble the relevant papers that you will have gathered on the basis of the suggestions in the sections 'At hiring' and 'On the job.' These include an up-to-date copy of your c.v.; a copy of your contract and any relevant memos about criteria for evaluation; the list of your institution's written criteria for contract renewal, promotion, or tenure; copies of students' evaluations of your teaching; copies of evaluations of your work from any point in your current job; and a list of potential referees who can write letters about your work.

3. Contact one or more people who recently received a contract renewal, promotion, or tenure (depending on what you are about to request for yourself), and ask if you can see the materials they submitted for their cases. Ask them such questions as what they have done about listing non-mainstream publications on their c.v.'s when they apply, since attitudes toward such publication vary by institution and by department.

4. Find out, from your department chair, who is to assemble the material and make the written case for your request. Also ask the chair to explain to you the process and the schedule for what steps are to be taken when. Most likely, you will be expected to prepare the materials and the case yourself. Then, the usual procedure is for you to submit your request and supporting documents to a committee. The committee may be appointed by an administrator, or some or all members may be chosen after discussion with you. At some institutions, the applicant is allowed to select one or more members of the evaluation committee. The committee usually meets, reviews your materials, and sends out some or all of your publications for review. Be sure to ask whether you are allowed to suggest reviewers, and if you are, be prompt about giving their names, academic positions, addresses, and telephone numbers to the chair of your committee.

5. Write your brief, assemble the supporting documents, and ask colleagues not on the committee to read and give you feedback about it. Remember to mention some of the work you have done that might otherwise be overlooked. For instance, if you have reason to believe that you spend more time than most faculty in helping students deal with the emotional issues that arise from your courses, or advising them on future careers, be sure to write about that under the appropriate category for your institution, such as 'Teaching' or 'Service to the institution and the discipline,' depending upon how your department or institution categorizes such work. Similarly, if you have served your department by creating and developing new courses to accommodate departmental needs, be certain to list this under a teaching or service category.[86]

6. Be creative about ways to increase your chances. A well-loved teacher anticipated being refused tenure because part of her work was in philosophy and part in women's studies, and as a result, she feared she had not published enough in either area. She also knew she was disliked by some faculty because she was a feminist. Her students, fearing that the university would lose her, nominated her for a prestigious teaching award, enclosing a strong brief, and she won the award. This became a powerful argument for granting her tenure.

7. If you get your contract renewal, promotion, or tenure, write notes to inform and thank those who wrote letters for you or helped you prepare your case.[87]

8. If your request for renewal, promotion, or tenure is denied, ask the chair of the evaluation committee to give you the reasons for the denial, and ask to see your file (the latter request may be denied, and you may want to explore the possibility of

filing a grievance or taking legal action to gain access to your file). Then try to evaluate the information to see what is reasonable and suggests areas in which you can improve, and also look for signs of bias, unfairness, and inappropriate procedures. Quina makes many helpful suggestions:

> Ask to see your file, and if there are inaccuracies or inappropriate comments, ask that they be corrected and/or write a response, documenting your concerns. Talk to other faculty, since you may find that one or two particular professors negatively evaluate everyone, or all women, or all feminists. Check your contract, to see whether there is a procedure for overturning a negative evaluation through a grievance procedure, for instance. Ask colleagues to help you with your weak areas, such as writing of papers or grant applications.
>
> At the time of the third-year review for tenure, ask yourself if you really want to stay at this institution, for now might be the time to get out, rather than waiting until your contract has fully run out, leaving you feeling desperate to find another job.[88]

9. If your request for promotion or tenure is denied, find out whether you have another chance to apply for it. If the request was for tenure, switching to a non-tenure-stream position may be an option for you, if you are comfortable with it.

10. If you are denied tenure, get your c.v. back into circulation, and 'keep up your morale, realizing that some of the best people have been the victims of unfair tenure decisions.'[89]

11. If you decide to fight a negative outcome, read what other women have to say about the process, check with your faculty association or union or the campus ombudsperson or affirmative-action officer about procedures within and outside the university, and perhaps ask a labour lawyer to advise you about extramural procedures.[90] Under no circumstances should you take action without reading Athena Theodore's book *The Campus Troublemakers: Academic Women in Protest*[91] and the American Psychological Association Committee on Women in Psychology's publication *Survival Guide to Academe for Women and Ethnic Minorities*. The latter includes a detailed section on 'Strategies for coping with a negative decision on promotion and tenure,' including the following advice:[92]

—   Recognize that negative psychological and somatic reactions are common and normal responses.
—   'Ask yourself what others could have done differently, particularly those in authority, such as the department chair, who has a responsibility to provide you with honest feedback concerning your performance.'
—   Do not expect to be able to go on doing 'business as usual.'
—   Consider taking a leave of absence to teach at another institution in a visiting capacity while your case is reviewed at your home institution.
—   Consider working outside of academia while your case proceeds.
—   Determine whether there have been procedural errors.
—   Correct inaccuracies and identify differential treatment (for example, have you been treated differently from white males, and were different standards used to evaluate your work?).
—   Try to disqualify evaluators who are unable to evaluate your work impartially.
—   Obtain letters from top scholars who know and respect your work and who can address the issues that were used to deny your application.
—   See whether the department chair will support you, if in your case the department recommended granting your request but higher-ups in the administration denied it.
—   'Reach out to powerful persons within the administrative structure who have a strong track record of support for the retention and promotion of women and ethnic minorities.'

In the same publication, detailed suggestions are given for determining whether there were procedural errors and for disqualifying persons unable to be impartial.

12. If you decide to dispute the decision, keep in mind that it is likely to be a lengthy, emotionally draining process.

13. If you dispute the decision, remember that you will need a great deal of support from friends and colleagues – and remember that that need is healthy and normal.

14. If you dispute the decision, realize that you may well lose the case, but if you win, your victory may make institutions more careful about allowing bias and impropriety to direct such evaluations in the future.[93] Familiarize yourself with the statistics on winning and losing, such as that, of more than 350 U.S. lawsuits filed since 1972 by college faculty claiming discrimination, white women suing as individuals have had a success rate of only 20 per cent, classes of women faculty filing suit have had a success rate of about 42 per cent, and 'racial minority men and women almost always lost.'[94] However, some of the victories have been impressive. These include the case of *Clark v. Claremont Graduate School*, in which an African-American professor was awarded $1 million for discrimination on the basis of his race, and the $1 million victory of Asian-American medical school Professor Jean Jew, whose case was determined to reveal racism and sexual harassment.[95]

15. If you dispute the decision, realize that if you win, you may not want to stay at or return to the institution that caused you so much grief, and if you do remain there, you may be the target of great hostility, the recipient of gratitude from others who appreciate your struggle, or some of each.

16. If you dispute the decision, realize that if you win and do not choose to stay at that institution, you may have great difficulty finding a job elsewhere, because people may think of you as a troublemaker.

17. Be sure to read the references cited in the notes for this section of this chapter as well as others in the bibliography.

At the top

Becoming a full professor, a departmental chair, a dean, or even a president can be exciting, but it does not bring utopia. Here are some suggestions for women at the top.

1. Beware: In some ways, even more demands may be made on your time and energy than when you were junior faculty. As you become more senior, especially if your teaching is well reviewed and you have published interesting work, more students will want to work with you and have you as a supervisor or a mentor. Your colleagues in your department will expect you to take on more committee work and administrative duties, since you presumably know the ropes. As a woman, and if you are a member of a non-dominant group other than 'women,' you will likely be in even greater demand by administrators who are increasingly pressured (or are choosing) to demonstrate that they strive for diversity in committees that deal with such issues as student recruitment, employment and pay equity, and general university administrative work.

As a woman administrator, you will probably be even more in the minority than as a woman professor. As a result, you may feel – and be – largely isolated from other women, unless you make special efforts to overcome this. Sandler and Hall point out other problems resulting from women administrators' heightened visibility, including that they are 'apt to be treated as tokens: overly visible, over-extended, sometimes given more responsibility than power, sometimes not really supported by those above them ... If she fails to measure up, many observers will regard this as proof that "a woman couldn't do the job." If, however, she succeeds, she is often seen as exceptional. For minority women, the issue of visibility is especially pertinent because visibility is heightened by race as well as by sex.'[96]

2. If you move into administration, you will have to decide how high you want to go. Some of the women administrators I interviewed advise women to *avoid* being the *top* administrator so they 'can float through the college unobtrusively, making the changes we want to make.' But others, such as Helen Breslauer of the Ontario Confederation of University Faculty Associations, warn that women are often kept in what she calls the 'A-team positions' – as assistant, associate, or acting deans, vice-presidents, and so on – and that this is frustrating in cases where they are used to 'prove' their institutions' commitment to employment equity but granted little real power. Be aware that being a successful senior administrator usually involves a major commitment of time and energy, an exquisite understanding of campus politics, and a rock-solid confidence in whatever stand you choose to take in the midst of those conflicting political forces.

And heed the warning of a top administrator I interviewed, who bemoaned the fact that, because she had been promoted quickly through the administrative ranks, she had little time to produce scholarly work; as a result, when she decided she wanted to switch to an academic job, or even simply do more teaching, she was told she was underqualified.

3. You may find you are becoming bored with your work – or you may discover that you love it more than ever. Some interviewees told me they were tired of the emotional drains that teaching and advising entail for them, but others said that, once they received tenure and had greater freedom to design and teach what they chose, they felt energized and happy. For many, tenure afforded the freedom to stop teaching required courses and instead to focus on 'courses the students take *only* because they really want to be there.' Similarly, although some women faculty were delighted to spend more time working with graduate students as they themselves became qualified to supervise theses and dissertations, others considered graduate-student supervisions to be so demanding that they had no time left to pursue their own research. The latter was particularly true of feminist faculty in departments that housed few feminist faculty and many feminist students, as well as of women in fields with mostly male faculties and traditions, since so many female students gravitate toward female faculty both as supervisors and as advisers for how to deal with their male teachers and peers.

One highly placed woman told me, 'As an administrator, at best I feel like the conductor of a symphony orchestra. And it's a hell of a lot of fun to have clout.'

4. Be on guard against displaying 'Queen Bee' behaviour. Many of the women I interviewed, at all levels of academia, made pleas along the lines of, 'Tell your readers not to forget other women once they get to the top.' Of course, this, too, is a matter for individual choice, since only some women want to invest time and energy in helping other women climb the career ladder. But the part of the plea that is most important is that even women who feel they themselves were not targets of negative treatment because of their sex recognize that many of the other women in their institutions may have been.

5. Be aware that, even though you do not regard yourself as being 'at the top' of the academic ladder, others may consider you to be right up there. Nearly every woman full professor or top administrator whom I asked, 'What advice would you give to women about being at the top?' replied, 'I don't know why you are asking me that. I'm not there.' How did they explain that feeling, in view of their official job titles? They could always find some explanation, such as never having written a book or feeling that students don't enrol in their courses in very large numbers. But almost to a woman, they expressed sentiments similar to one full professor of philosophy and women's studies, who explained: 'When I was promoted to full professor, I at last got a whiff of what I felt real power must be like. I seemed to have been given some sort of legitimacy. But then I learned that, except for now being given voting privileges in slightly more situations, I still function in an environment that does not welcome and respect women as fully as men.'

6. In spite of your substantial qualifications and achievements, if you want to change jobs, you may find it hard to do so. First of all, not many jobs become available in senior positions. Second, you may have learned so much in your current and previous jobs about what you want to avoid that you will have a terrible time making the decision to move to a place with many unknowns. Third, the better-known your work becomes, the more likely you are to have opponents in high places; thus, although some members of a department might want to hire you, they could be outvoted or overruled by those who disagree with your theories or who feel you have outshone them. Fourth, since a very senior job is a real plum, hiring committees often know exactly what personal characteristics and professional qualifications they want in that job. Thus, for instance, a woman who had received prestigious awards and published wonderful work wanted to move but kept finding that she was turned down for senior positions. After years of frustration, she discovered that the search committees for the interdisciplinary positions she sought were intent on hiring people who specialized in a particular, trendy type of methodology that she did not use. And finally, if you have substantial accomplishments, search committees may find your c.v. intimidating or assume (perhaps without bothering to investigate whether this is true) that you consider yourself a 'star' and won't be a team player in the department or program.

7. Some people will mistakenly assume that, because you are at the top, you got there easily, have an undemanding career and life, and control vast resources that you are reluctant to share with them. Some administrators and full professors told me that students and junior colleagues seemed not to understand that they might have research and writing projects they wanted to pursue, *even though* they had secure jobs and therefore didn't 'have to' continue publishing. As a consequence, the more junior people were often resentful, because they expected the senior women to put aside their own interests and needs to help them. This is a poignant situation, because it means that women are often set up against women and blame each other for their frustrations.[97] But we need to recognize that this happens predictably to any group with scarce resources and power: they begin to fight among themselves for what little is available, whether it is financial support, space, or social support. It is crucial both for women at the top and for more junior women faculty and students to remember that *most* women in academia feel overworked and inadequately supported.

Many women who have headed women's studies programs have described to me their intense frustration about the assumption many people have made, that they can provide quantities of space, time, and money but simply choose not to do so. Once you are head or director of an academic unit, there will be those who assume that, as an administrator, you have unlimited power, and when you try to tell them that that is not the case, some will remain as suspicious of you as they are of administrators in general.

8. Remember that being at the top in some ways does not guarantee being there in every respect. For instance, senior molecular biologist Shirley Tilghman reports that even women with outstanding accomplishments are often not invited to speak at conferences: 'In 1988, I ran a Gordon Conference on molecular genetics which was funded by the NIH. About 33% of the speakers and 45% of the attendees were women. Two years later, another conference on the same topic was arranged by some of my male colleagues. And only two of the speakers were women. I don't think you can attribute this to anything but an unconscious bias. In the biological sciences, there's been a tendency to think that we are doing so well that the problem is over. And most women would like to believe this. I believed it. But that is nonsense.

9. Be aware that the closer a woman gets to the top, the more people she is likely to encounter who are uncomfortable, or downright hostile, about her success. If this happens to you, remember that it does not prove that you are incompetent or wrongheaded. Some people will assume, for instance, that you got where you are because you tell the men at the top what they want to hear or that you make no efforts on behalf of anyone other than members of dominant groups, that you have no sense of responsibility to those who are treated unfairly. Another source of hostility may be your peers, or even those who are 'above' you in the hierarchy, since 'the culture of the senior administration is, in many respects, even more unapologetically masculinist/sexist than its critics imagine.'[99]

10. Be sure to read the references cited in the notes for this section of this chapter as well as others in the bibliography.

I hope that the descriptions of academia and the suggestions in this book give you a sense of some of the scope and variety of academic life for women. There is no denying that trying to cope with the difficult aspects of it can be like trying to lift 'a ton of feathers,'[100] but there is also much that is interesting and exhilarating. In your search for a campus that will meet your needs or in your efforts to change the one where you now work, you may find the check-list in chapter 8 to be of use.

8 Check-list for Woman-positive Institutions

The Commission [on Canadian Studies, Association of Colleges and Universities of Canada] recommends ... that universities and colleges approach the problems involved in correcting the current inequitable treatment of women in Canadian higher education as a question of central institutional policy which is properly the concern of the entire institution, and of everyone in it, and not simply the concern of those who are adversely affected by such discrimination. SYMONS and PAGE[1]

Do not assume that making women feel equally welcome with men in the university is women's responsibility. JOY PARR[2]

Here is a check-list[3] that is aimed at serving two purposes: (1) To guide you in your search for a woman-positive institution where you can study and work, and (2) To provide some suggestions for ways you can work to improve the situation for women at your institution, if you choose to do so. One can never compile a complete list of all possibilities, but it is hoped that these touch on some of the key issues. You will notice that some policies and practices listed here have rarely or never been implemented – but that does not mean they never *can* be. Some of the items listed under a particular heading may actually apply to more than one heading.

Does your institution have ...?

GENERAL

- a good record of hiring and promoting women and people of both sexes from non-dominant groups at all levels of the academic ladder
- a policy that discrimination on the basis of sex, race, age, disability, age, and sexual orientation is prohibited
- proactive and public measures that emphasize that the under-representation of non-dominant groups, as well as sexism, antifeminism, racism, ageism, and discrimination because of disability and sexual orientation are totally unacceptable, reflect on the character of the university as a whole, and must be dealt with collectively
- a policy that proven intent to discriminate or show bias may not be justified on the grounds of academic rights to freedom of expression
- active recruitment programs for attracting graduate students, postdoctoral students, and faculty from among women of all kinds
- a regular practice of informing all students, faculty, and other staff of their legal rights and responsibilities
- a formal affirmative-action or employment-equity and pay-equity policy, backed up by the staff, resources, and release time necessary to make them work, plus a solid record of actual achievements in these areas
- a status-of-women officer, especially one who has been 'allowed' to make or supported in making positive strides for women
- a standing committee on 'chilly climate' issues, to explore and report on those conditions, as well as to provide training and make recommendations to improve the situation
- an ombudsperson who can help women (and men) handle, in nonadversarial ways, problems related to sexism and other kinds of prejudice that arise

- undergraduate programs in women's studies, ethnic studies, and lesbian and gay studies, with library resources and speaker series
- chairs or professorships in women's studies, various ethnic studies, and lesbian and gay studies
- a high level of funding for women's studies, ethnic studies, and lesbian and gay studies and for a women's centre
- an office of race relations empowered to pursue the goal of improving intergroup relations on campus
- training sessions and educational resources on 'chilly climate' issues as ongoing aspects of staff and professional development within the college or university (note especially Sandler with Hall for a wealth of helpful details about how to plan such sessions[4])
- a requirement for department and search-committee chairs to attend sessions on affirmative-action recruitment and on the 'chilly climate' and the various forms of harassment and discrimination
- a program to reward departments or individuals who promote change regarding chilly-climate issues
- educational programs about the negative effects of holding prejudiced attitudes and behaving in discriminatory ways
- mechanisms to involve the students and staff who are the targets of discrimination and harassment in the process of change
- a course on multiculturalism and diversity, stressing the equality of all groups and cultures in the society, perhaps made compulsory for all graduating students
- institution-wide procedures to identify areas of possible systemic discrimination toward oppressed groups in courses being taught
- a requirement that departments develop affirmative-action plans
- a language policy – for both internal and external documents – that is free of bias in references to gender, race, age, disability, and sexual orientation, with guidelines to implement the policy and distribute it at all levels of the college or university

- formal guidelines for non-sexist research methods
- mentoring opportunities for women at all levels of the college or university, especially for re-entry women and members of non-dominant groups
- matching funds for departments inviting members of non-dominant groups as visiting scholars
- a program of regular analysis of internal funding practices, including which people and projects tend to receive funds
- regular safety audits
- a personal-safety-awareness officer
- a safety escort service, adequate lighting, and other safety measures for women on campus
- subsidized women's self-defence classes
- emergency shelters for women on campus
- resources devoted to analysing ways to attract and retain women students for science, engineering, and other non-traditional fields
- a status-of-women task force or commission
- a status-of-women office and officer
- a clear policy and resources for education about, prevention of, and dealing with harassment of all kinds, including sanctions against perpetrators and a range of options for the complainant
- mechanisms for people to express concerns about subtle forms of discrimination and deal with them
- a significant percentage of women in senior administrative posts
- a policy of not hiring top administrators who do not support affirmative action and pay equity
- departmental seminars on good faculty–student relationships
- an annual report of the institution including important statistics on students and faculty, specifying data about admissions, job types, funding, job offers and hires, salaries, ranks, and percentages of full-timers and part-timers, and analysed by sex, race, age, disability, and sexual orientation
- systematic collection of anecdotal, as well as statistical, information on women's status and experiences in the institution, and an annual report distributed publicly that outlines the

quantitative and qualitative findings of these studies
- mechanisms for correcting inequities found in the two kinds of data collection just described
- significant percentages of women faculty, administrators, trustees, and members of the most powerful committees from non-dominant groups
- workshops for teachers illustrating what behaviour is unacceptable to many women and members of other non-dominant groups
- campus-wide programs and publications for promoting respect for diversity
- peer-counselling programs for students and for staff
- responsiveness to the needs of the larger community in which the institution sits – the neighbourhood, the city, the rural county, and so on.
- workshops on how to recognize and eliminate sexist and other discriminatory behaviour in the classroom
- a program to identify and document systematically differential treatment of students, depending on sex, race, and so forth
- written and audiovisual resources about the professional climate, and publicizing of their availability for use by groups and individuals on campus
- audiotaping, videotaping, and other such services available to those who wish to analyse their own verbal and non-verbal behaviour in regard either to forms of bias or to teaching skills
- reviews of departmental policies and practices to ensure that these do not discriminate against women colleagues and colleagues from other non-dominant groups
- educational programs for administrators and administrative committees promoting equity
- a policy of permitting only 'equal opportunity' employers to recruit on campus
- a grievance procedure for dealing with complaints relating to sexism and other forms of discrimination and bias in the classroom
- mechanisms for analysing data from particular departments and disciplines to find out how their own brand of sexism

might be combatted, such as identifying reasons for graduate-student drop-outs
- mechanisms for faculty members to share a faculty appointment, including a tenure-track position
- a set of guidelines given to all search, promotion, and tenure committees to ensure that candidates are treated fairly on the basis of sex and other factors (see chapter 7 for many details suggested by Sandler with Hall and by Breslauer and West[5])
- evaluation of faculty's mentoring performance
- inclusion of mentoring ability and performance as a criterion for the hiring of new faculty and for tenure and promotions
- accessible, high-quality, reliable child care that is affordable and has flexible hours
- a campus culture that is supportive of students and staff with family responsibilities
- parental-leave policies and policies that recognize the demands of raising children and caring for aging relatives
- programs aimed at making the administration less hierarchical and more responsive to the needs of the people it is supposed to serve
- proactive programs aimed at promoting the integration into the mainstream curriculum of materials about people, especially women, of various races, ages, sexual orientations, and physical conditions
- a provincial or state ombudsperson to whom one can appeal if one's complaints about mistreatment on campus are not satisfactorily dealt with internally
- equal or equivalent athletic and recreational facilities for both sexes
- adequate health care and health insurance for women, including gynaecological services and contraceptive advice
- information about who (both students and staff) leaves that institution and why
- a good record of conferring honorary degrees on women and inviting women as commencement speakers – especially women who returned to university late in life and those from various non-dominant groups

FOR GRADUATE STUDENTS

- a welcoming climate for women's diversity
- a community feeling among graduate students and professors
- a sexual-orientation clause (prohibiting discrimination) in teaching and research assistants' unions' policies
- items about classroom-climate issues on student evaluation forms
- mechanisms for identifying possible sex biases in grading, advising, and counselling
- a handbook outlining students' rights and the services and forms of protection and redress available to them
- flexibility and adaptability of university programs for mature women students
- programs for part-time graduate study and accessibility of part-time study (for instance, in terms of the convenient scheduling of required courses for people who have full-time jobs and attend school part-time, financial aid, and so on)
- support groups, especially for women and men in non-traditional areas
- an international students' advisory centre
- special training to sensitize professors, graduate secretaries, and students to students' needs
- training for professors to serve as mentors and advisers in a Socratic manner
- assistance and guidance for students and faculty about publishing their first articles and applying for grants
- seminars for professors about important concepts in adult education (most research on education has been focused on children)
- rewards to professors for attracting students and penalties for driving them away
- regular studies of graduate students' progress, with a focus on the institutional causes of student attrition and results to be shared with both the public and other universities
- annual reviews of students' performance in all departments, with constructive feedback given to students

- informal meetings to discuss classroom climate and to stimulate awareness of the issues
- self-study of classroom-climate issues
- collection of data on gender and other differences in program-completion rates, funding, and professional-training opportunities (research assistantships, teaching assistantships)
- a maternity-leave policy for graduate students that is non-punitive and is free of academic and financial penalty
- explicit policies about maternity leaves in the collective agreements of teaching and research assistants
- a room or meeting place, possibly in connection with women's studies programs, where women graduate students can come together to study, relax, or discuss issues of common concern

FOR RECRUITMENT AND HIRING

- policies aimed at recruiting, hiring, and promoting more women at all levels of the institution and especially at the graduate faculty and senior administrative levels
- a policy of considering the success record of departments in meeting diversity goals as part of 'merit raise' decisions
- a 'cluster hiring program,' in which women and members of other non-dominant groups are hired in groups of two or more to minimize the burdens of 'tokenism,' especially in departments that house few or no such people
- an affirmative-action officer or advocate on every search committee
- a standard package of the kinds of items (space, lab equipment, and so on, with provisions tailoring this generic list to particular departments) considered negotiable after an initial employment offer has been made; the list is given to search committees, which show it to all job applicants
- careful scrutiny of current practices and criteria for promotion and tenure so that definitions of 'excellence' and 'academic freedom' are not allowed to conceal biases against women and other groups
- an explicit set of written criteria for search procedures

- a practice of informing search committees of their legal responsibilities
- a set of questions for search committees to use in determining 'if a candidate is aware of and responsible to women's issues'[6]
- a clear time-line for all steps in hiring, from publication of the job description through the recommendation to hire a particular candidate
- search committees whose members are respectful, supportive, and informative when candidates ask about such issues as those on this check-list
- a good record not only of hiring but also of promoting and granting tenure to women and to members of non-dominant groups of both sexes

WORKING CONDITIONS

- support groups or senior-junior pairings, especially for women and others in a minority in non-traditional areas, as sources of information and support for all graduate students and junior faculty (ideally, initiated by the senior person)
- mechanisms for examination of fairness regarding course loads, advisory responsibilities, committee membership, research, and access to teaching assistants and clerical support
- mechanisms to ensure that women and members of non-dominant groups of both sexes are not disproportionately burdened by committee work, advising, and teaching (perhaps even freeing them from all such responsibilities for one term, to allow them to concentrate on their research)
- inclusion of female colleagues and others in a minority in informal professional and social gatherings
- careful monitoring of salary differentials
- mechanisms to improve access to the university's research resources by women and others who are statistically less likely to obtain them
- programs to provide information and advice to women on practices in their particular disciplines; on dealing with issues such as current theoretical problems; on research and publica-

tion practices; on granting agencies; on conferences; on how to
prepare a curriculum vitae
- programs on improving one's skills in teaching, on the value of
  diverse teaching styles, on the acquisition of material and
  equipment, on strategies to cope with difficulties in the class-
  room/laboratory, and on revision of course and program content
- a policy that permits primary care-givers up to a one-year extension of the tenure decision (a 'stop-the-tenure-clock' policy)
- lower teaching loads at the beginning of a new appointment
- teaching relief for administrative work (course relief or leave
  time)
- mentoring system for grant-writing
- benefits for part-time faculty
- E-mail and fax support
- encouragement of interdisciplinary research within the university
- workshops on successful grant-getting
- programs to develop expertise in feminist methods and the
  way women approach grant proposals
- clear guidelines for office space and laboratory allotments, and
  the making of actual space and facilities allocations a matter of
  public record
- treatment of those in contractually limited positions as full-
  fledged members of the department, including access to travel
  funds for conferences and to small-scale research or study
  funds in the department and acceptance as regular voting
  members of the department
- a regular practice of having new faculty have a discussion with
  the chair of the department at the outset of their contract about
  the priorities of the department and the criteria likely to be
  used in determining their reappointment, promotion, or tenure

FOR PROMOTION AND TENURE

See also the General section above.

- an explicit set of written criteria for promotion and tenure committees

–   a practice of informing all promotion and tenure committees of
    their legal responsibilities
–   advocacy groups or committees that educate women faculty re-
    garding their contractual rights, and chilly-climate behaviour
    they might expect to encounter; a representative from the com-
    mittee accompanies women faculty members to all reappoint-
    ment, promotion, and tenure reviews as well as appeals of
    these reviews
–   administration- or personnel-department-sponsored ongoing
    seminars for faculty in regard to renewal, promotion, and ten-
    ure
–   mechanisms to determine whether there are differences in the
    stringency of the standards applied to evaluate women and
    men
–   provisions for junior faculty to view the promotion and tenure
    application files of all faculty who give their permission, to as-
    sist in preparing for their own promotion and tenure requests
–   a tenure ladder for part-time faculty
–   an affirmative-action officer or advocate on every promotion,
    tenure, and merit-raise committee
–   a mechanism of assigning a senior scholar (perhaps from a
    women's network) to the woman who is applying for promo-
    tion or tenure, to gather support letters, have respected schol-
    ars review the applicant's work, and ensure that proper
    procedures are followed

Does the faculty/association or union ...?

–   have proactive and public measures that emphasize that the
    underrepresentation of non-dominant groups, as well as sex-
    ism, anti-feminism, racism, ageism, and discrimination because
    of disability and sexual orientation are totally unacceptable, re-
    flect on the character of the university as a whole, and should
    be dealt with collectively
–   conduct educational programs for administrators and adminis-
    trative committees promoting equity
–   negotiate new criteria for pay and career advancement that are

aimed at eliminating bias based on gender and other categories
- make information about university personnel practices available to faculty women
- support status-of-women committees and give them a mandate to affect policy
- effectively represent women who hold part-time and sessional contracts
- include as negotiating clauses provisions about pay equity, day care, and maternity/paternity leaves
- lobby the institution's review committees to persuade them to consider the enormous amount of committee work done by women when deciding on renewal, tenure, and promotion
- bargain against criteria of merit (for raises, promotions, and tenure) depending on increased productivity, intensification of labour, and job speed-up
- insist that policies, collective agreements, and contracts address true equity issues and the effects of gender, race, age, or career patterns

Appendix 1:
The Data on Gender Bias in Academia[1]

The academic funnel

We have heard the statistics ... Women in the academy are NOT well represented in mere numbers and they are even less well represented at levels of power, decision-making and positions to influence or effect change in the organization ... The academy is a hostile world to women. The survival and access rates decrease as one progresses from the undergraduate to master's to doctoral to faculty levels. The ability and/or willingness to deal with the hostility reduces the ranks till only the exceptions get there.

MARTHA K. LAURENCE[2]

Although in both Canada and the United States at least 50% of undergraduates are women,[3] there is substantial attrition the higher one goes,[4] whether from the undergraduate through the master's to the doctoral level;[5] from the level of graduate student through new faculty, assistant and associate professor to full professor;[6] through comparison of staff with no administrative power to those who do have administrative power;[7] or through comparison of part-time and/or non-tenure-stream jobs to full-time and tenure-stream ones.[8]

Barinaga suggests that this funnelling process, or what she calls the leaking pipeline, is due to a combination of men's attitude (sometimes internalized by women) that women cannot be top achievers and the double burden of being a scientist while also being a wife and possibly a mother 'in a society that expects women, but not men, to put family ahead of career.'[9] As an important example of the way the funnelling continues, even though the number of women earning Ph.D.'s increases, Gibbons reports (in a special section on women in science in *Science* magazine[10]) the data for women in science and engineering. According to a National Science Foundation study, the number of women receiving Ph.D.'s grew from 21% to 28% in the period from 1979–89, but during that same time women only went from holding 5% to holding 7% of all tenured positions and from holding 6% to holding 8% of the full professorships.[11]

Barinaga offers a perspective, based on interviews with women neuroscientists, on some of the factors that contribute to the funnelling of women academics at different stages of their work lives: 'Deeply ingrained societal attitudes and expectations come into play early, undermining a woman's chance of seeking out and landing a tenure-track job. For those with enough persistence to get onto the tenure track, the mid-career period is dominated by a severe time crunch – especially for women with young children. Later, when a woman's career is in full flight, sexist attitudes return to center stage, keeping a woman out of the circles of power in her sub-field.'[12] How does the latter manifest itself? Writes Barinaga: 'Perhaps because these senior-level women are the ones who really do constitute a threat to the male establishment, many women neuroscientists believe they are being shut out of the real centers of power: the powerful university committees and the small groups that organize meetings ... When it is near the center of power ... the committee is likely to be all male ... A look at the foundation boards or the university committees that allocate funds and space ... will confirm that "the glass ceiling" for women is still very much intact.'[13]

Among students

According to Pyke,[14] women constitute 56% of all undergraduate enrolments in Canada but only 44% of all graduate enrolments,[15] and by the mid-1980s in the United States, women were earning nearly 50% of master's degrees but only between 32% and 35% of doctorates.[16] The percentages vary greatly depending on the particular field of study, so that men tend to be more highly concentrated in such disciplines as economics, engineering, philosophy, and computer science,[17] whereas 'women are poorly represented at the undergraduate and masters' levels in the applied and physical sciences, and badly represented in the applied and physical sciences at the doctoral level ... also less well represented than might be expected (on the basis of undergraduate enrolment) at the doctoral level in the life sciences.'[18] There are high concentrations of women students in such disciplines as nursing, education, translation, and library science.[19] According to the *Status of Women*

Committee Report,[20] for doctoral students, women make up 35.3% of the total for all fields combined in Ontario universities: 45.5% of those in the humanities, 43.3% of those in the social sciences, 17.5% of those in mathematics and the physical sciences, and 13.4% in 'graduate study' in all of Canada in engineering and applied science.[21]

Even in the fields where more women than men are enrolled as students, the higher the level, the more scarce do females become.[22] Dagg points out that the strikingly lower proportion of females among graduate students than among undergraduates 'is serious, especially for universities, whose professorate in the future, as largely in the past, will be made up of scholars with Ph.D.s.'[23]

The likelihood of a woman student who enters a doctoral program actually finishing that program varies greatly from one field to another. A study at one large, metropolitan university showed that, of those who enter, 79% of both sexes in the life sciences, 65% of women and 78% of men in the physical sciences and engineering, 59% of both sexes in education, 42% of both sexes in the social sciences, and only 37% of women compared with 51% of men in the humanities complete their doctorates.[24]

The funnelling of women students is particularly disturbing in light of the fact that 'on virtually every objective measure, women graduate students continue to score, on average, higher or the same as men.'[25] Although many factors may contribute to the funnelling of women in graduate study, one is that, at all levels and in most fields, women are more likely than men to be part-time students.[26] Part-timers have fewer chances to find mentors and supporters among faculty or other students and decreased opportunities to become involved in a generally supportive intellectual atmosphere, including faculty members' research projects. According to Pyke, 'of those attending university on a part time basis the proportion of women was 64%, 51%, and 39% for undergraduate, masters and doctoral levels respectively. The comparable percentages for the representation of women among full time students are all lower by several percentage points.'[27]

Hiring

Since the sexes have equal intelligence and roughly equal numbers as undergraduates, the huge preponderance of males as professors means they are 'staffed by men of lesser ability than that possessed by the many women who have not been hired.'

DAGG and THOMPSON[28]

Look at this department ... One female [in a specialty that I'm not in]. Come on! In this day and age! Oh yeah, but you can't say anything. They say there aren't that many qualified women, but the point is since I've started here, they have hired at least five profs. None of them have been women and you can't tell me that there aren't (enough qualified women). One-fifth of the PhDs in this field are women. So why do they hire five or six new profs and not one of them a woman?

Student quoted by ELLA HALEY[29]

After completing their graduate study, women are less likely than men to be hired by academic institutions. In Canada and in the United States, 27% of all faculty positions are held by women,[30] and in both countries far smaller and sometimes negligible percentages are held by women from non-dominant groups.[31] The proportions of Black, Hispanic, and aboriginal women have been tiny and slow-growing and often, at least in the United States, highest in historically Black or Catholic institutions.[32] According to the American Council on Education, in the mid-eighties 'African Americans represented only 2.2 percent of full professors in American universities.'[33] A similar pattern is found for men from non-dominant groups, but the numbers have been found to be even more dismal for Black women than for Black men[34] and for Chicanas than for Chicanos.[35] A study conducted by Deborah J. Merritt and Barbara F. Reskin revealed that, of 1104 professors who took law-school tenure-stream positions between 1986 and 1991, of the 'minority' professors, 97 were men and 84 were women, but in spite of their similarity in credentials, work experience, and family obligations, the women were hired at lower academic ranks and less prestigious institutions than the men.[36] Only 29% of the men started in non-tenure-track positions, in contrast to almost half of the women.

Hensel reports that there has been little or no increase in the proportions of women on faculties in recent decades, that some departments still have no women faculty at all, and that there are few or no women from non-dominant groups. 'At the current rate of increase [in the U.S.],' she writes, 'it will take women 90 years to achieve equal representation to men on American campuses,'[37] and the figure for Canada is estimated to be 100 years.[38] Mathematics departments have been described as some of the worst offenders: in 1990–1, the top ten U.S. math departments had approximately fifty men but only three women in tenure-track assistant professorships.[39]

Some statistics can be deceiving: for instance, it sounds encouraging to learn that, in the United States between 1975 and 1987, there was a 78% increase in the number of female full professors; however, what that means is that in 1975 only 2% of the entire faculty were women full professors, and in 1987 that figure was still only 3%, while *male* full professors accounted for 38% of all faculty members!

In addition, as Dagg and Thompson write, 'Universities produce thousands of women science graduates with graduate degrees but rarely, if ever, hire their own or from other universities as professors.'[40] And, 'While university administrators claim there aren't enough scientists to meet the demand, women science graduates unable to get jobs are upset.'[41] For instance, 15% of the women who received Ph.D.'s from Ontario universities in the spring of 1985 were unemployed one year later, nearly three times the rate for males.[42]

Even the increasing proportions of new doctorates awarded to women are not reflected in the hiring of faculty. According to Vetter and Babco, at the doctoral level in the life sciences, women receive 50% of doctorates but represent only 36% of those newly hired,[43] and according to Koshland, in chemistry women earned 10% of the doctorates but accounted for only 4% of new faculty hirings.[44]

The importance of these statistics is reflected in the difference in how most women feel walking into a mostly male meeting or conference, compared with one in which at least half of the people are female.

Moving up the faculty ladder – or not

Hensel reports that in the United States, women account for 50% of undergraduate students but only 1/4 of faculty members and 1/10 of tenured, full professors, [45] and Breslauer and Gordon note that, in Canada, more than half of full-time women faculty are found at the assistant professor rank and below, whereas more than three-quarters of the male full-time faculty are in the full and associate professor ranks.[46] Backhouse reports that in 1985, only 6.1% of the full professors in Canada were female.[47]

Indeed, only about 17% of *all* full-time faculty in Canada are female,[48] and in the United States, women make up only 27.1% of all tenured and non-tenured faculty at all levels of higher education, and minority women are 'virtually non-existent in all types of schools.'[49] According to Theodore, women are also the minority sex in U.S. religious colleges and colleges with a predominance of Black students.[50]

According to Paul Selvin, in the United States the top 10 math departments employ 300 tenured men but only 2 women, and even at the top 40 schools, women make up only 4.5% of tenured math faculty.[51] In Canadian medical faculties, only 8% of full-time full professors are women, as are only 12% of art professors in Canada.[52] In Canadian universities, as of 1985, women made up 8% of biology faculty at all ranks, 2% in chemistry, and 1% in geology and physics, with the percentages of women full professors in those fields being far lower still.[53] 'Even in education where two-thirds of the graduate students are women, only 26.5% of the faculty are women.'[54]

The prospects for women faculty in the future do not promise to improve much unless a great deal of pressure continues to be put on academic institutions. When top administrators at universities boast that they have hired a certain number of new women, the *percentage* of faculty accounted for by women may actually have decreased or remained the same, because so many already-employed women do not have their contracts renewed, are teaching only part-time, or do not receive tenure and therefore leave the institution.[55] So claims about increases in hiring of females cannot be taken automatically to indicate real progress. For example, at one institution that was cited for its pro-woman hiring.

> ... the numbers of women in the two career ranks of the University have actually declined over the past year ... Between 1990 and 1991 the number of female Associate Professors fell from 74 to 71. The number of male Associate Professors fell during the same period, by 10 – from 435 to 425 ... The males were promoted; the females were not promoted – they disappeared completely from the ranks of Associate and Full Professor. The number of male Full Professors ... increased in 1991 by 11, from 468 to 479. The number of female Full Professors ... decreased by 1, from 20 to 19.
>
> ... Thirty-five percent of all faculty members at [this university] who hold the ranks of Assistant, Associate or Full Professor are now *male* Full Professors. This group increased its percentage by 1% in a single year. *Female* Full Professors represent 1.38% of this same academic group. We note that this ridiculously low representation is barely more than the percentage increase in one year for male Full Professors![56]

Even in the heavily female-associated field of social work, where the majority of students are women, 61% of the faculty in Canada are male, as are 91% of the full professors.[57] Similarly, in Canada three-fourths of library-science students are women, but only two-thirds of the librarians employed by universities and fewer than one-third of library heads are women.[58]

Tenure and promotions

Women are funnelled out partly through being denied tenure or promotions,[59] and women faculty, administrators, and graduate students who are also members of non-dominant groups are the proportionately least represented among faculty in general, tenured faculty, and administrators.[60] According to Forrest, Hotelling, and Kuk,[61] women take 2 to 10 years longer than men to get promotions, and only 47% of women faculty are tenured, compared with 69% of the men.[62] Furthermore, even 'the rate of *increase* [my italics] for tenured male faculty has been greater than that of women. Between 1972 and 1981, the percentage of tenured male faculty increased by 17.7 percent; the percentage of tenured female faculty increased by 13.4 percent.'[63] Chused reports that the probability for any male faculty member to be tenured is 46.3%, but for any female faculty member only 7%[64] Chused also points out that, in institutions where tenured women account for at least 12% of the faculty, other women are more likely to receive tenure.

Even where *hiring* of women is on the increase, however, the overall rates at which they get promotion and tenure are actually *declining*.[65] For various reasons, women may also drop out before they come up for tenure.[66] Even when women and men are matched for experience, educational background, and academic discipline, women are still less likely to advance in academic rank.[67]

One cannot even safely assume these days that any improvement in such patterns will persist. For example, at one university, while 80% of the women reviewed for tenure during a recent three-year period had been approved, only 33% of the tenure decisions affecting women faculty during the next year were positive.[68] And the pattern is the same even in fields in which the majority of staff members are women; thus, for instance, 'the male librarians in Canadian universities have been promoted more rapidly than the women, even when men's abilities have been the same or lesser.'[63]

As Associate Professor of Sociology Mary Frank Fox wryly observes, 'You would think there was something mystical about the figure for the proportion of women at full professor, because it just doesn't change ... It just sits there stagnating – almost independent of the changing pool of female Ph.D.-level scientists.'[70]

Administrative power

Rarely are women made department heads, deans, or other top administrators, and, despite being placed on many working committees, infrequently do they hold positions on the powerful ones or on funding
bodies or editorial boards. In research universities, women are more
likely than men to be laboratory assistants without academic rank than
to be project directors.[71]

According to the Council of Ontario Universities, in 1991–2 in Ontario
universities, women occupied 46.2% of middle-management, but only
19.2% of upper-management, positions.[72] In the United States, 'it is
uncommon for women to be department chairs, and rarer still for them
to be academic deans,' and 'women administrators remain concentrated
in a small number of low-status areas that are traditionally viewed as
women's fields.'[73]

Job security – or not

Women are disproportionately found in the job categories with the least
security.[74] Breslauer and Gordon report that 'more than double the proportion of females than males were in non-tenure-stream positions.
Looked at another way, female faculty represented 13.2% of the tenured
faculty, 28.6% of those in probationary appointments and 32.4% of
those on contract.'[75] Dagg and Thompson have identified a trend, due
to universities' increasing financial problems, for more women to be
hired than before – but only for short-term or part-time appointments.[76]
Thus, some institutions point with pride to the larger numbers of women
they have recently hired, without disclosing that a large proportion of
these are only in marginal positions, with no benefits and no job security
and at significantly lower salaries because of the marginality of those
positions.

According to Hensel, in the United States nearly 40% of faculty at
accredited U.S. higher-education institutions are part-time or are full-
time but temporary (both sexes combined), and most part-timers are
women. Furthermore, the growth of the proportion of part-timers who
are women exceeded the increase in women doctoral graduates during
the same time period.[77]

Women: less and more

Information about a variety of other aspects of women academics' experiences reflects women's second-class status, some of it through the

ways in which women receive *less* – (less financial support as graduate students, lower salaries in academic jobs, and fewer jobs in high-status institutions) and some through the ways in which women have *more* (heavier teaching loads and more child-care or other family responsibilities while also attending graduate school or working in academia).

Less money

According to a study of one major Canadian university, women tend to receive less financial support than men in graduate studies: in the humanities, a larger proportion of men than women received full, three-term fellowships; in the social sciences proportionally more women received the smallest, or 'fractional' fellowships; and in the physical sciences and engineering, there was an overwhelming disproportion of awards to males (although in the last case, this may be at least partly because of the disproportionately high number of males in those programs). Only in the life sciences was the distribution of financial support close to equal for the sexes.[78] Furthermore, 'on average approximately 3 times as many men as women were awarded Differential Fee Waivers.'[79] The school of graduate studies at that university reported that 'in *every division* and in *both doctoral and master's degrees females receive less average support from all sources (including loans, teaching assistantships, etc.) than do their male counterparts.*'[80] As graduate students, women are also less likely than men to be hired to assist in professors' research, to find well-paid jobs of most kinds – including those unrelated to their academic work, and to receive financial support from their families of origin or their spouses. 'Financial security – or the lack of it – can make or break one's graduate student career: ... financial aid correlates inversely with lower attrition rates (Patterson & Sells, 1973; Feldman, 1974) and the time taken to complete a graduate degree (Girves & Wemmerus, 1988). Financial support helps the student's self-esteem and gives her status as a scholar within her department. In addition, freedom from financial worries allows students to devote more of their time and energy to their studies. Students employed as teaching or research assistants and/or as fellows are more likely to become involved in their graduate programs and their graduate degrees, particularly at the PhD level. Working closely with faculty aids academic socialization by providing informal contacts with faculty (Girves & Wemmerus, 1988).'[81] Furthermore, research has shown that women with fewer socio-economic resources encounter increased problems in the areas of housing, child care, health, and finances.[82]

In view of the role of such resources in increased problems, it is worrying that women in general tend to be found in disciplines that are underfunded, such as in the humanities and social sciences;[83] that women tend to finish undergraduate studies more deeply in debt than men;[84] that women have a harder time finding well-paid summer jobs and earn less after graduation than do men, a more severe problem for those who are single, sole-support mothers;[85] that Blacks and Hispanics of both sexes are more likely than whites to have their loan applications rejected;[86] and that, for various reasons, women are less likely than men to be able to get money from their parents, from loans, from getting their own grants, from working on a faculty member's grant, or from paid consulting jobs obtained through professors' recommendations. Even when they can find jobs, the continuing, dramatic lack of pay equity means that employed women are likely, on average, to earn between 2/3 and 3/4 of what similarly employed men earn. As a result, women often take patchwork jobs at various places, and even when the work is within their field of study, women students not infrequently find they have to support themselves by teaching one course at each of two or three institutions simultaneously.

Even within those fields in which substantial funding tends to be provided to graduate students, major granting bodies and universities do not provide funding for students who are registered as part-time while raising a family. 'Moreover,' notes Delisle, 'it is only recently that graduate schools have adopted maternity leave policies ... that allow women to go inactive and defer internal awards. The external granting bodies do not give consideration to the reduction in productivity (papers published) either during pregnancy leave or during part-time studies.'[88]

Dagg and Thompson point out that unmarried women are likely to have to finance their own graduate study, and married women are discouraged from taking money for themselves if their husband needs it.[89] Married women are also discouraged from taking time from household or child-care chores to do paid work. Dagg and Thompson conclude that neither unmarried nor married women are likely to have men to support them. A related concern is the practice, in some settings, of awarding financial aid on the basis of 'speedy progress and high marks,'[90] which puts women drained by existing debt and family responsibilities at a selective disadvantage.

Furthermore, many kinds of financial aid are simply not allowed to be given to part-time students.[91] As Haley points out,[92] this starts a vicious cycle, so that students who are working part-time *in order to afford attending graduate school* therefore are only able to attend school part-time; as a result of their part-time enrolment, they are denied the chance to compete for most or all scholarships or other forms of financial aid within the graduate school. This not only is detrimental for their financial situation but also means that their lives are fragmented, with some energy going into their graduate program, while their wage-earning energy may go into work totally unrelated to their field of study.

Some problems with financial aid are especially stark. For instance, Hall and Sandler report that women students are sometimes excluded 'from consideration for teaching assistantships in areas where women as a group are traditionally considered weak, for example, in statistics,'[93] and Breslauer and Gordon note that 'granting councils ... ask about career interruptions and a woman who takes time out for childbearing has to explain this gap,'[94] and 'age limits for some scholarships and research grants impede the progress of women whose education might have been interrupted by household responsibilities.'[95] Smith et al.[96] document the fact that students on parental leave are not allowed to defer certain fellowships, another policy that is more likely to penalize women than men. And since it is far more likely to be women than men who start graduate school later in life on account of family responsibilities, the age restrictions on some prestigious awards and postdoctoral fellowships hit women harder than men.[97]

At the faculty level, women tend to be paid less than men, and the pattern is even worse for racialized women. According to U.S. reports, 'At every rank, in every field, at every type of institution, women still earn less than their male counterparts.'[98] According to Canadians Breslauer and Gordon, 'In 1985–86 ..., for all ranks combined, there was close to a $10,000 difference in median salary between males and females,'[99] and Canadian professor Constance Backhouse notes that in 1985–6 the median salary for women in every academic rank was lower than that for men.[100] Part of the salary differential is due to the over-representation of men and underrepresentation of women in the higher-paid job levels, but even within the full professor rank, the median salary for males was $63,407, while for female full professors it was $60,154.[101] Among 'non-regular' instructors (part-timers, sessionals, and so on), too, women earn less than men.[102]

A recent study of the University of California at Berkeley has revealed that 'women, black and American Indian professors' are paid 'significantly less' than their white male counterparts,'[103] with greater disparities at higher professional levels. Specifically, white male full professors are paid 15% more than aboriginals, 8% more than Blacks, and 6% more than the category of 'women.'

The same sex difference is found among academic administrators:[104]

for instance, in the province of Ontario in 1991–2, 77% of male middle managers but only 50% of female middle managers received salaries of $50,000 and over.[105]

Still worse, women are paid less than men at all levels, *even when* their productivity and experience, their academic fields, and their academic institutions are controlled for.[106] In fact, in the United States the salary differential for females and males actually *increased* after 1978.[107]

Breslauer and Gordon remind us that 'underpayment of salary is accompanied by the added inequity of lesser pensions and benefits'[108] and go on to observe that 'sometimes women are offered starting salaries so low that inequities are created which persist for the entire career unless corrected by some form of anomalies payment or pay equity initiative. This can occur for a variety of reasons. Sometimes women cannot afford to turn down the position for personal reasons; sometimes they are unwilling or unable to negotiate for higher starting salaries. In some high-demand fields, good female candidates can be lost by low starting salary offers. Following such an experience, department chairpersons may be heard making perplexed or indignant remarks to the effect that they have "tried to hire a woman" but have not been successful.'[109]

Less prestige

Women are not only concentrated among the lower ranks of academic positions but are also more likely to be located in what are regarded as the 'lower-status' institutions: 'The more prestigious the school or department, the fewer the women.'[110] Women are more likely than men to enter junior-college teaching rather than college or university posts in the United States.[111] It is relevant that salaries in junior or community colleges tend to be significantly lower than those in the so-called 'higher-prestige' institutions.

More teaching responsibilities

Hiring, tenure, and promotion decisions for full-time faculty jobs and jobs with the promise (or reality) of employment security tend to be based, at most institutions, far more on one's record of publication than on one's teaching. Time spent teaching means time and energy spent away from research, writing, and publishing. Yet women are disproportionately likely to be involved in teaching, and to teach for more hours and to have larger student bodies than are men.[112] This is not because women freely choose to do more teaching; indeed, the Carnegie Foundation report revealed that women and men had similar *interests* in doing teaching and research.[113] Furthermore, women and members of both sexes from non-dominant groups are more likely to be assigned heavier committee and student-advising responsibilities than their white male counterparts,[114] so that this unfair distribution appears not only in terms of formal teaching *per se* but also in terms of teaching-related responsibilities.

More family-related responsibilities

Time spent doing child-care and household tasks also drains time, energy, and concentration from both teaching and publishing, and women remain far more likely to do the lion's share of family-related care.[115] In this context, it is important to know that nearly half the women who stay in academia are either single or childless; that married women are even less likely than other women to be hired into the tenure track; that the average professor works 55 hours a week but those who have major child-care and home responsibilities work 70 or more hours a week; and that marriage tends to be a depressant of women's academic productivity but a stimulant for men's.[116] Having on-site, high-quality, flexible, affordable child care can be a great help, but that is all too rare. According to Jane Beach, research associate at the Childcare Resource and Research Centre of the University of Toronto, although most colleges and universities in Canada now have *some* child-care programs, many do not take infants and toddlers, and many have very few spaces because their purpose is to serve as laboratory schools rather than to help mothers (or fathers) who work or study at the institution.[117] Furthermore, many have huge waiting lists, and often the centres are too expensive for many potential users and lack flexibility in regard to hours they are open, with requirements that a particular child always be in the centre for the same hours every day, and so on.[118]

Appendix 2:
The Maleness of the Environment

1. The relative lack of incentives for women

Sooner or later, academic women acquire the kind of information given in chapter 1 and appendix 1 about women's limited chances to find mentors, earn higher degrees, obtain financial support in graduate school, and get teaching or research jobs followed by promotions and tenure. As a result, in Dagg's words, there is 'less incentive for women than men to earn Ph.D.s because they know their chances of becoming tenured professors are slim.'[1]

2. Sexist language, 'jokes,' and comments

It is my contention that I am not a crank, I am not a freak, I am not a totalitarian fascist determined to impose my will on others, I am not sexually deprived, I do not seek revenge on men, but I am labelled as these (and worse) to my face and behind my back, because of my lack of deference and my persistent failure to accept my 'proper place' as a subordinate female in a patriarchal, competitive and hierarchical system. C. RAMAZANOGLU[2]

Examples of anti-woman language, 'jokes,' and remarks in academia are depressingly abundant. We shall look first at some of the varied forms they take and then at the effects they have on academic women. Keep in mind that these comments come variously from faculty, other staff members, and students.

The forms

Roberta Hall and Bernice Sandler, pioneers in the description and analysis of how it feels to be a woman in academia, have listed a number
of forms of sexist language on campus; these include 'inappropriately
personal or sexual references, in order to annoy or distract women, or
to trivialize women's contributions, especially in circumstances where
performance is being evaluated; ... the use of generic HE; ... calling
women by first names and men by their last; addressing the class as if
no women were present (Asking a question with, "suppose your wife
...''); crediting men's comments to their author ("as Bill said") but not
women's; and phrasing classroom examples in a way which reinforces
a stereotyped and negative view of women's physiological traits (such
as describing a female character as typically weak and irrational).'[3] Sandler and Hall further point out that 'minority women may be subject to
even more "joking" remarks, especially about their sexuality, about preference given to minority women, and about how "they've got it made.'' '[4]
   Other general, common forms include the use of sexist language such
as 'man' or 'mankind' in class (when research has shown that the use
of sexist language perpetuates sexist beliefs and thoughts[5]); calling women
faculty Miss or Mrs, not Prof. or Dr;[6] the telling of sexist 'jokes' during
lectures; the use of only-female sexuality or body parts as the subjects
of mocking comments or to spice up lectures and slides; the practice of
referring to women as 'babes,' 'broads,' or even 'bitches'; spoken or
written (even in official letters of recommendation) evaluations of women
students' or faculty members' appearance or speculations about their
private lives; and comments that imply that women cannot be truly
serious about their work. Then, too, 'the naming of our degrees, the use
of the pronoun "he" in official university documents, courses which are
described as "Man and his Environment" all convey to women that they
are not a part of the university.'[7] Gloria Steinem has asked, 'How would
you feel if you got a spinster of arts degree when you graduated? ... Or
then got a mistress of science and had to work very hard to get a sis-
tership?'[8]
   It is helpful to know not only the general categories of sexist comments
but also some examples, because only such specifics can actually prepare
us for what we may encounter. Listed below are examples, some blatant
and some more subtle, that I was told in interviews or read in the
literature.

-   Professors called a woman with a 17-year-old son a 'good girl' because she did an excellent report, and then they warned that their sexist comments in class must not be censored.[9]
-   A faculty member said to a woman, 'I know you're competent and your thesis advisor knows you're competent. The question in our minds is are you *really serious* about what you're doing.'[10]
-   A faculty member remarked, 'The admissions committee didn't do their job. There's not one good-looking girl in the entering class.'
-   A male professor told a woman, 'I hear I'm supposed to stop looking at you as a sex object.'[11]
-   A woman professor reported, 'I remember having to correct at least two of my young male students because they addressed me as "dear."'[12]
-   In a medical school, a male clinician starts rounds daily with, 'Gentlemen, we shall begin.' When someone pointed out that a woman was part of their group, the professor said, 'You could have fooled me – she has no tits.'[13]
-   Comments from members of hiring committees, such as 'Why do we need another woman, we've already got one,'[14] or, from a male professor, 'I hope they don't put a woman on the de-canal selection committee.' And when a woman colleague, as-tonished by this remark made in her presence, demanded of him, 'How do you think that makes me feel?' he replied that in his eyes she was not a woman.[15]
-   A woman professor 'attempted to persuade the chair of her de-partment to stop referring to the secretaries as "girls" in his departmental correspondence. When she pointed out to him that even the publication style guidelines within their disci-pline encouraged the use of non-sexist language, he blew up.'[16]
-   'When I told my wonderful male dissertation chair I was getting married, he asked if I'd be dropping out of the pro-gram.'[17]
-   A 50-year-old woman faculty member was told by the dean that she was senile.[18]

Some of the most vicious forms of verbal harassment in recent years have included hostile responses such as 'No means more beer'[19] to an anti-date-rape campaign on a campus, such graffiti as 'Woman equals Nazi'[20] at a law school, vandalism perpetrated against a women's studies program,[21] and of course, most horrifying, the murder of fourteen women at l'Ecole polytechnique in Montreal.[22]

The effects

What does it do to women to be subjected to these sexist comments and behaviour or to be attacked for using non-sexist language or feminist material? As Backhouse et al. note, often there is clearly an intention to make women feel excluded: 'Often part of the fun seems to be to see how faculty women will respond.'[23]

In academic settings, where men's gender has rarely been used as a reason to exclude them or question their competence but where women's often has, it can be demoralizing and is certainly sexist simply to call attention repeatedly (even in allegedly harmless ways) to a woman's gender. As Backhouse reports, 'In some departments simply being female and a faculty member is enough to invite unwelcome comment.'[24] One woman told her, 'I don't think that there's a day goes by that some kind of comment isn't made about my being a woman.' This makes women feel that, in their work setting, their sex rather than their competence and their efforts is salient and important.

Faculty women report that it makes them feel helpless, displaced, alienated, singled out and conspicuous, unfeminine, excluded, trapped, deserving of blame, distanced, out of place, and chosen as a target for anger and resentment.[25]

The ways in which sexist language and remarks can have most of the above effects is self-evident, but some examples will help to clarify some of the more subtle or complex mechanisms. For instance, Backhouse et al. describe the ways that women may make varied and valiant efforts to respond to sexist jokes but nevertheless end up feeling helpless and displaced; they report one woman's 'three strategies for coping [with sexist jokes]: ignoring it (which doesn't stop it), joking back (which was ironically considered offensive by male faculty members), or assertiveness (which was criticized because it suggested that one was "too sensitive" or "didn't like men." One result of this was that women felt displaced from lounges and coffee rooms, thus missing opportunities for academic debate and discussion.'[26] Similarly, 'sometimes a joke may be prefaced with "You girls probably won't like this joke," perhaps as a way of excusing one's self. However, such a comment makes it difficult for a woman and others to oppose the joke. It also communicates to women that the speaker does not care if they are offended ... When women indicate their displeasure at joking remarks that express aggression toward individual women or toward women as a group, the rejoinder is often, "Can't you take a joke?" or "Don't you have a sense of humor?" – remarks aimed at making the woman feel that *she* is at fault, rather than the person who offended her.'[27]

Sometimes it seems that there is no good way to cope – and that very no-win set-up for women is a powerful contributor to the maleness of the academic environment.

An example of the way that sexist remarks can make women feel conspicuous in a negative way, as well as unfeminine, is given by Franklin et al.: 'One woman earned high grades in a traditionally male field. Her professor announced to a mostly male class that this represented an unusual achievement "for a woman" and was an indication, first, that the woman student was probably not really feminine, and second, that the males in the class were not truly masculine, since they allowed a woman to beat them.'[28] The feeling of exclusion caused by sexist comments and jokes was expressed by one assistant professor in the following way: 'I feel like I have just walked into a men's locker room.'[29]

3. The frequency of sexual harassment and the lack of safety for women

How many academic men have had their knee patted while discussing departmental affairs, been advised to seek therapy for their sexual problems after a stormy staff meeting, had the size and desirability of their bottom discussed in public by colleagues?

C. RAMAZANOGLU[30]

In many college and university policies about sexual harassment, the sexist comments described in the previous section are explicitly included in the term 'sexual harassment.' Whereas 'sexual harassment' initially was defined fairly stringently as a demand for sexual contact, backed by the threat of reprisals from someone who had the power to do so, the term has been expanded in most settings to include gender-based harassment and the creation of a hostile or discomfitting work environment, such as by the displaying of photographs of nude women.[31]

Harassment has been and still is a particularly difficult problem for women to know how to handle, because the very naming by women of some behaviour as 'sexual harassment' is often treated as though it were a form of violence against men, an intrusion on men's rights.[32] As a consequence, a woman who dares to apply this label risks incurring still more wrath and harassment in addition to being treated as though *she* is the problem.

In this section, we shall look at the kinds of gender-based abuses of power that go beyond the level of sexist remarks, as well as at the most extreme end of the harassment continuum: lack of physical safety for academic women because of their gender.

Gender-based mistreatment and harassment

First, we shall look at the incidence of sexual harassment, then at some of the reasons that it is directed at women graduate students and faculty, next at the forms it takes, and finally at some of the effects it has on its targets.

Incidence

Women graduate students are at greater risk as targets for sexual harassment than are undergraduates, since they have more at stake, needing positive recommendations from professors in their programs in order to get jobs in their chosen fields.[33] Furthermore, they are exceptionally vulnerable because they must work individually and closely with their supervisors, most of whom are men.[34] Disturbingly, research has shown that women graduate students are even more likely than female undergraduates to be harassed. In various studies, it has been reported that 36%, 61%, and 'about three-quarters'[35] of female graduate students have been the targets of sexual harassment, usually by male faculty. In a Harvard University study, 32% of faculty women with tenure and 49% of untenured women reported having been sexually harassed.[36] Furthermore, one study showed that nearly one in five women graduate students on one campus had had their safety threatened or violated on campus while graduate students,[37] and 4% of students on another campus had been sexually assaulted.[38]

These types of treatment do not appear to be significantly related to either age, marital status, or academic department, but for students the incidence does appear to increase with level; that is, it is significantly worse of Ph.D. than for master's students.[39]

Reasons

Because so little work has been done with perpetrators of sexual harassment, it is not known for certain why graduate-student and faculty women would be such likely harassment targets. However, some suggestions have been made both about the motivations of individual harassers and about the laissez-faire attitudes of administrators who run the institutions in which the harassment takes place.

One might speculate that male faculty find it easier to rationalize their harassment of women in those two groups than, say, of undergraduate women, because the graduate-student and faculty women are older and therefore presumably better able than undergraduate women to choose whether or not to have sexual contact. In fact, of course, it could be argued that higher-status women have even fewer degrees of freedom, because their chances for employment, tenure, promotion, and winning of funding in their chosen fields are so closely tied to the men on the faculty and in the administration. It is certainly true that, since graduate students are more likely than undergraduates to work closely with faculty, potential harassers have far more opportunities to harass the former.

Morris also suggests that sexual harassment is a way some men deal with what they perceive as threats to 'male supremacy,' threats they believe to be stronger from higher-status women.[40] Thus, such men resist women's power and devalue them through harassment. Furthermore, Morris notes, 'most PhD programmes have relatively few women, and as the status of women as doctoral students becomes increasingly inconsistent with social expectations, more effort can be expected to devalue them as students.'[41]

At a different level, sexual harassment in general persists in part because the university 'doesn't take responsibility for the climate that normalizes [sexual harassment] ... They don't have a clue what systemic discrimination is, so they're constantly dealing with events as if they're aberrant.'[13] McIntyre gives the example of one administration's lack of response to the joking that took place in its law school the day after the massacre of fourteen women students on a Montreal campus. She says the administration was insensitive: 'It was a scary time to be a feminist ... in the face of really evident fear by women, they didn't get it. Nobody spoke for women and said how awful, on this of all days.' Instead, the university tried to protect itself. 'They act as if the worst that can happen in the gender wars is that your school gets pointed at as one where this happens.'[43]

Added to both individual perpetrators' motives and academic institutions' permissive attitudes toward harassment are the general, pervasive sexism and condoning of violence throughout our culture that
have been shown to perpetuate both violent and demeaning behaviour
and the acceptance of women in particular as targets for that type of
behaviour.[44]

Forms

The forms that overt sexual harassment or threats to women's safety
may take include the following:

–   Faculty and internship supervisors 'hitting on' female graduate
     students[45]
–   Unwanted touching, male faculty members draping their arms
     around women faculty, hugging, 'bum patting,' patting the
     stomachs of pregnant women, lifting women up bodily by the
     shoulders and moving them when faculty men want to pass
     them in the hall, and male faculty – even married ones – prop-
     ositioning women[46]
–   Sexual staring or sexual remarks, through to sexual advances
     and sexual assaults[47]
–   Accosting or attacks, 'peeping,' or physical threats[48]
–   'Men tending to claim more physical space than women, using
     touching as a way to assert power or dominance; tenured pro-
     fessors having more trouble remembering the women graduate
     students' names than the men's; ... dismissing a woman who
     doesn't understand something but offering more attention and
     help to a man who doesn't; not answering women's questions;
     ... instructors who can't answer questions say[ing] the women
     or "girls" don't understand; ... coaching men but not women
     students in working toward a fuller answer by probing further;
     waiting longer for men than women to answer a question; re-
     sponding more extensively to men's comments than to
     women's'[49]
–   A parking-lot security guard telling a woman faculty member
     who reported that a man was lying across the floor in front of
     the elevator on the level where she had parked her car, 'Oh,
     that's just Fred. Don't pay any attention to him,' and then re-
     fusing her request that the guard accompany her to her car (in-
     terview)

- A male faculty member insisting that each of his female graduate students come to his office individually, allegedly so that
  he could approve their paper topics, then holding and rubbing
  his penis while talking to them (interview)

Effects

The women against whom these kinds of behaviour have been directed
have experienced serious negative effects, including the following:

- 'Uncomfortable' feelings[50]
- Anger, frustration, depression, and anxiety[51]
- Negative effects on academic standing[52]
- Withdrawal from the university[53]
- Impairment of 'the freedom of women to work late, take eve-
  ning courses, attend extra-curricular events, or accept night
  jobs on campus'[54]
- For lesbians, racialized women, and disabled women in particular, all of whom are even more frequent targets of harassment
  and sexual assault than are white, heterosexual, able-bodied
  women, there are intensified concerns for intellectual safety,
  political safety, and physical safety (for instance, if males in a
  course you teach have harassed you and you have to leave
  your office after class at 10 PM)[55]
- Fear of teaching courses that might arouse harassing students'
  or colleagues' wrath; fear of speaking one's mind as a student
  or faculty member and exercising one's academic freedom; and
  especially the fear of lecturing and writing from a feminist
  perspective[56]
- Dropping of courses, avoidance of discussion groups[57]
- Fear of receiving bad recommendations from harassers whose
  advances were rejected[58]
- The undermining of self-confidence as an intellectual from
  wondering, 'Does he think I'm smart or just want to sleep with
  me?'[59]

4. The devaluing of women

On account of their gender, it is not uncommon for academic women
to be suspected of not taking their work seriously[60] and even of not
doing their own work.[61] Theodore recounts the story of a woman who

was explicitly asked, when applying for an academic job, 'Are you really serious?'[62] Systematic research has shown that neither otherwise left-wing, progressive people nor religiously conservative nor 'antiminority' university personnel are either more or less likely than others to consider women to be dedicated to their academic work.[63]

Even more insulting and destructive are the comments baldly made to racialized women academics. As one Black female doctoral student reported, 'Many professors believe that blacks in general cannot write; consequently, many black students realize that certain professors will never give an A to a black student, even though she or he may deserve it.'[64] This statement was substantiated with several examples, such as, 'A black student turned in a research paper to a professor, and in returning the paper to the student, the professor commented, "I did not know blacks could write like that." '[65] And still another black female student, who had received only A grades and positive feedback throughout her doctoral studies, was accused of not writing her dissertation and was required to prove to her adviser and committee that she had done the work.[66]

Women report being frequently insulted and demeaned in various ways,[67] including having their work undervalued in the peer-review process because they are women;[68] being dehumanized; being ignored; being discouraged, even in the face of obvious and substantial accomplishments; and being patronized.[69]

As an example of women facing blatant insults, according to one woman, 'At times, the *loathing would strike me* – e.g., when I was hired into a tenure-track position and was told (jokingly) that the only reason I was hired was that nobody else who was a qualified clinician had applied.'[70] Ironically, with affirmative action's arrival, it is often charged that the person was hired *only* because she is a woman or a member of another non-dominant group. And, according to another faculty woman, 'there had been one predictably vitriolic review [of my work] in one of the Toronto newspapers, by a journalist who "trashed" it for its feminist perspective. My first day in the faculty, I arrived in the faculty lounge ... To my surprise and discomfort, someone had tacked the column up on the bulletin board ... the most vicious passages were underlined in red. In some other context, I wouldn't have minded. I'm not afraid of criticism, and I actually thought some of the more far-fetched parts of the article were rather funny. But I didn't really know a soul in the faculty yet.'[71]

The following incident illustrates the way women are ignored: 'where the external assessments of the unit in question had specified the lack of women as an issue to be addressed by the new selection committee, [a woman faculty member on the committee] waited and waited to see if *anyone* else would raise the question [of how do we recruit women] ... When it was clear that no one else would take responsibility for these issues, she finally raised the question herself.'[72] Women have also had their authority subverted, 'whether directly or through foot-dragging': one woman administrator, for example, reports that a male subordinate would go over her head to a higher-level administrator and come back with 'Bill and I have talked about this, and we've decided ...' In another instance, when a woman chair attempted to institute a mandated faculty-evaluation policy in her all-male department, she faced comments to the effect that the department 'got along well enough without this kind of mothering,' coupled with department members' refusal to take her directives seriously and 'forgetting' to follow the procedures.[73]

5. The devaluing of much of women's work[74]

Although some women faculty fit the traditional academic model of claiming to do objective research, working on their own and within a single academic discipline on theoretical research in traditional ways on traditional topics, many women do not. Increasingly, women academics are questioning the whole notion that there can be such a thing as objectivity, and as Naomi Black points out, 'any questioning of objectivity is likely to receive a hostile response when voiced by women, however non-feminist, simply because their presence challenges the male monopoly that produced the illusion of objectivity.'[75] Women are also increasingly likely to do interdisciplinary and team research and to have their work devalued because of that.[76] Similarly devalued are the kinds of academic endeavours that involve applied, practical, action-oriented, 'relevant,' 'political,' or community-based work, as well as work that calls into question the academic status quo, mainstream research, or even the power distributions in the wider society[77] – and it is precisely these kinds of work that many women academics undertake, rather than the type that's 'aimed at the small, select audience who read academic journals ... This perspective has not always been well received by assessment committees. The Academic Freedom and Tenure Committee of the Canadian Association of University Teachers reports the number of cases it handles from women is about double their representation in the university. Many of these involve women who have challenged academic orthodoxy.'[78] Since, according to one study, about 70% of women do non-mainstream work that often 'differs from and ultimately challenges established scholarly patterns,'[79] this constitutes a major problem, for it is difficult to get such work published in the mainstream, refereed journals that count so much in decisions about hiring, tenure, and promotions;[80] and even if it is published in those highly respected journals, the hiring, tenure, and promotions committees within one's own college or university may devalue it or even use it against the applicant because of the nature of the topics, the approach, or both. Cummings et al. note that 'senior faculty members, who are usually male, are inclined to see fresh perspectives as less than serious, perhaps even frivolous, and a personal challenge to them.[81] Thus, women are frequently criticized for lacking in originality, not taking their work seriously, not working on mainstream research and not publishing in established journals.[82]

In the so-called hard sciences, it is apparently even easier than in other academic disciplines for biases against women and non-traditional work to come into play, because most journals in the hard sciences do not use blind review: instead, the reviewers know the identities of the authors whose work they evaluate.[83] This means, for instance, that women have to think long and hard about the risks to their career of teaching such non-traditional courses as 'Philosophy of Human Sexuality,' 'Psychology of Sex and Gender,' or 'Social and Political Factors in Research on the Biology of Gender.' Even one's extracurricular work can affect the decisions one's evaluators make about one's career. One woman I interviewed told me that when she started a birth-control clinic that offered abortion counselling in the town where she had an academic job, she 'naively assumed' that that wouldn't affect her university standing. But powerful faculty members who got wind of that extracurricular work used it to brand her academic work as unscholarly, presumably because it was too closely related to the 'real world' and perhaps because they objected to abortion counselling altogether.

According to Aisenberg and Harrington, women are less likely than men to feel comfortable 'throwing out data just to yield or keep to a neat theory.'[84] This is probably partly becuase women are more likely than men to be accustomed to dealing with the complexities and 'messiness' of feelings and interpersonal relationships and partly because so many women's terribly low self-esteem[85] makes them less likely to feel they have the right to toss out information that is difficult to explain. It is easy to understand how the association of women academics with 'messy,' subjective, unscholarly work is perpetuated, when the pattern just described is combined with women's greater tendency than men to teach courses that deal with emotional and personal issues, as well as to spend time outside of class listening to students talk about personal problems. This is a powerful instance of the operation of the catch-22 that women cannot deal both with issues of feelings or nurturance and with issues requiring intellectual rigour.

As a result of this devaluing of the work that many academic women choose to do, 'women's self-esteem is undermined and their authority and credibility subverted in ways which ensure that they will not have an opportunity to realize their potential.'[86]

6. The exclusion and isolation of women

It has been said that, because of the 'chilly climate' for women on campus,[87] women feel isolated and excluded from the collegial networks that are at the heart of academia.[88] Haley has observed that academic 'women in particular lead marginal lives as compared to other women their age,'[89] and as Theodore has pointed out, women who also belong to other groups that are targeted for discrimination have been told outright that they simply 'don't fit.'[90]

This exclusion generates 'a strong sense of uncertainty, frustration and alienation ... that plagues most women academics at one point or another in their careers and sometimes throughout their professional lives.'[91] Indeed, feelings of isolation and bitterness were reported in one study to be expressed even more by senior faculty women than by faculty women at more junior levels,[92] perhaps in part because their numbers are even smaller at higher levels.

Both intentional and unintentional 'oversights'[93] can lead women graduate students, women in the academic hiring process, and women faculty on the job both to feel and to be marginalized or excluded.

Women graduate students

In a variety of ways, women graduate students have been made to feel they don't belong in academia. Some department heads say freely that they don't like to take women as students because they won't complete their degree programs but will marry and make home their primary responsibility (interview) – and, ironically, some deny women funding because they assume their husbands will support them.[94] Male faculty have been known to say, 'We didn't ask women to come here'; to help men but not women students get part-time jobs while they are still in school; to take longer to give women than men students feedback on drafts of their work; to ignore women selectively in class; to welcome the same comment or question from a man that they ignored when it came from a woman; to offer spontaneously to write letters of reference for men students but not for equally competent women students; and to be more likely to invite men than women to assist them in giving workshops, go on out-of-town trips with them to meet colleagues at other institutions, encourage them to write grants for financial support, and ask them to co-author publications with them.[95]

Some specific, nightmarish stories told by Theodore[96] include male faculty giving women bad course grades despite their having received A's in all their work throughout the term, withholding information about scholarships from women, giving women false questions to prepare for their preliminary or general examinations while pretending they were real questions, and giving them bogus job referrals. Theodore also describes the experience of a woman research assistant whose male boss had her run 120 experiments but had his two male assistants run only between 20 and 40 experiments apiece. The professor became 'furious' when she asked him about this.

In the hiring process

In spite of the recent emphasis on affirmative action or employment equity that has brought improvements to some settings, many administrators are defensive about the still slow rate at which most institutions continue to hire women and especially those from other non-dominant groups for faculty positions. Not uncommonly they say, 'We *really want* to hire women, but there just aren't good ones around.' A bit of investigation often reveals, however, that when women do apply, they aren't even asked to come in for interviews.[97]

The fact that a job is advertised is certainly no guarantee that the search will be fairly and openly carried out. Jobs are often advertised when a search committee has either explicitly or tacitly already decided whom to hire – and since most search committees are primarily white and male, white men are most likely to have been informed of the search or given encouragement in response to their initial inquiries. Such committee members then tend to recruit white, male candidates informally, through the old boys' network. Furthermore, 'the official policy of giving preference to internal candidates is often given only lip-service and in practice well-qualified women are passed over.'[98]

My own experience is an example of the latter. I had accepted a one-year teaching position late one summer, begun teaching some of the program's core courses in September, and had received excellent evaluations from my students. When, during that year, the same job was advertised but this time as a tenure-stream one, I hastened to apply, knowing my curriculum vitae fit the job description to a T. The top administrator had chosen a search committee, mostly of men from a somewhat different branch of psychology from my own – and not the branch named in the job description. When I was the only suitable candidate to apply, the committee decided to widen its search. In principle, it's fair enough to widen a search; however, at a time when the Canadian government was only allowing hiring from outside of Canada if no one living or working in Canada was suitable for the position, this group short-listed four white males who were U.S. citizens residing in the United States. In contrast, as a landed immigrant, I was already allowed to work in Canada. To add insult to injury, all four came from the same branch of psychology as the majority of the search committee members, and only one could conceivably have fit the job description.

Nevertheless, my institution paid to fly all four men to Toronto, put them up at a fancy hotel, took them out for meals at expensive restaurants, and scheduled them to present colloquia. They forgot to schedule my colloquium and to invite me to lunch – until I raised the subject myself. Determined to avoid hiring me, the committee made no clear recommendation, and no one got the job. In fact, not until June – extremely late for a position that was due to begin in September – did the powers-that-be notice that they had no one to teach their core courses, and they hastily asked me if I would do it for another year. I said I would accept if I got a promotion and a raise, and to my surprise, they agreed. Incredibly, the following year, something very similar happened – although ultimately, I got the job, because no one else remotely qualified applied. I have since learned how common such experiences are for women, and it makes us feel neither secure nor welcomed when we are treated in these ways.

Lest women believe that if they *are* flown in for a job interview they will be well treated, consider this story: 'During her interview for a position, ... [a woman] was picked up from her hotel by a male faculty member, dropped off in his office and left by herself with the [newspaper] for an hour. "What was so astonishing about this," she said, "was that he left without saying anything. I discovered shortly that all this time he was chatting next door with a male colleague. I guess his discomfort with a prospective female faculty member was such that he just couldn't bear to sit down and exchange pleasantries with me that morning.'[99] And even when a woman is actively recruited for a one-year job, the department may well refuse to consider her for reappointment, thus rapidly shifting her from the status of insider to that of isolate.[100]

Naturally, male academics sometimes have similar experiences, but it can be more painful and confusing for women for three reasons: (1) if we become assertive when ignored, we know we risk being considered too hard-driving; (2) we are already likely to feel – consciously or not – less welcome in academia than are men, so such experiences compound the feeling of exclusion; and (3) our frequently terrible low self-esteem usually leads us to conclude that we deserve such unspeakable treatment rather than that our hosts are simply unsocialized fellows!

On the faculty

Once a woman has an academic job, she may well continue to be isolated and excluded, either formally or informally. Formally, for instance, because of anti-nepotism rules in some institutions, only one member of a married couple can be tenured or hold a position above a certain rank, and as a matter of practice, the member of the couple most likely to suffer from such rules has been the woman.

Also in formal proceedings, women faculty who complain to the administration about being harassed (on the basis of sex, race, age, sexual orientation, or physical ability) by a male colleague typically find that, if the harasser fights the charge, he will be defended by the faculty association or union to which they both belong.

Less formally, Cummings et al. have described the lack of support women faculty receive for 'addressing problems related to teaching, research or personal matters,'[101] thus preventing them from fully becoming colleagues and instead treating them as inadequate, incompetent, insecure, or lacking in 'collegiality.' Such walls, encountered daily as part of the routine that seems to emerge as part of the normal process in many areas, make any new pitfall or obstacle particularly daunting.[102]

Faculty women's descriptions of the informal ways they are excluded are many and varied. They include the following:[103]

– Men talking less to women than to other men
– Men rarely including women in informal activities
– Men stopping talking when a female colleague enters the faculty lounge or lunch-room
– Men during a coffee break shifting the subject when a woman approaches
– Men changing the subject to 'solicitous inquiries about her children or husband' when a woman colleague approaches
– Men ignoring a woman's attempt to join a conversation

- Men ignoring women's comments
- Men not notifying women when meetings are scheduled
- Men briefing other men, but not women, routinely in informal ways prior to meetings
- Men maintaining an extremely male-oriented social life, such as fishing trips, racquetball, and poker, which women are rarely invited to join
- Men being collegial with women, but only when no other men are present
- Men on a search committee discussing, in the presence of a woman colleague, how they could avoid hiring a woman
- Men postulating in the presence of female colleagues that employment equity will lower standards

As Pyke has said, academics function to a great extent 'through colleague or networking systems through which the informal and unwritten rules of the profession are disseminated and insider information shared.'[104] When women are excluded from these systems, they both *feel* marginalized and *are in fact* marginalized, kept ignorant of the 'rules' that really count.

Some of my interviewees who work in the humanities or social sciences said they wished they worked in the 'hard sciences,' because they felt that there, objectivity, fairness, and equality would surely reign, with the work taking precedence over everything else. However, according to Jessie Bernard, 'Women scientists are less likely than men to be invited to participate in situations making for opportunities for informal communication ... Fewer women were editors, associate editors, or members of professional panels and committees which would bring them into contact with confreres from other laboratories.'[105] Indeed, the sciences have traditionally been more disproportionately male than the other fields, and in fields with relatively few females, 'there are some indications that overt sexist behavior is more prevalent,'[106] that the men are more likely to isolate and exclude women, if only because they are not sure how to behave with females who are their potential or actual colleagues.[107]

What helps

As with so many elements of academic life that intensify the maleness of the environment, my informants and those who have published their own work in this field report (and I have also noted) that the greatest

antidote to feelings of alienation and isolation is the company and support of other women.[108] As one woman told me: 'I was hired as the
only woman in my department and one of the few in the whole, geo-
graphically isolated college. I was so busy that it took me a year to link
up with other women, but when I did, it really helped. I realized that
my own feelings and experiences were not weird and that I was not
crazy.'

7. The even greater harassment and exclusion of women from non-dominant groups and of feminists

'Minority women, by race, ethnicity, sexual orientation, or disability
have often felt a double isolation – from mainstream, male relationships
and from white female networks, as well. One black faculty member
stated: "I've been here since September 1969 ... I never have and I never
will be part of the inner circle and I've always recognized that." '[108]
Academic women readily learn that even more risky than being a woman
faculty member per se is being a woman who is also a member of another
non-dominant group or being known to be a female member of the
women's studies faculty or a feminist.

According to the Ontario Confederation of University Faculty Associations, such groups as the disabled and First Nations peoples have
been even 'more effectively excluded than others':

> When one considers the number of First Nations women in Can-
> ada, and their conspicuous absence from campuses either as
> students, staff or faculty, the drastic effects of being doubly dis-
> advantaged are clear. For the heroic few doubly or triply disad-
> vantaged who do squeeze through gaps in the ivory walls, the
> chilly environment, the additional burdens placed upon them
> merely by virtue of who they are, the loneliness and isolation,
> the lack of role models, etc., ensure that this number remains a
> marginalized and silent minority.
>
> As for the disabled, their omission from university participation
> is compounded by societal attitudes which see the differently
> abled as unabled, by physical barriers ..., and by lack of financial
> resources to provide assistance (counselling services, health care
> facilities, etc.). Those who are academically qualified are inhib-
> ited/excluded by these barriers.[110]

The Committee on Women in Psychology has detailed a variety of the forms that racism takes in academia,[111] and recent empirical research reveals that 15% of 'visible minority students' experience 'unpleasant racial experiences' on campus,[112] and another 18% report having seen racial graffiti and hate literature there. A majority of the students polled 'believed that professors, administrators and staff are not as caring about the problems of the visible minorities as they are about majority race students,' and two of the most serious problems they reported facing were those 'relating to cultural differences' and racial discrimination.[113] In another study, 20% of students from all races reported having witnessed at least one racist incident on campus during the previous year, and 17% said that racism on campus was prevalent.[114]

In their respective papers, Rothblum, Barale, and Rohrbaugh carefully explore some of the forms of exclusion and mistreatment to which lesbians and gay men in academia are subjected;[115] *Lilith* magazine documents a variety of incidents of campus harassment in which the form of racism displayed was anti-Semitism;[116] and Farrell and Jones write about different manifestations of racism in higher education.[117] In a recent U.S. study, of 125 lesbians and gay males at university, three-quarters had experienced verbal abuse, 26% had been threatened with violence, and 17% had had personal property damaged.[118] Furthermore, as Kitzinger notes, 'We also confront blatant heterosexism systematically built into conditions of employment and contractual arrangements: relocation expenses, for example, often apply to the prospective employee plus legally defined "spouse" only, and superannuation schemes rarely cover a same sex partner so that there are privileges for people who enter into heterosexual marriages which lesbians and gay men (as well as single people) are prevented from sharing.'[119] Thus, graduate students and faculty who are not only female but who also belong to other non-dominant groups often have to cope with both sexual harassment and other types of harassment as well.

For feminists of any stripe, harassment because of their politics is a risk. Kitzinger reports that 'one sympathetic (male) member of a psychology department which had rejected my application for a lectureship told me that his department already had a feminist and that, as far as some members of the department were concerned, she was "one too many."' [120] Dagg and Thompson have said that 'many women fear to talk about or recognize sexism because they fear they will be treated worse.'[121] This scenario is related to the catch-22 that working with other women for change means you risk being perceived as threatening, but not doing so can mean you remain isolated and powerless. Here, we encounter another catch-33 – that, although by *not* teaching women's studies you may remain isolated from a potential, important source of support, by *teaching* women's studies 'you risk remaining an outsider.'[122]

Simply feeling like an outsider is by no means the worst consequence of taking, majoring in, or teaching women's studies or being known as a feminist. As Backhouse et al. found, 'Feminist faculty who teach in the field of women's studies reported an intrusive institutional preoccupation with their sexual orientation ... When [one instructor] included academic materials on homosexuality and lesbianism in her courses, the students complained to the chair that she was "gay" ... Many women are intimidated by the pervasive scrutiny of their sexuality, and some find themselves deterred from teaching or researching in areas that are commonly viewed as challenging to heterosexual or male-dominant stereotypes. The implications for academic innovation are staggering.'[123]

In addition to preoccupation with their sexuality or sexual orientation, known feminists or women's studies faculty risk incurring uninhibited displays of wrath, mostly but not always from men. Examples include a male professor who said, 'You should be teaching this [women's studies] stuff on street corners'[124] and male students accusing a professor of 'shoving [her] politics down students' throats.' And law professor Sheila McIntyre reported that, when she simply used the phrase 'women and men' instead of 'men and women,' she was the target of angry behaviour.[125]

Other common displays of anger include verbal attacks, shouting down, and mockery for using non-sexist language or lecturing from a feminist perspective.[126] Even behaviour one might expect to have been left far behind by the time students reach university can reappear: Theodore reports spitballs being thrown at a feminist lecturer.[127]

Here is an incident I witnessed first-hand. When a department chair announced in a faculty meeting that she had requested that the new dissertation guidelines include a requirement that non-sexist language be used, a male colleague became red in the face, began to shake with rage, and shrieked, 'Does this mean that when my students are writing about a man, they will have to call him "she?!" '

Such informal, unofficial displays of hostility and ostracism are not always the only forms in which negative attitudes toward feminists are expressed. Some places simply will take great pains to avoid hiring you if you are known to be a feminist.[128] Or, once hired, you may encounter trouble. The committees that make tenure decisions are usually mostly or entirely composed of men, and not infrequently male faculty members undervalue or devalue feminist research and publications,[129] sometimes by labelling them as propaganda or as political *rather than* scholarly – as though conservative, traditional forms of research are free from propaganda or political implications. Since not getting tenure often ends one's academic career, many women who wish to do either scholarly or political work for women avoid such undertakings until after they have tenure.[130] 'Women involved in scholarship on women and gender [have] frequently commented that their research was not recognized as legitimate in their home department, and they felt that their scholarly efforts in this area were not given equal weight with research on non-gender related topics.'[131]

Racialized women faculty report that this dilemma can be even worse for them than for other women: 'Women of color found themselves in a double bind: their involvement in teaching and research on gender and race was perceived as insufficient by their students and as excessive by their chairs.'[132]

Laurence relates the following story of a woman's exclusion because of her association with women's studies: 'a woman ... had just completed her Ph.D. in business: she was called in by the department head where she was in the second year of a term contract and now hoping for a tenure track appointment and told she did not fit in with the group, that they did not like her participation on the university Women's Studies committee and she was advised to resign; they did not like the feminist content in her courses and if she said nothing to anyone about this interview she would get a good recommendation in her application for a position at another university. Her teaching evaluations were good ... She has since left academia and gone into the private sector.'[133]

Women even report being denied their most basic rights because of what or how they choose to teach. For instance, Backhouse et al. relate the story of a woman whose department chair refused to allow her to identify her (feminist) area of research in the departmental graduate brochure.[134] This same woman was refused permission to teach graduate courses, and the situation persisted until the university formally stepped in to stop it.

As students, women are not infrequently discouraged from majoring in women's studies. In the undergraduate women's studies program in which I teach, we were informed that a faculty adviser was telling his students, 'If you want to get into the law school here, be sure you don't major in women's studies.' When I phoned the dean of the law school to check this out, he told me that not only was that not true but that their admissions committee was then headed by an ardent feminist.

Similarly, at the institution where I teach graduate students, at least two male professors in my own department regularly warn women students not to take courses from feminist faculty. Sometimes they say that students will be pressured to take part in lesbian sexual activities if they enrol in our courses, and sometimes – when the students indicate that they know some of us are heterosexual – the professors simply look menacing and vaguely suggest that it would not be in the students' interests to be associated with us.

Faculty women who work to improve the status of women are often disparaged not only to students but also to committees who are reviewing their performance, as well as being marginalized from decision making in their department and faculty.[135] Not only being publicly known as a feminist or teaching women's studies but even venturing to raise an issue related to women can elicit outbursts of rage, as in this example: '[I was the sole woman serving on a committee.] The job of the committee I was told was to assure the quality and standards of graduate training ... During one of the first meetings that fall, I noted the lack of women or mention thereof in accounting for the programs, faculties, students, and consultants. The male on my immediate left turned to me, rose up in his chair, looked down his nose at me and stated venomously and emphatically – "oh god, don't tell me you're one of those women's libbers! don't tell me we are going to have to hear about the woman thing!" and turned back to the group to get on with the business, having taken care of the miscreant.'[136]

8. The existence of a double standard

In an important sense, most of chapters 1 through 5, as well as this appendix, are about the sex-based double standard in academia, the existence of one set of rules and standards for women and a quite different set for men. In this section, however, we shall use some examples to illustrate the range of situations in which the double standard has its impact.

Evaluation

Different standards for women and men operate when their work in academia is evaluated. Research shows that, regardless of academic discipline, work is rated higher when allegedly produced by a man than when allegedly produced by a woman.[137] Other research reveals that racialized women academics are more critically evaluated by students of both sexes than are other academics and that male students are more critical of women academics than of men in technical fields such as math and science.[138] Not only are women faculty from non-dominant groups evaluated by some people more harshly than other women and than men, but the same appears to be true for women *students* from non-dominant groups. For instance, a student who had received all A's on her papers had her grades changed to B's when the professor discovered she was Black.[139]

Double standards for evaluation come into play when individuals are considered for jobs, tenure, and promotion; for instance, a man's non-academic experience may be regarded as 'enriching,' while that of a woman may be regarded as revealing a 'lack of focus.'[140] And women's accomplishments may be downgraded when they are equal or even superior to those of their male peers:

–   A man is described as 'serving on two departmental commit-
     tees and *even* on one institutional committee,' while a woman
     with identical experience is noted as 'serving on two depart-
     mental committees but *only* on one institutional committee.'[141]
–   A woman dean with two years' experience is said to be 'mov-
     ing too fast,' whereas a man with comparable experience is
     seen as appropriately 'on the fast track.'[142]

Common practices in regard to the authorship of papers and books have often made the double standard for evaluation hard to question. Typically, the wife (or woman student or faculty colleague) is listed as second author when she and her husband publish together – or, even if she is first author, it is assumed that the real creativity behind the work was his.[143] Indeed, one woman-man pair wrote a book together, and partly on the basis of that book, he was awarded tenure. She, however, was refused tenure on the grounds that she had 'done no work of her own' (interview).

Labelling

Labelling is heavily shaped by a double standard. Backhouse et al. say that 'male faculty might be viewed as eccentric, they might be ridiculed or imitated, but they would never be attacked as incompetent. For women, the connotation of incompetence is always tacked on.'[144] It is poignant, then, that women faculty who feel inadequate and long for advice, in-formation, or support dare not go to colleagues for help, for fear that

that will be seen as proof of their incompetence – whereas a man who asks for help is more likely to be regarded as taking the appropriate initiative in adjusting to his new setting.[145] Women who turn down committee assignments often are called 'ungrateful' or 'not interested in advancement,' whereas a man will more likely be treated with respect for refusing to sacrifice research time for busy-work.[146]

Even the very labels 'part-time' and 'full-time' are based on spurious, gender-based double standards about what constitutes such work: 'As Everett C. Hughes has pointed out, academic men in fact work part-time at their supposed jobs, spending the rest in committee meetings, office sociability, and other activities; but by social definition this is full-time work. The woman, however, who teaches regularly and intensively during the hours her children are in school is defined as a part-time worker, even though she actually puts in as many hours as the men.'[147]

Student–faculty interactions

Student–faculty interactions are another arena in which the double standard is evident. These include the following:

–   Some faculty ask women ' "lower order" factual questions ("When did Wordsworth write the first version of *The Prelude*?") and reserve "higher order" critical questions for men ("What do you see as the major thematic differences between the 1805 and 1850 versions?").'[148]
–   Some professors interrupt women more often than men students or allow women to be easily interrupted by others in class discussion.[149]
–   Male students tend to interrupt faculty of both sexes more than do female students.[150]
–   Male students tend to interrupt female professors significantly more often than male professors.[151]
–   'Students accept high standards, discipline and toughness from their male teachers and deeply [resent] any such behaviour from their women teachers.'[152]
–   Students evaluate female professors more harshly than male ones.[153]
–   A male professor tells a female doctoral student he cannot give her much direct supervision, because he has a jealous wife – although he did not do the same with his male students.[154]
–   A female student is considered aloof if she refuses to go out for

a beer with her male adviser but is considered seductive and loose if she does go (while the same does not apply to male students).[155]

In hiring

When academic staff are hired, the double standard can lead to women being started at lower ranks and salaries than men who are equally qualified.[156] Similarly, a woman who had taught at a university on a sessional basis for several years while completing her doctorate learned that another sessional, a man also without a Ph.D., had just been hired – and at a rank above hers while her rank was *decreased*.[157] A double standard can be revealed in other ways related to hiring. For instance, a male colleague contested the hiring of a woman faculty member, 'intimating that her position in the department was entirely due to her "relationship" with a senior member of the department ... In addition to these insinuations being completely without basis, the senior male faculty member with whom she had been linked routinely functioned as a mentor for junior men. In fact, given his prominence in the field, his support of them was usually treated as an important indication of their competence and promise.'[158]

Salary and rank are not the only arenas in which a double standard based on gender appears at the time of hiring. Women are more likely to be made to share offices than are men, as well as being more restricted to undergraduate teaching; then later in their careers they are more likely than men to be denied their requests for sabbatical leave.[159]

After hiring

Only a few examples of the vast array of double-standard manifestations on the job will be mentioned here. Backhouse et al. describe a department that often hired new faculty who had not yet received their Ph.D.'s, where 'the faculty was much more forthcoming with assistance in the form of "time off" for research leave and scheduling adjustments for men than for women' to finish their doctoral requirements.[160] The double standard also operates when women faculty who ask to switch from teaching courses unrelated to their fields of specialization to courses that *are* related are greeted with extreme hostility about their 'selfishness,' while similar requests from men are more likely to be greeted as normal ambition.[161] And within the work environment, when men and women have the same qualifications and rank, women may be given lower-status committee work or less powerful positions by administrators.[162]

Women who become pregnant while holding faculty jobs are often treated with irritation, chided for being unprofessional or for 'letting down the discipline' if they take *any* time off when the baby comes, and are regarded generally as sources of embarrassment; in contrast, as Backhouse et al. note, 'men at the same age and stage of their careers ... are often roundly congratulated when they get tenure and are seen to be starting a family. This is seen as solid evidence that they are settling down and making a permanent commitment to live in [the university city].'[163] Indeed, in Sandler and Hall's view, people with the same marital and parental status are regarded very differently depending on their sex, since it is often presumed that women's family responsibilities will interfere with their academic work, whereas for men it is often presumed that being married and having children are signs of their general stability. Thus, 'should a woman leave a meeting early or request a change in meeting time, colleagues may assume that she must attend to children or a household matter, and her request is often resented. When man does the same, the more common assumption is that he has some important matter to attend to, and that his request is justified.'[164]

Two final examples give a flavour of how extreme can be the manifestations of the double standard. One relates to the very different ways a president of a major university dealt with one of his female and one of his male professors. Responding to a question from media reporters about why he allowed a male professor to continue to do research that was both appallingly racist and methodologically sloppy, the president said that academic freedom includes this man's right to teach and publish as he does. In stark contrast, when a female professor from the same university published a painstakingly documented report revealing the sexism within that university, the president denounced her to the media, claiming she was destroying the institution's good name and ought not to be allowed to do so.

The other story was told to me by its central character. As a graduate student, she had been chosen to represent the graduate students' association on a powerful university committee and was surprised to be chosen to chair it. During the meetings, a male professor sat overly close to her and continually cursed and muttered in her face during the meetings, but no one made any attempt to stop him. Having seen the committee function when a man had chaired it, she conducted the meetings much as he had done; thus at one point she said, 'Since I want to make that motion, I'm momentarily stepping down from my post as chair,' just as the previous chair had regularly done. But this time, a man who had long been a member of the committee hit the roof and told her she was out of order. The men on the committee immediately decided that they· needed more procedural rules and adopted stringent ones on the spot. After her term as chair was over, another man took over, and they threw out the new rules.

The effects

If these stories are demoralizing to read about, we can only imagine how depressing they were for the women who experienced them first-hand. Hall and Sandler report some of the negative consequences of such differential treatment:[156]

- Discouraging classroom participation
- Preventing students from seeking help outside of class
- Causing students to drop or avoid certain classes, to switch majors or subspecialties within majors, and in some instances even to leave a given institution
- Minimizing the development of the individual collegial relationships with faculty that are crucial for future professional development
- Dampening career aspirations
- Undermining confidence

Instead of sharpening their intellectual abilities, women may begin to believe and act as though

- their presence in a given class, department, program, or institution is at best peripheral, or at worst an unwelcome intrusion;
- their participation in class discussion is not expected, and their contributions are not important;
- their capacity for full intellectual development and professional success is limited; and their academic and career goals are not matters for serious attention or concern.[166]

9. The expectation that women will fit feminine and racial stereotypes

Black women faculty and administrators at one university were told to 'keep Blacks in line' on anti-apartheid issues – as if it were

their job to control other Blacks on campus in order to protect the
institution from embarrassment or disruption.
                                              SANDLER with HALL[167]

Often ... I am the only woman in whatever setting I find myself. It
means that I am often called upon to be THE WOMAN. I am
asked to speak from the Woman's Perspective, as if I knew all
women and their views.   ANNETTE ATKINS[168]

The above incidents illustrate the way that members of non-dominant groups are often treated as though they can speak for, control, or represent *all* the members of the groups to which they belong. They also illustrate the way that a stereotype – such as women as protectors and peacemakers – can be hauled into play in ways that unfairly burden those to whom the stereotype is applied.

Perhaps even more likely to be subjected to preconceived notions than 'the woman' in a department is 'the feminist,' one of whom relates that she 'was often treated as a "single-issue person," as if her sole concern was women and the position she took on any issue must reflect her feminist commitments. [People] assume[d] that they knew already what she would say.'[169] Indeed, although many women graduate students are not even familiar with feminist scholarly work, some people expect them to know that work and defend it, simply because they are women: 'I remember a horrible oral examination in which my male colleagues put on the spot a student they had trained, asking her to compare Plato and St. Augustine on the topic of women – questions they had never previously suggested to her were important.'[170]

It is at best unsettling and at worst infuriating when someone assumes they know what we think and feel (or ought to think and feel) simply because of our sex – or race, class, age, sexual orientation, or physical conditions. Of course, those assumptions are usually restricting or otherwise negative when the target groups are not white, middle-class, able-bodied, heterosexual, and male. We don't want to spend our work hours trying to fit within the stereotypes (speaking softly, being supportive, and so on) *or* trying to *avoid* doing anything that people could use to justify the stereotypes.

What most of us want is to be perceived realistically and respected for who we are. However, academic women have reported upsetting experiences that involved criticism of them both for fitting stereotypes and for *not* fitting them (see also chapters 4 and 5). For instance, as discussed in chapter 4, because of the myth that academic work is solidly based in objectivity, women faculty who do not fit the model of rational, objective researcher are criticized for that failure; however, when women *do* fit that model, it is assumed that they cannot be truly feminine, so they are '*accused* of being rational and ambitious rather than commended for it.'[171]

Racialized women confront both the stereotypes about women and those about the racial or ethnic group in which they are classified, so that women from some groups may be assumed to be naturally good at, say, math and science; thus, if they do well they are not assumed to deserve credit, because it 'comes naturally' to them, and if they do not do well, they are assumed to be unnaturally deficient. 'On the other hand,' say Sandler and Hall, it is often assumed 'that minority women are less likely to be capable than other students, to lack certain skills, or to have certain personality traits ... [People] seem to expect them either to be academically incompetent or to be academic superstars who are "exceptions to the rule." '[172] Other stereotypes that come between racialized women's actual behaviour and what others make of it include a professor's assumption 'that a black woman's silence is due to "sullenness," ' or 'an Asian American woman's silence to "natural passivity." '[173]

In a crazy-making paradox, in some ways women from non-dominant groups are ignored, but in some ways they are the subjects of intense attention 'not as individuals, but as representatives of their particular ethnic group – as when a minority woman is called upon the give the "black woman's view" of an issue or problem rather than her own view.'[174]

Many women graduate students who had not fit the mould of the dependent female who needs to check in continually with her thesis supervisor for guidance told me stories of their supervisors' rage about their *lack* of 'feminine' neediness and their concomitant independence from these allegedly omniscient men. Some such men went beyond stating their anger and treated the students in a variety of punitive ways, including delaying their progress and humiliating them in their final oral examinations. One woman told me, 'I handed in my draft to my chair, and he said, "Too late. I'm gone for the summer. And the rest of the committee's angry at you because you went away and wrote it without checking with us." ' On the other hand, a woman who had regularly checked with her committee in the same department had been berated for being too 'dependent.'

So many stereotypes have been used against academic women. The assumption that women are constantly nurturant (see chapter 4) is often the basis for intensely angry objections from students who choose to take courses taught by women – or women's studies courses – because they believe that they will require little work and that high grades will be easy to obtain. A young man majoring in commerce stormed into my office after receiving a low grade on a short paper for my undergraduate women's studies course. 'You've got to realize,' he yelled, 'that as a commerce student I have a heavy workload. I just took your course because I thought it would be easy – and now I'm getting lousy marks in it!' He expected me to apologize to him for the trouble I had caused him. I found it hard to imagine that he would have had the gall to berate a male professor in that way. Surely he would have realized that what he said would have been deeply offensive to a man, but either he was unaware that it was equally offensive to me, or else he simply didn't care because I was female.

Students who are female can be taken to task for failing to be nurturant, even when it is clearly not their responsibility. The expectation that women will be nurturant leads many men to feel stunned and upset when a woman criticizes their work, although they feel it is appropriate when a man does so.[175] Consider the woman graduate student in clinical psychology who said to a male psychiatrist, 'I see in your letter that you felt the patient you referred to me is psychotically depressed. What was it about her behaviour that was psychotic?' The psychiatrist became uncomfortable in trying to answer and finally said, 'Well, she had had a hysterectomy, but I didn't think she should have been *that* depressed!' and the student realized that the psychiatrist had been careless in initially describing the woman as psychotic. Several days later, the student's supervisor, another male psychiatrist, took her to task; the other psychiatrist had called him to complain about the student 'backing him into a corner,' and the supervisor told the student, 'Your role should have been to build up his male ego.' In this case, too, it is hard to imagine that the supervisor would have said the same thing to a male student.

Colleagues and administrators often indulge in the 'good ole girl' phenomenon, asking women to take on excessive amounts of thankless, low-status, or non-credit work (for example, some administrative tasks or committee functions) on the assumption that they won't say 'no' and indeed *ought not* to refuse because women are supposed to be compliant.

Since another part of the feminine stereotype is that women are not supposed to put themselves forward,[176] a woman whose department chair asked her if he could nominate her for a teaching award said she couldn't give him an answer for three months. Although some people would mislabel her behaviour as evidence of women's 'fear of success,'[177] the real problem was instead her fear of *how she would be treated if she won the award*. She feared she would be considered immodest, hard-driving, or other things regarded as inappropriate in a woman professor.

Certainly, there is abundant evidence that successful academic women are often regarded as legitimate targets of unfounded attacks. Take, for instance, the following example, which is not particularly unusual: 'A long-time member of [a faculty] related how, after winning her tenure, she faced public comments from colleagues to the effect that the only reason she got tenure was because she must have slept with [the faculty member who had been chair at the time she was hired]. The bizarre twist here was that the individual cited as responsible for her ultimate success had not been particularly helpful in pursuing her case.'[178]

Perhaps the most ironic of the stereotypic expectations in academia is that women are not assumed to be intelligent. Thus, a woman who does well 'may be praised for "thinking like a man" – a back-handed compliment which implies that there is something wrong with "thinking like a woman," which she is ... She may also feel confused, because what seems a "petty" incident has sparked in her such a strong response ... [Her professor's] comment has linked her academic performance to her sex by communicating a perception of her **not** primarily as an individual **learner**, but as a **woman** who, like "all women," is of limited intellectual ability, operating outside of her "appropriate" sphere, and likely to fail.'[179]

In regard to the stereotypic but still current expectation for women to shoulder most family and household responsibilities,[180] women are taken to task when such responsibilities interfere with their career progress, even while academic institutions do little to ease or redistribute women's double burden. As seen in appendix 1, day care for children is often not available on campus; even when it is, its hours may not be ample or flexible, it may be costly, and there may be long waiting lists. In some settings, students' children may not be placed in child-care centres. Assistance from academic institutions with the care of elderly or ill relatives is virtually non-existent. As Klodawsky writes, these limitations make it hard for women to be 'able to pursue an idea or argument until its logical conclusion; research, discussion, and writing all become bounded by a set of demands of quite a different order, tied to "family responsibilities" and the financial pressures associated with them.'[181]

When women want to have both family *and* a career, that is often called 'having it all,' which 'calls up images of a child hogging all the toys or eating all the ice cream,'[182] although no such images are called up for men who want both family and career. Women wanting to do both often choose to start one early, but if creating a family is the one they do first, they walk into the biases against older women when they do begin their academic careers. Women trying to do both find that, rather than beautifully interweaving the two as they had longed to do, they end up trying to lead two, separate, full-time lives and feeling they are failing at both. Indeed, when a woman *does* succeed in filling both roles, it tends to be because she has extra money or help coming from elsewhere.

Unforeseen emergencies, such as financial problems or a family member suddenly becoming ill, are serious threats to academic women's work, as to women's paid work of any kind. What if a child or an elderly parent falls ill just when you are due at a job interview, or what if they need surgery during a semester when you are lecturing and being scrutinized for a possible tenure-stream job? And, as Aisenberg and Harrington point out, the informal arrangements that might help women out are more likely to be supportive of men: 'Women wouldn't dream of having secretaries in the department babysit kids on spring vacation, but men do.'[183] Similarly, when women divorce, they try never to mention it at work, but men get lots of sympathy when their marriages end. And at home, as countless women told me in our interviews, they lack support: their male partners are often threatened by the fact that the women consider their academic work to be a major commitment. 'When a woman told a man her husband was threatened because her work 'was going great guns ... he said, 'Well, what do you expect?'' '[184] Men, say Aisenberg and Harrington, often say outright that they expect women to revolve around them.

10. The general maleness and heterosexism of the environment

The culture of the academy ... is not presently one that necessarily respects or supports women ... active hostility to [women's] presence is too often a fact. CUMMINGS et al.[185]

The general maleness and heterosexism of most academic environments include 'the full range of overt and covert discriminatory behavior'[186] and overt and covert stereotyping.[187] Insofar as academia is a seat of enlightenment, we would expect that the higher one goes on the academic ladder, the fewer such problems one would find; however, research shows that in fact the reverse is true: the environment becomes more male (in terms of both proportions of males and a wealth of other factors; see appendix 1) as one goes from the undergraduate to graduate level and from there into and up the faculty and administration ladder.[188]

Structures and clocks

One of the most fundamental aspects of the maleness and heterosexism of academia is the 'academic clock,' the schedule of achievements that faculty are expected to follow in order to be hired, to have one's contract renewed, to be promoted, and to receive tenure. This clock is male and heterosexual because the schedule is far easier to keep if one is a man who has a wife or female partner to fill the traditional roles of taking care of all household and child-care work, as well as typing and editing his papers for him.[189] Indeed, it has been pointed out that the university as an institution functions partly on the assumption that 'the family' (read: 'wife') will expend a great deal of physical and emotional energy in order to make it as easy as possible for the male professor to concentrate on his work.[190] Not uncommonly, wives 'provide the unpaid labour of research or teaching assistants.'[191]

Hochschild vividly illustrates this point in the following description of the route to a successful academic career: 'Most important, put your all into those crucial years after you get your doctorate – in your twenties and thirties – putting nothing else first then. Take your best job offer and go there no matter what your family or social situation. Publish your first book with a well-known publisher, and cross the land to a slightly better position, if that comes up. Extend your now-ambitious self broadly and deeply into research, committee work, and editorships, to make your name in your late twenties and at the latest early thirties.'[192]

The academic clock was constructed without consideration of the fact that the period in which faculty are usually expected to work hardest to demonstrate their abilities is the very time when women are most likely to have infants and young children; and while many institutions now grant maternity leave, paternity leave is both rarer and shorter, thus perpetuating male academics' tendencies to minimize their household responsibilities.[193] Furthermore, the fact that women faculty may be granted maternity leave usually does not stop the academic clock; that is, if a male and a female faculty member started as assistant professors at the same time, all but a handful of institutions simply count publications in refereed journals, failing to allow for the fact that, since hiring, the woman has spent nine months pregnant (perhaps feeling tired or nauseated) and then serving as primary caretaker of an infant and young child. Furthermore, 'women report that even taking what is presently available to them leaves them stigmatized and vulnerable to the charge of not being serious about scholarly work. Research grants and indeed research work itself are not always adaptable to maternity leave interludes.'[194] Similarly, sabbaticals – which can be prime times for doing important research – are often best taken in locations other than one's academic setting; however, women are disadvantaged in that respect because it is considered more acceptable for a man than for a woman to expect the family to move in order to accompany them on a sabbatical.[195]

Responsibilities for caring for elderly parents, which women are considerably more likely than men to shoulder, are even more unlikely than child care to be accorded respect or consideration.

The academic schedule usually considered ideal includes high productivity from the beginning of one's career (a difficult task for women, who are more likely to lack the self-confidence and comfort with self-promotion that make that possible) and the focus on one or two major research themes,[197] which may be all the more true for faculty in the sciences than in other fields. However, many of my interviewees from the whole range of academic disciplines told stories similar to my own: when I was being interviewed for my current job, the search committee asked me what my ten-year research plan was. At the time, I was exhausted from having the major responsibility for raising very young children, and I also had little self-confidence about my ability to garner major research grants; therefore, the luxury of even *considering* a ten-year plan had never entered my mind. Men are more likely than women to assume that they will be able, during the next five or ten years, to put their work ahead of household responsibilities, since they are more likely to assume correctly that one or more women in their lives will pick up the slack.

As Breslauer and Gordon write, 'The concept of a career as a continuous progression, with regular and distinct stages, disadvantages women whose other obligations often stream them into part-time faculty positions or contractually-limited appointments, which are unlikely to be entry points into faculty ranks.'[196] Furthermore, in spite of media tales about the alleged plethora of 'new men' who do half of the housework and child care, 'empirical studies do not show any significant changes in the amount of time [most men] spend on household work.'[199]

Appendix 3:
Suggested Guidelines for Hiring, Promotion, and Tenure Committees

Here is Sandler and Hall's start on a list of guidelines proposed for ensuring that job candidates are treated fairly regardless of their sex:

– Are all candidates asked roughly the same questions and given the same information?
– Do all candidates meet with people at the same level?
– Are men and women entertained in a similar manner and at the same level?
– Are late offers made more often to women than to men?
– Are dissenting voices noted?[1]

Further, they suggest that members of such committees

– *Be aware of differences in discussions about women's and men's qualifications and background, and take steps to remedy inequities.* Be aware of the pattern of focusing on the *potential* of male candidates and the *deficiencies* of female candidates.
– *Examine criteria – including those that seem fair on their face – to ensure that they do not inadvertently discriminate against women, and that they indeed related to the position.* Some institutions give substantial weight to particular kinds of experience or accomplishments from which women have been excluded, such as having been a Rhodes scholar in the days when women were not considered.
– *When professional women are invited to campus as guest lecturers, have them meet with [graduate] students specifically to discuss the climate barriers they may have faced and how they approached them.*[2] (The University of Western Ontario's 'chilly climate' videotape is an important resource in this regard.)

You might add items from the list suggested by Breslauer and West, who suggest that we remind colleagues that in the hiring process fair treatment requires that

- questions of the same type, posed in the same tone, be addressed to male and female candidates
- women and men should meet members of the university of similar rank
- similar tolerance for deviation from the advertised preferences in rank, start date, and teaching load be accorded women and men candidates
- discussions appraising men and women candidates do not confuse differences in their genders with differences in their quality, for example, by focusing upon the potential of male candidates and the deficiencies of female candidates, by assuming that family responsibilities will distract women and 'settle' men, by assuming that the partners of male candidates will follow them to the job site and that the relationships of female candidates will be destabilized by a job offer
- community social and cultural activities attractive to both women and men be presented to all candidates
- 'exit' interviews be conducted with women candidates who are not hired to evaluate whether they have been treated differently in introductions, interviews, presentations, and related settings;
- similarly, exit interviews be conducted with women who leave for other jobs or because they do not get tenure, in order to find out to what degree climate issues may have been involved.[3]

And the authors of Ohio State University's *Handbook for Faculty Searches with Special Reference to Affirmative Action* provide a list of questions one may and may not ask of a candidate.[4]

Notes

Works cited here are found in full in the Bibliography. Those with a simple year reference (1988) are listed in the opening General section. Those with a small-capital suffix (1992B, 1988E) are listed in one of the specialized sections that follow the General section (as outlined in the introduction to the Bibliography).

Preface

1 Many women who have been called 'women of colour,' 'minority women,' or 'non-whites' have expressed their dislike for these terms. Nayyar Javed drew my attention to the term 'racialized women,' which reflects the fact that the division of people into races is a sociopolitical act that is wrongly assumed to be scientifically justified. Nikki Gerrard suggested the term 'women from non-dominant groups,' which also underlines the political nature and consequences of such divisions. Therefore, I most often use these terms in the rest of this book.

2 Nerad 1988

Chapter 1

1 Caplan 1981
2 University of Western Ontario manual for videotape 1991
3 Wine 1988E: 49
4 Ibid.
5 1988
6 Feldman 1974; Sandler with Hall 1986
7 1982
8 El-Khawas 1982
9 1983E: 144
10 Simpson 1979E
11 Johnson et al. 1989: 42
12 Quoted by Simeone 1987: 64
13 Sandler with Hall 1986
14 Hall and Sandler 1982
15 Aisenberg and Harrington 1988

16 Sandler with Hall 1986: 13
17 Backhouse et al. 1989
18 Davenport 1982E, quoted by Simeone 1987: 95
19 Sheinin 1987
20 Rich 1979a: 132
21 Feldman 1974
22 Ibid.
23 1979a: 132
24 Aisenberg and Harrington 1988: 139
25 de Beauvoir 1974
26 Washington and Harvey 1989E; Hensel 1991
27 Raymond 1991: A31
28 Amato 1992: 1372
29 Selvin 1992: 1383
30 Sandler with Hall 1986: 13
31 Backhouse 1990
32 Ibid.: 39
33 Russell et al. 1988
34 1984: 209
35 1991: 20–1
36 1992: 1365
37 Selvin 1992: 1383
38 For the data and references on which this section is based, see appendix 1 and the notes for it.

Chapter 2

See Simeone 1987, chap. 6, on family responsibilities.
1 1992B: 33
2 1989: 68
3 Selvin 1992: 1382
4 1991: F1
5 Caplan 1981
6 E.g., Cohen and Gutek, 1991
7 Dagg and Thompson 1988
8 Wine 1988E: 49, 52

9 Wine 1988E
10 Wine 1988E: 50
11 Wine 1988E
12 Dagg and Thompson 1988
13 Dagg and Thompson 1988; Hay 1991; Smith et al. n.d.
14 Aisenberg and Harrington 1988
15 Ibid.
16 Hay 1991
17 Ibid.: 3
18 Pyke 1991A; Hall and Sandler 1982
19 Sandler with Hall 1986
20 Theodore 1986B: 58
21 Ramazanoglu 1987I: 71
22 Dagg and Thompson 1988; Hall and Sandler 1982: 4; see also Parr 1989C
23 Dagg and Thompson 1988: 94
24 1986B: 12
25 Johnson et al. 1989: 2 (executive summary)
26 Johnson et al. 1989: 7

Chapter 3

In general, for this chapter, see Salancik's (1987) fine chapter on power and politics in academia.
1 1989: 10
2 1988: 41
3 Smith et al., n.d.: 15–16
4 1989: 22
5 1991: 5
6 E.g., see Backhouse et al. 1989
7 1989: 25
8 Johnson et al. 1989
9 Ibid.
10 Breslauer and Gordon 1989
11 Johnson et al. 1989

12 Theodore 1986B: 4, 47, 50
13 Ibid.: 50
14 Theodore 1986B; Johnson et al.
   1989
15 Ibid.
16 Theodore 1986B
17 Johnson et al. 1989
18 Theodore 1986
19 1988
20 Sandler with Hall 1986: 15
21 Johnson et al. 1989: 9 (executive
   summary)
22 Theodore 1986
23 Ibid.
24 Ibid.; Johnson et al. 1989
25 1989: 3
26 Briskin 1989
27 Theodore 1986B
28 Ibid.: 103
29 Ibid.: 103
30 Ibid.
31 Ibid.
32 Ibid. 219
33 Richardson 1991: 4

Chapter 4

1 Hensel 1991
2 Thomas et al. 1982E; Breslauer
   and Gordon 1989
3 1988: 52
4 Reid 1987
5 Aisenberg and Harrington 1988
6 Simeone 1987: 28
7 Theodore, 1986B: 46–7
8 Theodore 1986B
9 E.g., Theodore 1986B; Ontario
   Confederation of University
   Faculty Association 1989
10 1989: 10
11 Ibid.

12 Breslauer and Gordon 1990: 20
13 Pleck 1986; Hochschild 1975
14 1989
15 Breslauer and Gordon 1990: 19
16 1989: 10
17 Parr 1989C: 1
18 1988E: 47
19 Ramazanoglu 1987I: 68
20 Aitken and Walker 1989: 2
21 Gibbons 1992b: 1386
22 1991: 3
23 1989: 25
24 Briskin 1989
25 Ibid.: 10
26 Breslauer and Gordon 1989: ii
27 White 1980
28 Wine, Moses, and Smye 1980;
   Smye, Wine, and Moses 1980;
   Caplan 1989
29 Sanford and Donovan 1984
30 1985
31 Caplan 1989
32 Ibid.
33 Caplan 1981, 1989
34 Caplan 1981
35 David Riesman in Introduction
   to Bernard 1964: xxiv
36 Caplan 1985
37 (Susan Mann) Trofimenkoff
   1989A: 115
38 Burger 1986I; Cammaert 1985I;
   Glaser and Thorpe 1986I; 'Harvard Releases Sexual Harassment Report' 1984I; MacKenzie
   and Lussier 1988I; Morris 1989
   I; Paludi 1990I
39 Breslauer and Gordon 1989: 19
40 Dagg and Thompson 1988
41 Chesler 1986; Caplan 1989
42 Theodore 1986B
43 Caplan 1989

Chapter 5

1 E.g., Chesler 1973; Canadian Mental Health Association 1987; Stoppard 1988; Caplan 1985, 1991, 1992
2 Hay 1991: 5–6
3 Aisenberg and Harrington 1988
4 1986B
5 1991: 10
6 Sandler with Hall 1986: 3
7 1988
8 1991: 8; see also Sandler with Hall 1986
9 1989: 32
10 1990
11 Personal communication, 1992
12 1988: 65
13 Tidball 1974
14 Aisenberg and Harrington 1988: 12
15 1986
16 Thomas et al. 1982E: 47
17 Hay 1991: 5
18 Personal communication, 1992
19 1989: 23
20 1986B
21 Siegel 1990a/G, 1990b/G, 1990c/G
22 Delisle 1989A: 74
23 Sandler with Hall 1986: 9
24 Caplan 1989

Chapter 6

In regard to many issues in this chapter, see Ackerman 1986 on middle-aged women and career transitions for material on styles of coping.
1 Nedelsky 1991: 9

2 Stark-Adamec and Adamec 1981H
3 Cited by Rich 1979a: 131
4 Hay 1991
5 The first two from Sandler with Hall 1986: 20–1; the rest from Vartuli 1982A: 54–6
6 Vartuli 1982A: 56
7 Aisenberg and Harrington 1988: 58–9
8 See Nedelsky 1991 on how absolutely crucial it is to make contacts with other women; see also Rose 1986 and Tracey 1982 on women helping and supporting other women.
9 1979a; 145
10 Caplan 1980, 1989
11 1992
12 Siegel 1990b/G
13 Thomas et al. 1982E
14 Sandler with Hall 1986: 9
15 1986: 20
16 Johnson et al. 1989
17 See University of Western Ontario's Caucus on Women's Issues 1991
18 Sandler with Hall, 1986
19 Briskin, 1990b: 3
20 1991: 12
21 Ibid.
22 On mentors, see Simeone 1987, chap. 5; Hall and Sandler 1983, for detailed suggestions on how to decide if you need mentoring, what to look for in mentors, and how to get mentors to choose you, as well as on how to be a mentor, groups of women who may have special mentoring needs and special

problems finding mentors (women in non-traditional fields, older women, 'minority' women, and disabled women), and problematic aspects of mentoring for women; Symons 1977; and Gilbert et al. 1983.

23 Rowe, 1981D; Hall and Sandler 1983

24 Thomas et al. 1982E; Dagg 1989

25 Breslauer and Gordon, 1989: 13

26 Ibid.: 14

27 Goldstein 1979D

28 Laurence 1989D

29 Gordon and Breslauer 1990: 14

30 Ibid.: 14

31 Vartuli 1982A: 46

32 Morris 1989

33 Thomas et al. 1982E

34 Aisenberg and Harrington 1988

35 Ibid.

36 Eichler 1989A: 75–7

37 Haley 1989A

38 Tidball 1974

39 1992b/D

40 See Caplan 1981, 1989.

41 Sethna and Lampi 1991A

42 Nielsen 1982

43 Sandler with Hall 1986: 20

44 Cummings et al. 1991

45 1989A: 32

46 Johnson et al. 1989: 71–2

47 Dagg 1989

48 Hall and Sandler 1982: 2

49 1986

50 Ibid.

51 Dagg 1989

52 1990b: 3

53 1989: 84

54 Haley 1985A: 161

55 Described by Caplan 1992

Chapter 7

1 You will find enormously helpful, practical, step-by-step advice from graduate students themselves in the book edited by Vartuli (1982A), including chapters by Vartuli, Bolig McConnell, and Smith on how it feels to be a graduate student and specific suggestions about comprehensive examinations and dissertation writing; by Levy, on surviving in a predominantly white male institution; by Barnett, on stress during the Ph.D. period; by Tracey, on women supporting and helping women; by Williams, on relationships for the woman doctoral student; by Levstik, on balancing Ph.D. work and family responsibilities; and by Wells, on the older woman's Ph.D. experience. Along similar lines, see the chapter by Rogers (1986) on the graduate-school experience. Also, see *Get Smart! A Woman's Guide to Equality on Campus*, by Katz and Vieland (1988), especially pp. 36–7, 64–5, 100, 130, and 131–42 for a host of useful, practical, and often simple-to-implement suggestions for women students in regard to the classroom, faculty-student relations, self-esteem, and avenues of complaint and redress for problems. And the two chapters by Zanna and Darley (1987a, 1987b) on doing

research – including writing proposals, writing articles, orally presenting results, and managing the faculty-graduate student research relationship – are extremely good. So is Bem's (1987H) chapter on writing journal articles.

2 1989
3 1991A
4 Vartuli 1982A
5 Rogers 1986A
6 Aisenberg and Harrington 1988: 70
7 Sheinin 1989
8 McCurdy-Myers 1991A: 20
9 Delisle 1989A
10 Ibid.
11 See Nedelsky 1991.
12 1989A
13 Nedelsky 1991; OCUFA 1989: 1
14 1982: 13
15 Dagg 1989: 29
16 Bronstein 1986C
17 1988
18 Haley 1985A
19 For good general information, see Bronstein 1986C; McNairy 1982C; Darley and Zanna 1987C; Heiberger and Vick 1992C.
20 Bronstein 1986C
21 Ibid.
22 Ibid.
23 In general, see Darley and Zanna 1987C
24 See Bronstein 1986C; Committee on Women in Psychology 1992.
25 In general, see Darley and Zanna 1987 – they also discuss

in detail the presentation of a talk in the context of a job interview.

26 Bronstein 1986C
27 Ibid.: 20
28 Ibid.: 21
29 Rogers 1986A
30 In general, see Darley and Zanna 1987C
31 1991: 4
32 Johnson et al. 1989: 8 (executive summary)
33 Menges and Exum 1983
34 Breslauer and Gordon 1989: 22
35 1989: 15
36 1986C: 23
37 Bronstein 1986C
38 1989: 29
39 Ibid.: 30
40 Personal communication, 1992
41 Cadet 1989
42 Theodore 1986B
43 Backshouse et al. 1989
44 1990: 15
45 1992: 117
46 Bronstein 1986C
47 Ibid.
48 Bronstein 1986C
49 Ibid.
50 See Taylor and Martin 1987, who write in detail about the first years of the job, teaching, administrative work, research, faculty colleagues, working with students, financial issues, writing, self-promotion, time management, establishing priorities, and life outside of work; McKeachie 1987 for a whole, detailed chapter on teaching; Zanna and Darley 1987a for

suggestions about doing research (including proposal writing, writing articles, and oral
presentation of results) and
Zanna and Darley 1987b for
advice on managing faculty–
graduate student research relationships; Baron 1987H for a practical guide to writing research
grants; Bem 1987H on writing
journal articles; Gibbons 1986
for advice to junior faculty;
Yoder 1986 on the transition
from graduate student to assistant professor; and Quina 1986
on 'lessons from my first job.'

51 1991: 20
52 Theodore 1986B
53 Briskin 1990a; McMullen 1991
54 Briskin 1990a; 3
55 Aitken and Walker 1989: 3;
    McMullen 1991
56 Committee on Women in Psy-
    chology 1992
57 Ibid.
58 Ibid.
59 Sandler with Hall 1986
60 1988
61 Ibid.
62 1982H
63 Cummings et al. 1991
64 Stake 1986
65 Gibbons 1986
66 Nielsen 1982
67 1986: 20
68 Johnson et al. 1989: 35
69 Committee on Women in Psy-
    chology 1992: 11
70 Ibid.: 17
71 Ibid.
72 Parr 1989C

73 Quina 1986: 91
74 n.d.: 22–3
75 Backhouse et al. 1989
76 Committee on Women in Psy-
    chology 1992: 16
77 Johnson et al. 1989: 83
78 Ibid.
79 1991H: 7–8
80 Johnson et al. 1989
81 Smith et al., n.d.
82 Johnson et al. 1989
83 In general, see Quina's (1986)
    chapter, which is chock-full of
    practical, detailed suggestions.
84 1986
85 Committee on Women in Psy-
    chology 1992
86 Johnson et al. 1989
87 Quina 1986
88 Ibid.: 43
89 Ibid.: 44
90 See Gray 1985a, 1985b (H);
    Farley 1985; LaNoue and Lee
    1987B; Vladeck 1981B; Davies
    and Davies 1981B. See also the
    excellent book, *Rocking the Boat:
    Academic Women and Academic
    Processes*, edited by DeSole and
    Hoffman (1981). There, you will
    find fine chapters on the indi-
    vidual experiences of Black and
    white women, and full- and
    part-time faculty, who filed law-
    suits or grievances, as well as
    material on the contexts and
    processes of these legal and
    quasi-legal proceedings. See
    also the book by Theodore
    (1986B) and the chapters by
    Cheatum (1982) and Boring
    (1982B).

91 1986B
92 Committee on Women in Psychology 1992: 25–42
93 Committee on Women in Psychology 1992
94 Lee 1991, cited by Committee on Women in Psychology 1992: 37
95 Committee on Women in Psychology 1992
96 1986: 13
97 See Caplan 1980, 1989
98 Morell 1992: 1369
99 Backhouse et al. 1989: 25
100 University of Western Ontario manual for videotape 1991

Chapter 8

1 1984: 211
2 1989C: 2
3 The items on this check-list are taken or adapted from Backhouse 1990, Backhouse et al. 1989, Bogart et al. (n.d.), Bogart (1984), Briskin 1990b, Committee on the Status of Women 1989, 1991, 1991A, and 1991F, Council of Ontario Universities 1990, Cummings et al. 1991, Dagg 1989, Dagg and Thompson 1988, Delisle 1989A, Haley 1985A and 1989A, Hall with Sandler 1982, Hyde 1992, Johnson et al. 1989, Justus et al. 1987, Klodawsky 1989, Larkin et al. 1991, McMullen 1991, Newsletter of the Teaching Resource Office 1981, Ontario Confederation of University Faculty Associations 1989, Patterson and Sells 1973, Project on the Status and Education of Women 1986 and 1988, Pyke 1990, Rich 1979a, Richardson 1991H, Sandler with Hall 1986, Selleck and Breslauer 1989, Sheinin 1989, Silvia 1990, Smedick 1989, Smith et al. (n.d.), University of Western Ontario 1989E, University of Western Ontario's Caucus on Women's Issues 1991, University of Wisconsin 1988, and Wine 1988.

The reader is particularly urged to see Bogart et al., *Institutional Self-study Guide for Sex Equity*, a superb guide, with a wealth of detailed suggestions for students, faculty, administrators, and staff (e.g., directors of research and development, of library services, of counselling services). It can be obtained from the Project on the Status and Education of Women, Association of American Colleges, 1818 R Street N.W.; Washington 20009. Also, Ohio State University's *Handbook for Faculty Searches* 1987 is recommended as a fine reference for institutions to use in learning how to do faculty searches that maximize the chances that women and people of both sexes from non-dominant groups will be considered equally with others, from the beginning to the end of the search, and also that these people, once hired, will be retained.

4 1986
5 Sandler with Hall 1986; Breslauer and West 1989C; see also Dagg 1989.
6 Sandler, Hughes, and DeMouy 1988

Appendix 1

1 Some of the data given in this appendix are from Canadian studies and some from U.S. ones, but as Sheinin has noted, there is great similarity between universities in the two countries (1989).
2 1989D: 62–3
3 Hensel 1991; Dagg 1989; Macmillan 1989
4 Sandler with Hall 1986
5 Feldman 1974; Dagg 1989; Macmillan 1989
6 Macmillan 1989
7 Dagg and Thompson 1988; Sandler with Hall 1986
8 Breslauer and Gordon 1989
9 1992: 1366
10 1992b
11 Ibid.
12 1992: 1366
13 Ibid.: 1367
14 1991A
15 Statistics Canada 1991a
16 Hensel 1991; Sandler with Hall 1986
17 Macmillan 1989; Yeates 1989
18 Macmillan 1989: 2
19 Macmillan 1989
20 Status of Women Committee 1990
21 Pyke 1991A

22 Department of Secretary of State of Canada 1992; Council of Ontario Universities 1990; Touchton and Davis with Makosky 1991
23 1989: 28
24 Sheinin 1989: 103–4
25 Simeone 1987: 9
26 Breslauer and Gordon 1989; Selleck and Breslauer 1989; Macmillan 1989; Pyke 1991A; Dagg and Thompson 1988
27 Pyke 1991A: 4
28 1988: 65
29 1985A: 57
30 Department of the Secretary of State of Canada 1992; United States Department of Education 1990b
31 Simeone 1987
32 Harvey 1986E; Astin and Burciaga 1981E; Aguirre 1985E; Office of Minority Concerns 1985E
33 *The Women's Review of Books* 1992: 13
34 Menges and Exum 1983
35 Aguirre 1987E
36 *Chronicle of Higher Education* 1992
37 1991: 11
38 Dagg and Thompson 1988
39 Selvin 1992
40 Dagg and Thompson 1988: 15
41 Ibid.: 18
42 Ibid.: 10
43 1987
44 1988
45 1991
46 1989
47 1990
48 Statistics Canada 1990;

Breslauer and Gordon 1989;
Pyke 1991A
43 Theodore 1986B: xix
50 1986B
51 1992
52 Statistics Canada 1991b, table
    2e
58 Dagg and Thompson 1988
54 Pyke 1991A: 11
55 Cummings et al. 1991
56 Ibid.: 5–6
57 Dagg and Thompson 1988
58 Ibid.
59 Ibid.; Sandler with Hall 1986
60 Sandler with Hall 1986
61 1984
62 Sandler with Hall 1986
63 Ibid.: 2
64 Cited by Angel 1988
65 Hensel 1991; Coordinating
    Committee for the Status of
    Women 1989
66 Coordinating Committee for the
    Status of Women 1989
67 Etaugh 1986
68 Johnson, Timm, and Merino
    1989
69 Dagg and Thompson 1988: 45
70 Gibbons 1992b: 1386
71 Theodore 1986B
72 1992
73 Sandler with Hall 1986: 2
74 Rajagopal and Farr 1991F
75 Breslauer and Gordon 1989: 25
76 1988
77 1991
78 Sheinin 1989
75 Ibid.: 108
80 School of Graduate Studies,
    University of Toronto 1990A: 14
81 Haley 1989A: 37

82 Haley 1989A
83 Haley 1989; Smith et al., n.d.;
    Macmillan 1989
84 Dagg 1989
85 Ibid.
86 Wiseman 1991E
87 Vartuli 1982A
88 Delisle 1989A: 73
89 1988
90 Haley 1989A: 37
91 McCurdy-Myers 1991A; Haley
    1989A; Wise 1989A
92 1989A
93 Hall and Sandler 1982: 11
94 1989: 19
95 Ontario Confederation of Uni-
    versity Faculty Associations
    1986: 2
96 N.d.
97 Delisle 1989A
98 Sandler with Hall 1986: 2
99 1989: 22
100 1990
101 Breslauer and Gordon 1990
102 Committee on the Status of
     Women 1991
103 New York Times 1991E: 71
104 Pounder 1989
105 Council of Ontario Universities
     1992
106 Barbezat 1987, 1988
107 Williams, Williams, Anderson,
     and Roman 1987
108 1990: 12
109 Ibid.: 13
110 Sandler with Hall 1986: 2
111 Feldman 1974; Bernard 1964
112 Theodore 1986B
113 1989
114 Ohio State University 1987: 35
115 Pleck 1986

116 Hensel 1991; Committee on the Education and Employment of Women in Science and Engineering 1979; Reskin 1980
117 1992
118 Dagg and Thompson 1988

Appendix 2

1 Dagg 1989: 28
2 Ramazanoglu 1987I: 62
3 1982: 8–9
4 Sandler with Hall 1986: 10
5 E.g., Miller and Swift 1977
6 Theodore 1986B
7 Breslauer and Gordon 1989: 3
8 Cohen 1988: 370
9 Dagg and Thompson 1988
10 Women's Caucus 1970: 101
11 Ibid.
12 Backhouse et al. 1989: 21
13 Dagg and Thompson 1988: 37
14 Backhouse et al. 1989: 26
15 Ibid.: 26
16 Ibid.: 27
17 Theodore 1986B: 7
18 Theodore 1986B
19 Kierans 1990
20 Landsberg 1990I
24 Dagg and Thompson 1988
22 Pyke 1990A
23 1989: 34
24 Ibid.: 26
25 'helpless' – Backhouse et al., 1989, Sandler with Hall 1986; 'displaced' – Backhouse et al. 1989; 'alienated ... unfeminine' – Hall and Sandler 1982; 'excluded' – Morris 1989, Sandler with Hall 1986, Johnson, Timm, and Merino 1989; 'trapped ...

blame' – Sandler with Hall 1986; 'distanced ... place' – Johnson, Timm, and Merino 1989; 'and chosen' – Sandler with Hall 1986, Benokraitis and Feagin 1986
26 1989: 34–5
27 Sandler with Hall 1986: 10
28 Franklin et al. 1981I: 20
29 Johnson, Timm, and Merino 1989: 37
30 Ramazanoglu 1987I: 73
31 Dagg and Thompson 1988
32 Ramazanoglu 1987I
33 Pyke 1991A
34 Dagg 1989
35 Cammaert 1985I; Burger 1986I; Morris 1989I
36 'Harvard Releases Sexual Harassment Report' 1984
37 Morris 1989I
38 Burger 1986I
39 Morris 1989I
40 Ibid.
41 Ibid.: 16
42 Law professor Sheila McIntyre, cited by Govier 1990I: 8
43 Quoted by Govier 1990I: 8
44 E.g., Caplan 1985
45 Stark-Adamec 1991: 4
46 Backhouse et al. 1989: 34
47 Burger 1989I
48 Morris 1989
49 Hall and Sandler 1982: 7–9
50 Morris 1989
51 Cammaert 1985I
52 Ibid.
53 Ibid.
54 Dagg and Thompson 1988: 111
55 Interviews
56 Interview

57 Theodore 1986B
58 Ibid.
59 Ibid.
60 Theodore 1986B; Vartuli 1982A; OCUFA 1989
61 Vartuli 1982A
62 Theodore 1986B: 12
63 Vartuli 1982A: 112
64 Ibid.: 52
65 Ibid.
66 Ibid.
67 McMullen 1991; Cummings et al. 1991; Backhouse et al. 1989
68 Gordon and Breslauer 1990
69 'dehumanized' – Haley 1989A; 'ignored' – Backhouse et al. 1989; 'discouraged' – Sandler with Hall 1986: 11; 'patronized' – Dagg 1989, Backhouse et al. 1989
70 McMullen 1991: 2
71 Backhouse et al. 1989: 17–18
72 Ibid.: 28–9
73 Sandler with Hall 1986: 11
74 Kitzinger 1990
75 Black 1989: 70
76 Johnson, Timm, and Merino 1989; Aisenberg and Harrington 1988
77 Aisenberg and Harrington 1988
78 Breslauer and Gordon 1989: 26–7
79 Aisenberg and Harrington 1988: 86
80 Richardson 1991H; Kitzinger 1990
81 Cummings et al. 1991: 5
82 Parr 1989C
83 Bleier 1987, 1988
84 Aisenberg and Harrington 1988: 95

85 Sanford and Donovan 1984
86 Backhouse et al. 1989: 5
87 Hall and Sandler 1982
88 Haley 1989A
89 Ibid.: 86
90 Theodore 1986B: 53
91 Johnson et al. 1989: 18 (executive summary)
92 Johnson et al. 1989
93 Parr 1989C: 2
94 Dagg 1989
95 Theodore 1986B: Hall and Sandler 1982: 11; Vartuli 1982A
96 Theodore 1986B
97 Dagg and Thompson 1988
98 Smith, Cohen, Staton, Drakich, Rayside, and Burt (n.d.): 15–16
99 Backhouse et al. 1989: 7
100 Theodore 1986B
101 Cummings et al. 1991: 8–9
102 Ibid.: 9
103 Sandler with Hall 1986; Johnson et al. 1989; Theodore 1986B; OCUFA 1989; American Institutes of Research (n.d.)
104 1991A: 11
105 Bernard 1964: 272
106 Sandler with Hall 1986: 17
107 Sandler with Hall 1986
108 Johnson et al. 1989
109 Simeone 1987: 94; for more good material about the devaluation of work not about or produced by white males, see hooks 1990.
110 OCUFA, 1990: 2
111 1992
112 Ramcharan, with Chacko and Baker, 1991E: 7
113 Ibid.: 8, 11

114 University of Western Ontario 1989E
115 Rothblum (n.d./E); Barale 1988E; Rohrbaugh 1986E
116 Chayat 1987E; Rubenstein 1987E; Schnur 1987E; Spencer, Chayat, and Rubenstein 1987E
117 1988E
118 Kitzinger 1990E
119 Ibid.: 392
120 Kitzinger 1990: 125
121 Dagg and Thompson 1988: 9
122 Aisenberg and Harrington 1988: 103; see also Richardson 1991H on the marginalization of feminist/women's research.
123 Backhouse et al. 1989: 32
124 Theodore 1986B: 77
125 Cited by Dagg and Thompson 1988
126 Dagg and Thompson 1988
127 1986B
128 Ibid.
129 Breslauer and Gordon 1989
130 Dagg and Thompson 1988
131 Johnson et al. 1989; 8 (executive summary)
132 Ibid.
133 Laurence 1989D: 64–5
134 1989
135 Parr 1989C; American Institutes of Research (n.d.)
136 Laurnece 1989D: 66
137 Nieva and Gutek 1980
138 Peck 1978
139 Vartuli 1982A
140 Parr 1989C: 2; American Institutes of Research (n.d.)
141 Carter 1985A
142 Shavlik 1986
143 Sandler with Hall 1986

144 Backhouse et al. 1989: 21
145 Backhouse et al. 1989
146 Sandler with Hall 1986; Richards 1986
147 Riesman 1964
148 Hall and Sandler 1982: 3
149 Hall and Sandler 1982
150 Sandler with Hall 1986
151 Hall and Sandler 1982
152 Friedman 1985
153 Basow and Silberg 1986; Briskin 1990C; Friedman 1985
154 Pyke 1991A
155 Delisle 1989A
156 McMullen 1991
157 Backhouse et al. 1989
158 Ibid.: 28
159 Theodore 1986B
160 Backhouse et al. 1989: 12
161 Backhouse et al. 1989
162 Theodore 1986A
163 1989: 16
164 1986: 5
165 1982
166 Ibid.: 3
167 1986: 13
168 1983, cited by Sandler with Hall 1986: 3
169 Backhouse et al. 1989: 28
170 Black 1989: 70
171 Aisenberg and Harrington 1988: 12
172 1986: 12; based partly on Simpson 1979E and Noonan 1980
173 Sandler with Hall 1986: 12
174 Ibid.
175 Sandler with Hall 1986
176 Aisenberg and Harrington 1988
177 See Caplan 1985 for a critique of this concept.
178 Backhouse et al. 1989: 30

179 Hall and Sandler 1982: 4–5
180 See Simeone 1987, chap. 6, on family responsibilities.
181 Klodawsky 1989: 52
182 Aisenberg and Harrington 1988: 111
183 Ibid.: 120
184 Ibid.: 127
185 1991: 3, 5
186 Laurence 1989D: 64
187 Haley 1989A
188 Pyke 1991A; Morris 1989
189 Breslauer and Gordon 1989; Gordon and Breslauer 1990; Smith et al (n.d.)
190 Gordon and Breslauer 1990
191 Ibid.: 22
192 1975: 49

193 Gordon and Breslauer 1990
194 Nova Scotia Confederation of University Faculty Association 1987, cited by Gordon and Breslauer 1990: 18
195 Gordon and Breslauer 1990
196 Ibid.
197 Richardson 1991H
198 1989: ii
199 Gordon and Breslauer 1990; see also Pleck 1986.

Appendix 3

1 1986: 19
2 Ibid.: 19–20
3 1989: 1–2
4 1987; see p. 21

Bibliography

Cited below are, first, one source that has many useful listings in it, even though some may now be out of date; then a lengthy list of general references; and finally references pertaining to specific categories (in alphabetical order):

A Graduate students
B Grievances and legal proceedings
C Job searches and hiring
D Mentors, supervisors, and role models
E Non-dominant groups
F Non-regular instructional personnel (e.g., part-time, sessionals, etc.)
G Older women
H Research, writing, publishing, and obtaining grants
I Sexual harassment and safety

In Mary L. Spencer, Monika Kehoe, and Karen Speece, eds. *Handbook for Women Scholars: Strategies for Success* (San Francisco: Center for Women Scholars, Americas Behavioral Research Corporation 1982), see:

- For list and description of advocacy organizations, both general and discipline-specific, pp. 31–40
- For list of women's caucuses and committees of professional organizations, pp. 61–8 (but since this list was compiled for 1982 publication, also check your own organization, which may well have a women's caucus or section by now)
- For list of women's research and resource centres, pp. 107–12
- For list of career resources, p. 128
- For list of financial resources, pp. 128–31

General

Abel, Elizabeth, Marianne Hirsch, and Elizabeth Langland. 1983. ' "They Shared a Laboratory Together": Feminist Collaboration in the Academy.' *Women's Studies International Forum* 6: 165–8

Abramson, Joan. 1979. *Old Boys – New Women: The Politics of Sex*. New York: Praeger

– 1975. *The Invisible Woman*. San Francisco: Jossey-Bass

Academe. 1991. Special issue. The annual report on the economic status of the profession, 1990–1. March/April

Acker, Sandra. 1983. 'Women, the Other Academics.' *Women's Studies International Forum* 6: 191–202

Adams, Harriet Farwell. 1983. 'Work in the Interstices: Women in Academe.' *Women's Studies International Forum* 6: 135–42

Ahmed, Maroussia, et al. 1989. *Integration of Female Faculty at McMaster*. Hamilton, Ont.: Status of Women Committee, McMaster University Faculty Association

Aisenberg, Nadya, and Mona Harrington. 1988. *Women of Academe: Outsiders in the Sacred Grove*. Amherst: University of Massachusetts Press

Aitken, Johan, and Gillian Walker. 1989. 'Language Counts When Gender Matters: Excellence and Merit.' *OCUFA Forum* 'Supplement' 6(18): 2–3

Amato, Ivan. 1992 'Profile of a Field: Chemistry – Women Have Extra Hoops to Jump Through.' *Science* 255: 1372–3

American Institutes of Research. n.d. 'Social-educational Climate Affecting Sex Equity.' Sec. V of *Institutional Self-study Guide on Sex Equity for Postsecondary Educational Institutions*, 1–2. Repr. by Association of American Colleges, Washington

Anderson, Mary R., and Gloria N. Wilson. 1985. 'Faculty Women's Association: An Instrument for Change.' *Journal of Social Issues* 41: 73–84

Angel, M. 1988. 'Women in Legal Education: What It's Like to Be Part of Perceptual First Wave, or, The Case of the Disappearing Woman.' *Temple Law Review* 61(3): 799–846

Astin, Helen. 1973. 'Career Profiles of Women Doctorates.' In *Academic Women on the Move*, A.S. Rossi and A. Calderwood, eds, 139–61. New York: Russell Sage Foundation

Astin, Helen, and Alan Bayer. 1972. 'Sex Discrimination in Academe.' *Educational Record* 53: 101–18

Astin, Helen and Diane Davis. 1985. 'Research Productivity across the Life and Career Cycles: Facilitators and Barriers for Women.' In *Scholarly Writing and Publishing*, Mary Frank Fox, ed., 147–60. Boulder, Colo.: Westview Press

Astin, Helen, and Laura Kent. 1983. 'Gender Roles in Transition: Research and Policy Implications for Higher Education.' *Journal of Higher Education* 54: 309–24

Astin, Helen S., and Mary Beth Snyder. 1982. 'Affirmative Action 1972–82: A Decade of Response.' *Change* 14: 26–31, 59

Atkins, Annette. 1983. 'The Camels Are Coming, the Camels Are Coming.' *St. John's Magazine* (Collegeville, Md.), Winter: 9

Backhouse, Constance B. 1990. 'Women Faculty at the University of Western Ontario: Reflections on the Employment Equity Award.' *Canadian Journal of Women and the Law* 4: 36–65

Backhouse, Constance, Roma Harris, Gillian Michell, and Alison Wylie. 1989. 'The Chilly Climate for Faculty Women at UWO: Postscript to the Backhouse Report.' Unpublished paper, University of Western Ontario. London, Ont.

von Baeyer, P.L., D.L. Sherk, and M.P. Zanna. 1981. 'Impression Management in the Job Interview: When the Female Applicant Meets the Male (Chauvinist) Interviewer.' *Personality and Social Psychology Bulletin* 7: 45–51

Bannerji, Himani, Linda Carty, Karl Delhi, Susan Heald, and Kate McKenna, eds. 1991. *Unsettling Relations: The University as a Site of Feminist Struggles.* Toronto: Women's Press

Barbezat, D. 1988. 'Gender Differences in the Academic Reward System.' In *Academic Labor: Markets and Careers*, D.W. Breneman and T.I.K. Youn, eds, 138–64. New York: Taylor and Franklin

– 1987. 'Salary Differentials or Sex Discrimination?' *Population Research and Policy Review* 6(1): 69–84

Barinaga, Marcia. 1992. 'Profile of a Field: Neuroscience – The Pipeline is Leaking.' *Science* 255: 1366–7

Basow, Susan A., and Nancy T. Silberg. 1986. 'Student Evaluations of College Professors: Are Males Prejudiced against Women Professors?' *Journal of Educational Psychology* 79(1): 308–14

Beach, Jane. 1992. Personal communication. 7 May

Beck, Evelyn Torton. 1983. 'Self-disclosure and the Commitment to Social Change.' *Women's Studies International Forum* 6 (special issue on women in academe): 159–64

Belenky, M.F., B. McV. Clinchy, N.R. Goldberger, and J.M. Tarule. 1986. *Women's Ways of Knowing.* New York: Basic Books

Benditt, John. 1992. 'Women in Science – Pieces of a Puzzle.' *Science* 255: 1365

Bennett, S.K. 1982. 'Student Perceptions of and Expectations for Male and Female Instructors: Evidence Relating to Questions of Gender Bias in Teaching Evaluation.' *Journal of Educational Psychology* 74(2): 170–9

Benokraitis, Nijole V., and Joe R. Feagin. 1986. *Modern Sexism: Blatant, Subtle and Covert Discrimination.* Englewood Cliffs, NJ: Prentice-Hall

Berg, Helen, and Marianne Ferber. 1983. 'Men and Women Graduate Students: Who Succeeds and Why?' *Journal of Higher Education* 54: 629–48

Bernard, Jessie. 1964. *Academic Women.* New York: New American Library

Berry, Margaret. 1979. *Women in Educational Administration.* National Association of Women

Bird, Rose, California Supreme Court Justice. 1986. Quoted in *Washington Post*, 8 April, C4

Black, Naomi. 1989. 'Man Is the Measure ...' In *Proceedings of a Conference on Women in Graduate Studies in Ontario*, Carolyn Filteau, ed., 68–71. Toronto: Ontario Council on Graduate Studies

Bleier, Ruth. 1988. 'Science and the Construction of Meaning of the Neurosciences. In *Feminism within the Sciences and Health Care Professions*, S.V. Rosser, ed., 91–104. New York: Pergamon

– 1987. Presentation in symposium on 'Bias in Sex Differences Research.' American Association for the Advancement of Science Convention, Chicago

Bogart, Karen. 1984. *Toward Equity: An Action Manual for Women in Academe.* Washington: Project on the Status and Education of Women, Association of American Colleges

– 1981. *Technical Manual for the Institutional Self-study Guide on Sex Equity*, appendix C, 'Illustrative Problems and Proposed Solutions for Inequities.' American Institutes for Research, Washington

Bogart, Karen, Judy Flagle, Marjory Marvel, and Steven M. Jung. n.d. *Institutional Self-study Guide for Sex Equity for Postsecondary Educational Institutions.* Washington: Project on the Status and Education of Women, Association of American Colleges

Breslauer, Helen J. 1985. 'Women in the Professoriate: The Case of Multiple Disadvantage.' In *The Professoriate: Occupation in Crisis*, 82–104. Toronto: Ontario Institute for Studies in Education

Breslauer, Helen J., and Jane Gordon. 1990. 'Redressing the Imbalance: The Public Policy Agenda and Academic Women.' Presented to Canadian Society for the Study of Higher Education, University of Victoria

– 1989. 'The Two-Gender University: Catching up to Changes in the Clientele.' Presented to Canadian Sociology and Anthropology Association and Canadian Society for the Study of Higher Education, Laval University, Quebec City

Briskin, Linda. 1990a. 'The Pressure to Create Representative Structures within Universities Is Taking a Toll on Women.' *OCUFA Forum*, March: 3

– 1990b. 'Under-representation of Women, Anti-feminism and Affirmative Action.' *OCUFA Forum*, April:3

- 1990c. 'Gender in the Classroom.' *CORE: Newsletter of the Centre for Support of Teaching (York)* 1(1), September: 2–3
- 1989. 'A Feminist Politic for the University: Beyond Individual Victimization and Toward a Transformed Academy.' *CAUT Status of Women*, March: 10

Brooks, V.R. 1982. 'Sex Differences in Student Dominance Behavior in Female and Male Professors' Classrooms.' *Sex Roles* 8: 683–90

Cadet, Nancy. 1989. 'Marginalia: Women in the Academic Workforce.' *Feminist Teacher* 4: 16–18

Cambridge University Women's Action Group. 1989. 'Forty years on ... The CUWAG Report on the Numbers and Status of Academic Women at the University of Cambridge.' *Cambridge Review*, October: 135–42

Camilleri, Jennifer, Alison Davidson, Kelly Kane, and Donna McDonagh. 1991. 'Tyranny and Solidarity in the Feminist Classroom.' Paper presented at Eighth Annual Meeting of Community Psychology, New Britain, Conn.

Canadian Association of University Teachers. 1989. *Employee Benefits Survey for Faculty in the Western Provinces.* Ottawa

- 1987. *CAUT Policies Concerning the Status of Women.* Ottawa
- 1986. *Employee Benefits Survey for Faculty in the Atlantic Provinces.* Ottawa

Canadian Mental Health Association, Women and Mental Health Committee. 1987. *Women and Mental Health in Canada: Strategies for Change.* Toronto: Canadian Mental Health Association

Caplan, Paula J. 1992. 'Driving Us Crazy: How Oppression Damages Women's Mental Health and What We Can Do about It.' *Women and Therapy* 12: 5–28

- 1991. 'How *Do* They Decide Who Is Normal? The Bizarre, but True Tale of the *DSM* Process.' *Canadian Psychology/Psychologie Canadienne* 32: 162–70
- 1989. *Don't Blame Mother: Mending the Mother-Daughter Relationship.* New York: Harper and Row
- 1986. 'Psyching Women Out: How the Women's Movement Has Affected My Work.' *Popular Feminism Papers*, no. 1. Centre for Women's Studies in Education, Ontario Institute for Studies in Education, Toronto
- 1985. *The Myth of Women's Masochism.* New York: E.P. Dutton
- 1981. *Between Women: Lowering the Barriers.* Toronto: Personal Library
- 1980. *Between Women: Lowering the Barriers.* Toronto: Personal Library

Caplan, Paula J., Joan McCurdy-Myers, and Maureen Gans. 1992. 'Should "Premenstrual Syndrome" Be Called a Psychiatric Abnormality?' *Feminism and Psychology* 2: 27–44

Caplow, Theodore, and Reece J. McGee. 1965. *The Academic Marketplace.* New York: Doubleday and Company

Carnegie Foundation for the Advancement of Teaching. 1989. *The Condition of the Professoriate: Attitudes and Trends*. Princeton, NJ: Carnegie Foundation

Chamberlain, M. 1988. 'Faculty Women: Preparation, Participation, and Progress.' In *Women in Academe: Problems, Progress, and Prospects*, 255–73. New York: Russell Sage Foundation

Cheatum, Billy Ann. 1982. 'Protective Strategies for Change-makers.' In *Handbook for Women Scholars*, Spencer, Kehoe, and Speece, eds, 122–4

Chertos, Cynthia H. 1983. 'Hard Truths for Strategic Change: Dilemmas of Implementing Affirmative Action.' *Women's Studies International Forum* 6: 231–42

Chesler, Phyllis. 1986. *Mothers on Trial: The Battle for Children and Custody*. New York: McGraw-Hill

– 1973. *Women and Madness*. New York: Avon

Christiansen-Ruffman, Linda. 1991. 'Bridging the Gap between Feminist Activism and Academe.' In *Women and Social Change: Feminist Activism in Canada*, Jeri Dawn Wine and Janice L. Ristock, eds, 258–82. Toronto: Lorimer

Chronicle of Higher Education. 1992. 'In' box, 6 May: A19

Clance, Pauline Rose. 1985. *The Impostor Phenomenon: When Success Makes You Feel Like a Fake*. New York: Bantam Books

Clark, Shirley, and Mary Corcoran. 1986. 'Perspectives on the Professional Socialization of Women Faculty: A Case of Cumulative Disadvantage? *Journal of Higher Education* 7: 20–43

Clifford, Geraldine Joncich, ed. 1989. *Lone Voyagers: Academic Women in Coeducational Institutions, 1870–1937*. New York: Feminist Press

Cohen, Aaron Groff, and Barbara A. Gutek. 1991. 'Sex Differences in the Career Experiences of Members of Two APA Divisions.' *American Psychologist* 46: 1292–8

Cohen, Marcia. 1988. *The Sisterhood: The True Story of the Women Who Changed the World*. New York: Simon and Schuster

Cole, J.R. 1979. *Fair Science*. New York: Free Press

Committee for Advancement of Women in Scholarship. 1989. *Plan for Advancement of Women in Scholarship*. Ottawa: Royal Society of Canada

Committee on the Education and Employment of Women in Science and Engineering. 1979. *Climbing the Academic Ladder: Doctoral Women Scientists in Academe*. Washington: National Academy of Sciences

Committee on the Status of Women. 1991. 'Summary Report on Checklist Surveys: Undergraduate Students, Non-academic Staff and Faculty.' Toronto: Council of Ontario Universities

– 1989. *Women's Studies Programmes in Ontario Universities*. Toronto: Council of Ontario Universities

Bibliography 243

- 1988. *Employment Equity for Women: A University Handbook.* Toronto: Council of Ontario Universities

Committee on Women in Psychology. 1992. *Survival Guide to Academe for Women and Ethnic Minorities.* Washington: American Psychological Association

Concordia University Office on the Status of Women. 1991. *Inequity in the Classroom / En toute galité.* (Video; Deborah d'Entremont, director.) Montreal

Coordinating Committee on the Status of Women. 1989. *Report of the C.C.S.W.* Berkeley: University of California

Copas, Ernestine M., Helen H. Mills, Patricia L. Dwinell, Louise McBee, and Betty J. Whitten, eds. 1983. *Shaping our Destiny: Techniques for Moving Up in Higher Education.* Athens, Ga.: University of Georgia Center for Continuing Education

Council of Ontario Universities. 1992. *Full-time Non-academic Staff: 1990–91 by Abella Group, Salary Range, and Gender.* Toronto: Council of Ontario Universities

- 1990. *Annual Report 1989–90, Committee on the Status of Women.* Toronto: Council of Ontario Universities

Council of Ontario Universities Committee on the Status of Women. 1990. *A Statistical Glance at the Changing Status of Women in the Ontario Universities.* Toronto: Council of Ontario Universities

Crawford, Mary. 1982. 'In Pursuit of the Well-Rounded Life: Women Scholars and the Family.' In *Handbook for Women Scholars*, Spencer, Kehoe, and Speece, eds, 89–96

Creswell, John, Daniel Wheeler, Alan Seagren, Nancy Egly, and Kirk Beyer. 1990. *The Academic Chairperson's Handbook*, Lincoln: University of Nebraska Press

Cummings, Anne, Regna Darnell, Lousie Forsyth, Elizabeth Harvey, Raija Koski, Diana Majury, and Genese Warr-Leeper. 1991. 'Support for UWO Women as Academic and Professional Persons (SWAPP).' University of Western Ontario, London, Ont.

Curby, Vicki. 1980. *Women Administrators in Higher Education.* National Association of Women

Dagg, Anne Innis. 1989. 'Tenure and Promotion.' *OCUFA Forum* ('Supplement') 6(18): 4

Dagg, Anne Innis, and Patricia J. Thompson. 1988. *MisEducation: Women and Canadian Universities.* Toronto: OISE Press

Deaux, K., and T. Emswiller. 1974. 'Explanations of Successful Performance on Sex-linked Tasks: What Is Skill for the Male Is Luck for the Female.' *Journal of Personality and Social Psychology* 29: 80–5

Deaux, K., and J. Taynor. 1973. 'Evaluation of Male and Female Ability: Bias Works Two Ways.' *Psychological Reports* 32: 261–2

de Beauvoir, Simone. 1974. *The Second Sex*. New York: Vintage

Department of the Secretary of State of Canada / Secrétariat d'Etat du Canada. 1992. *Profile of Higher Education in Canada*. Ottawa

DeSole, Gloria, and Lenore Hoffman, eds. 1981. *Rocking the Boat: Academic Women and Academic Processes*. New York: Modern Language Association of America

DeWine, S. 1986. 'Breakthrough: Making It Happen with Women's Networks.' In *Women in Organizations: Barriers and Breakthroughs*, J.J. Pilotta, ed., 85–101. Beverly Hills, Calif.: Sage

Dudovitz, Resa L. 1983. Editorial (special issue on women in academia). *Women's Studies International Forum* 6: 129–30

Ehrhart, Julie Kuhn, and Bernice R. Sandler. 1990. *Rx for Success: Improving the Climate for Women in Medical Schools and Teaching Hospitals*. Washington: Association of American Colleges

– 1987. *Looking for More than a Few Good Women in Traditionally Male Fields*. Washington: Association of American Colleges

Elgin, Suzette Haden. 1980. *The Gentle Art of Verbal Self-defense*. Englewood Cliffs, NJ: Prentice-Hall

El-Khawas, Elaine H. 1982. 'Differences in Academic Development during College.' In *Men and Women Learning Together: A Study of College Students in the Late 70's*. Providence: Office of the Provost, Brown University

Elmore, P.B., and K.A. LaPointe. 1975. 'Effect of Teacher Sex, Student Sex, and Teacher Warmth on the Evaluations of College Instructors.' *Journal of Higher Educational Psychology* 67(3): 368–74

– 1974. 'Effects of Teacher Sex and Student Sex on the Evaluations of College Instructors.' *Journal of Higher Education* 66(3): 386–89

Etaugh, C. 1986. 'Women Faculty and Administrators in Higher Education: Changes in Their Status Since 1972.' In *Strategies and Attitudes: Women in Educational Administration*, P. Farrant, ed. Washington: National Association of Women Deans, Administrators, and Counselors

Evaluating Courses for Inclusion of New Scholarship on Women. 1988. Washington: Association of American Colleges

Farley, Jennie. 1985. 'Women versus Academe: Who's Winning?' *Journal of Social Issues* 41: 111–20

– ed. 1981. *Sex Discrimination in Higher Education: Strategies for Equality*. Ithaca: New York State School of Industrial and Labor Relations

Feldman, Saul. 1974. *Escape from the Doll's House: Women in Graduate and Professional Education*. New York: McGraw Hill

Ferber, M.A., and J.A. Huber. 1975. 'Sex of Student and Instructor: A Study of Student Bias.' *American Journal of Sociology* 80(4): 949–62

Financial Aid: A Partial List of Resources for Women. 1989. Washington: Association of American Colleges

Finch, Janet. 1983. *Married to the Job.* London: George Allen & Unwin

Finkelstein, Martin. 1984. 'The Status of Academic Women: An Assessment of Five Competing Explanations.' *Review of Higher Education* 7: 223–46

Florentine, R. 1988. 'Increasing Similarity in the Values and Life Plans of Male and Female College Students? Evidence and Implications.' *Sex Roles* 18: 143–58

Forrest, L., K. Hotelling, and L. Kuk. 1984. 'The Elimination of Sexism in University Environments.' Paper presented at Second Annual Symposium, Student Development Through Campus Ecology, Pingree Park, Colo.

Frank, H.H., and A.H. Katcher. 1977. 'The Qualities of Leadership: How Male Medical Students Evaluate Their Female Peers.' *Human Relations* 30: 403–16

Friedman, Susan. 1985. 'Authority in the Feminist Classroom: A Contradiction in Terms?' In *Gendered Subjects*, Margo Culley and Catherine Portuges, eds, 203–8. Boston: Routledge & Kegan Paul

Fuehrer, Ann, and Karen Maitland Schilling. 1985. 'The Values of Academe: Sexism as a Natural Consequence.' *Journal of Social Issues* 41: 29–42

Galbraith, John Kenneth. 1990. *A Tenured Professor: A Novel.* Boston: Houghton Mifflin

Gibbons, Ann. 1992a. 'Key Issue: Two-career Science Marriage.' *Science* 255: 1380–1

– 1992b. 'Key Issue: Tenure – Does the Old-boy Network Keep Women from Leaping Over This Crucial Career Hurdle?' *Science* 255: 1386

Gibbons, Judith. 1986. 'Pitfalls on the Way to Tenure.' In *Career Guide for Women Scholars*, Suzanna Rose, ed., 27–35. New York: Springer

Giddings, Paula. 1984. *When and Where We Enter: The Impact of Black Women on Race and Sex in America.* New York: Mirror

Gilbert, L., J. Gallessich, and S. Evans. 1983. 'Sex of Faculty Role-model and Students' Self-perceptions of Competency.' *Sex Roles* 9: 597–607

Glick, P., C. Zion, and C. Nelson. 1988. 'What Mediates Sex Discrimination in Hiring Decisions?' *Journal of Personality and Social Psychology* 55: 178–86

Goldhor, Susan. n.d. *How to Get a Job* and *How to Keep a Job.* Pamphlets. Amherst, Mass.: Center for Applied Regional Studies

Gordon, Jane, and Helen J. Breslauer. 1990. 'The Model of an Academic Career: Implications for Female and Male Academics.' Presented to Canadian Sociology and Anthropology Association, Victoria, BC

Graham, Dee L.R., Patricia O'Reilly, and Edna I. Rawlings. 1985. 'Costs and Benefits of Advocacy for Faculty Women: A Case Study.' *Journal of Social Issues* 41: 85–98

Graham, Patricia Albjerg. 1973. 'Status Transitions of Women Students, Faculty, and Administrators.' In *Academic Women on the Move*, A.S. Rossi and A. Calderwood, eds, 163–72. New York: Russell Sage Foundation

Gutek, B.A. 1985. *Sex and the Workplace: The Impact of Sexual Behavior and Harassment on Women, Men and Organizations.* San Francisco: Jossey-Bass

Hall, Roberta M., and Bernice R. Sandler. 1984. 'Out of the Classroom: A Chilly Campus Climate for Women?' Washington: Project on the Status and Education of Women, Association of American Colleges

– 1982. 'Out of the Classroom: A Chilly Campus Climate for Women?' Washington: Project on the Status and Education of Women, Association of American Colleges

Hallon, Charles J., and Gary R. Gemmill. 1976. 'A Comparison of Female and Male Professors on Participation in Decision-making, Job-related Tension, Job Involvement, and Job Satisfaction.' *Education Administration Quarterly* 12: 80–93

Harnett, R. 1981. 'Sex Differences in the Environment of Graduate Students and Faculty.' *Research in Higher Education* 14: 211–30

Hay, Deborah. 1991. 'Pollyanna Ph.D. Goes into Academia.' Presented in Section on Women and Psychology symposium on 'Fear and Loathing in Academia,' Canadian Psychological Association, Calgary

Heins, Marjorie. 1987. *Cutting the Mustard: Affirmative Action and the Nature of Excellence.* Boston: Faber & Faber

Henley, Nancy. 1977. *Body Politics: Power, Sex and Nonverbal Communication.* Englewood Cliffs, NJ: Prentice-Hall

Hensel, Nancy. 1991. *Realizing Gender Equality in Higher Education: The Need to Integrate Work/Family Issues.* ASHE-ERIC Higher Education Report no. 2. Washington: George Washington School of Education and Human Development

– 1989. 'Resolving the Conflict: Parenting and Professorship.' *Thought and Action* 5: 71–84

Heyer, Patricia. 1985. 'Affirmative Action for Women Faculty: Case Studies of Three Institutions.' *Journal of Higher Education* 56: 282–99

Heyman, Ira M. 1977. *Women Students at Berkeley: Views and Data on Possible Sex Discrimination in Academic Programs.* Office of the Chancellor, University of California, Berkeley, June

Hochschild, Arlie Russell. 1975. 'Inside the Clockwork of Male Careers.' In *Women and the Power to Change*, Florence Howe, ed., 47–80. New York: McGraw-Hill

Holmstrom, Engin. 'Barriers to Women in Graduate School.' In *Graduate and Professional Education of Women*. American Association of University Women (ed.) Conference Proceedings, Washington

hooks, bell. 1990. *YEARNING: race, gender, and cultural politics*. Toronto: Between the Lines

Howard, Suzanne. 1978. *But We Will Persist: A Comparative Research Report on the Status of Women in Academe*. Washington: American Association of University Women

Howe, Florence. 1984. *Myths of Coeducation*. Bloomington: Indiana University Press

Howe, Florence, and Carol Ahlum. 1973. 'Women and Social Change. In *Academic Women on the Move*, A.S. Rossi and A. Calderwood, eds, 393–423. New York: Russell Sage Foundation

Howe, Florence, Suzanne Howard, and Mary Jo Boehm Strauss, eds. 1982. *Everywoman's Guide to Colleges and Universities*. New York: Harper and Row

Howe, Karen Glasser. 1985. Personal communication

Huber, Joan. 1973. 'From Sugar and Spice to Professor.' In *Academic Women on the Move*, A.S. Rossi and A. Calderwood, eds, 125–35. New York: Russell Sage Foundation

Hunter, M.S., and C. Shannon. 1987. 'Women in Academia: Career Orientation, Satisfactions, and Stress.' *Affilia* (Spring): 39–49

Hyde, Janet Shibley. 1992. 'Stop the Revolving Door, I Want to Get In: Improving Efforts to Tenure Women at the University.' Presented at Harvard University, Cambridge, Mass.

Jacobs, Lucy. 1981. 'Problems Encountered by Women and Minority Students at Indiana University.' *Indiana Studies in Higher Education*

Johnson, Kathryn K., Lenora A. Timm, and Barbara J. Merino. 1989. *Academic Women at the University of California, Davis: Institutional Barriers to Retention and Promotion and Recommendations for Action*. Davis, Calif.: University of California

Johnson, Liz, with Roberta M. Hall. 1984. Selected activities using 'The Classroom Climate: A Chilly One for Women?' Washington: Project on the Status and Education of Women, Association of American Colleges

Justus, Joyce Bennett, Sandria B. Freitag, and L. Leann Parker. 1987. *The University of California in the Twenty-First Century: Successful Approaches to Faculty Diversity*

Kahn, Ethel D., and Lillian Robbins. 1985. 'Social Psychological Issues in Sex Discrimination.' *Journal of Social Issues* 41: 135–54

Kanter, R.M. 1977. 'Some Effects of Proportions on Group Life: Skewed Sex Ratios and Responses to Token Women.' *American Journal of Sociology* 82: 965–90

Karttunen, Frances. 1992. 'Academia's Leaky Pipeline.' *The Radcliffe Quarterly*, December: 30–2

Katz, Montana, and Veronica Vieland. 1988. *Get Smart! A Woman's Guide to Equality on Campus*. New York: Feminist Press at the City University of New York

Kaufman, D.R. 1978. 'Associational Ties in Academe: Some Male and Female Differences.' *Sex Roles* 4: 9–21

Kelly, Gail P., and Sheila Slaughter, eds. 1991. *Women's Higher Education in Comparative Perspective*. Norwell, Mass.: Kluwer Academic Publishers

Kierans, T. 1990. 'Where Were the Guardians?' *Globe and Mail Report on Business Magazine*, May: 47

Kitzinger, Celia. 1990. 'Resisting the Discipline.' In *Feminists and Psychological Practice*, E. Burman, ed., 119–36. London: Sage

Klodawsky, Fran. 1989. 'Parental Leave and Child Care Issues.' In *Proceedings of a Conference on Women in Graduate Studies in Ontario*, Carolyn Filteau, ed., 52–9. Toronto: Ontario Council on Graduate Studies

Klotzburger, Kay. 1973. 'Political Action by Academic Women.' In *Academic Women on the Move*, A.S. Rossi and A. Calderwood, eds, 359–91. New York: Russell Sage Foundation

Koshland, D.E. 1988. 'Women in Science.' *Science* 239: 1473

Kriegel, Leonard. 1972. *Working Through: A Teacher's Journey in the Urban University*. New York: Saturday Review Press

Landsberg, M. 1991. 'This University Doesn't Waste Female Minds.' *Toronto Star*, 18 May: F1

Larkin, June, Kathryn Morgan, and Joan McCurdy-Myers. 1991. 'Still outside the Sacred Grove of Academe.' Unpublished paper, University of Toronto

Larsen, Max, and Joan Wadlow. 1982. 'Affirmative Action: A Dean's Role.' *Journal of Educational Equity and Leadership* 2: 274–81

Lattin, Patricia Hopkins. 1983. 'Academic Women, Affirmative Action, and Mid-America in the Eighties.' *Women's Studies International Forum* 6: 223–30

Laws, Judith Long. 1975. 'The Psychology of Tokenism: An Analysis.' *Sex Roles* 1: 51–67

Lee, B.A. 1991. 'Improving Faculty Employment Decisions.' *Thought and Action* 7: 73–90

Levstik, Linda S. 1982. 'The Impossible Dream: The Ph.D., Marriage, and Family.' In *The Ph.D. Experience: A Woman's Point of View*, Sue Vartuli, ed., 93–104. New York: Praeger

Levy, Phyllis Saltzman. 1982. 'Surviving in a Predominantly White Male Institution.' In *The Ph.D. Experience: A Woman's Point of View*, Sue Vartuli, ed., 45–59. New York: Praeger

Lieberman, Marcia R. 1981. 'The Most Important Thing for You to Know.' In

Rocking the Boat: Academic Processes, Gloria DeSole and Lenore Hoffman, eds, 3–7. New York: Modern Language Association of America

Lipe, M.G. 1989. 'Further Evidence on the Performance of Female versus Male Accounting Students.' *Issues in Accounting Education* 4: 144–52

Lott, Bernice. 1985. 'The Devaluation of Women's Competence.' *Journal of Social Issues* 41: 43–60

McIntyre, Sheila. 1987–8. 'Gender Bias in the Law School.' *Canadian Journal of Women and the Law* 2: 362–407

McKeachie, W.J. 1987. 'Tips on Teaching.' In *The Compleat Academic: A Practical Guide for the Beginning Social Scientist*, Mark P. Zanna and John M. Darley, eds, 87–113. New York: Random House

MacMillan, Brian. 1989. 'The Flow-through Hypothesis: A Review of the Data.' In *Proceedings of a Conference on Women in Graduate Studies in Ontario*, Carolyn Filteau, ed., 1–12. Toronto: Ontario Council on Graduate Studies

Mangan, Katherine S. 1988. 'Women Seek Time off to Bear Children Without Jeopardizing Academic Careers.' *Chronicle of Higher Education* 34(21): A1, 16–17

Martin, M. 1984. 'Power and Authority in the Classroom: Sexist Stereotypes in Teaching Evaluations.' *Signs: Journal of Women in Culture and Society* 9(3): 482–92

McMillen, Liz. 1986. 'Legal Experts Eye 2 Sex-bias Lawsuits Brought by Women's Studies Scholars.' *Chronicle of Higher Education*, 9 April

McMullen, Linda M. 1991. 'Fear and Loathing in Academia: Women's Experience in the University.' Presented in Section on Women and Psychology symposium, 'Fear and Loathing in Academia.' Canadian Psychological Association, Calgary

Menges, Robert J., and William H. Exum. 1983. 'Barriers to the Advancement of Women and Minority Faculty.' *Journal of Higher Education* 54(2): 123–44

Miller, Casey, and Kate Swift. 1977. *Words and Women*. Garden City, NY: Anchor

Mitchell, J.M. 1987. 'The Association of the Old Boy Network with Productivity and Career Satisfaction of Women Academics and Antecedents to the Old Boy Network.' Ph.D. dissertation, University of California, Los Angeles

Moglen, Helene. 1983. 'Power and Empowerment.' *Women's Studies International Forum* 6: 131–4

Moore, Kathryn M. 1987. 'Women's Access and Opportunity in Higher Education: Toward the Twenty-first Century.' *Comparative Education* 23: 23–4

Morell, Virginia. 1992. 'Speaking Out: Shirley Tilghman.' *Science* 255: 1369

Morlock, Laura. 1973. 'Discipline Variation in the Status of Academic

Women.' In *Academic Women on the Move*, A.S. Rossi and A. Calderwood, eds, 255–312. New York: Russell Sage Foundation

Morris, Ramona. 1989. 'Safety Problems and Sexual Harassment on Campus.' In *Proceedings of a Conference on Women in Graduate Studies in Ontario*, Carolyn Filteau, ed., 13–27. Toronto: Ontario Council on Graduate Studies

Murch, Kem (writer and director). 1991. *The Chilly Climate for Women in Colleges and Universities*. (Videotape.) University of Western Ontario, London, Ont.

National Child Care Information Centre. 1988. *Status of Day Care in Canada 1988: A Review of the Major Findings of the National Day Care Study*. Ottawa: Health and Welfare Canada

National Women's Studies Association (U.S.). 1982. Constitution

Nedelsky, Jennifer. 1991. 'Inadequacy and Disentitlement: Internal Barriers to Women's Equality.' Paper presented to American Political Science Association

Nerad, Maresi. 1988. 'The Vicious Cycle of Gender and Status at the University of California at Berkeley, 1918–1954.' Paper presented at annual meeting of the Association for the Study of Higher Education, St Louis

Newsletter, Center for Continuing Education of Women, University of Michigan. 1982. Report of 'Self-image versus Professional Image: The Rules for Success,' presentation by Ellen Henderson reported in this issue, vol. 15, no. 1 (Spring): 3–4

New York Times. 1991. 'Race and Sex Tied to Disparities in Professors' Pay.' 8 December: 771–2

Nielsen, Linda L. 1982. 'Alchemy in Academe: Survival Strategies for Female Scholars.' In Spencer, Kehoe, and Speece, eds, *Handbook for Women Scholars*, 113–20

Nieva, Veronica F., and Barbara A. Gutek. 1980. 'Sex Effects on Evaluation.' *Academy of Management Review* 5: 267–76

Noonan, John F. 1980. 'White Faculty and Black Students: Examining Assumptions and Practices.' Cited by Hall and Sandler 1982

Nova Scotia Confederation of University Faculty Associations. 1987. Workshop on academic life, March, Halifax

Office on the Status of Women, Concordia University. 1991. (Produced and directed by Deborah d'Entremont.) 'Inequity in the classroom / En toute galité. (Videotape)

Ohio State University. 1987. *Handbook for Faculty Searches with Special Reference to Affirmative Action*. Columbus: Ohio State University

Ontario Confederation of University Faculty Associations (OCUFA). 1990. Special report: 'Employment Equity for Academics.' *OCUFA Forum* ('Supplement') 6(25): 2–4

- 1989. 'The Hiring and Retention of Female Faculty: An Introduction to Resource Materials.' *OCUFA Forum* ('Supplement') 6(18)
- 1986. 'Employment Equity for Women Academics: A Positive Action Strat-
  egy.' *OCUFA Forum* ('Supplement'): 2–3
Paludi, M.A., and L.A. Strayer. 1985. 'What's in an Author's Name? Differen-
  tial Evaluations of Performance as a Function of an Author's Name.' *Sex
  Roles* 12: 353–61
Patterson, M. 1973. 'Sex and Specialization in Academe and the Professions.'
  In *Academic Women on the Move*, A.S. Rossi and A. Calderwood, eds,
  313–32. New York: Russell Sage Foundation
Patterson, M., and L. Sells. 1973. 'Women Dropouts from Higher Education.'
  In *Academic Women on the Move*, A.S. Rossi and A. Calderwood, eds,
  79–91. New York: Russell Sage Foundation
Peck, T. 1978. 'When Women Evaluate Women, Nothing Succeeds like Suc-
  cess: The Differential Effects of Status upon Evaluations of Male and Fe-
  male Professional Ability.' *Sex Roles* 4: 205–13
Peller, Gary. 1991. 'Espousing a Positive View of Affirmative-action Policies.'
  Chronicle of Higher Education, 18 December: B1–2
Perry, Gloria R., and Judith A. Chaney. 1987. *Coping with Multiple Demands:
  A Study of Women Faculty in Schools of Nursing* (ERIC document no. ED289-
  087)
Pfeffer, Jeffrey, and Alison Davis-Blake. 1987. 'The Effect of the Proportion of
  Women on Salaries: The Case of College Administrators.' *Administrative
  Science Quarterly* 32: 1–24
Pleck, Joseph. 1986. 'Employment and Fatherhood: Issues and Innovative
  Policies:' In *The Father's Role: Applied Perspectives*, Michael E. Lamb, ed.,
  385–412. New York: John Wiley and Sons
Pounder, Diana G. 1989. 'The Gender Gap in Salaries of Educational Admin-
  istration Professors.' *Educational Administration Quarterly* 25: 101–201
Project on the Status and Education of Women. 1988. *Evaluating Courses for
  Inclusion of New Scholarship on Women*. Washington: Association of Ameri-
  can Colleges
- 1986. *Guide to Nonsexist Language*. Washington: Association of American
  Colleges
- 1982. 'Two Surveys, One Conclusion: Across the Board, Women Faculty
  Still Earn Less than Men.' *On Campus with Women* 12: 7
- 1981. *Nontraditional Careers*. Washington: Association of American Colleges
- 1980. *Sexist Biases in Sociological Research: Problems and Issues*. Washington:
  Association of American Colleges
Pyke, Sandra (Chair of Committee on Status of Women in Ontario Universities). 1990. 'A Message to Council.' In Council of Ontario Universities, *An-*

nual Report 1989–90. Committee on the Status of Women, Toronto: Council of Ontario Universities

Quina, Kathryn. 1986. 'Helping Yourself to Tenure.' In *Career Guide for Women Scholars*, Suzanna Rose, ed., 36–45. New York: Springer

– 1986. 'Lessons from My First Job.' In ibid., 89–93

Rao, Aruna, ed. 1991. *Women's Studies International: Nairobi and Beyond*. New York: Feminist Press

Rausch, Diane K., et al. 1989. 'The Academic Revolving Door: Why Do Women Get Caught?' *CUPA Journal* 40: 1–16

Raymond, Chris. 1991. 'Continuing Shortage of Women in Science Decried: Many Drop Out.' *Chronicle of Higher Education*, 11 December: A31–2

Raymond, Janice. 1982. 'Mary Daly: A Decade of Academic Harassment and Feminist Survival.' In Spencer, Kehoe, and Speece, eds, *Handbook for Women Scholars*, 81–8

Reid, Pamela Trotman. 1987. 'Perceptions of Sex Discrimination among Female University Faculty and Staff.' *Psychology of Women Quarterly* 11: 123–8

Relating to Each Other: A Questionnaire for Students. 1989. Washington: Association of American Colleges

Relating with Colleagues: A Questionnaire for Faculty Members. 1989. Washington: Association of American Colleges

Reskin, B.F. 1980. *Sex Differences in the Professional Life Chances of Chemists*. New York: Arno Press

– 1979. 'Academic Sponsorship and Scientists' Careers.' *Sociology of Education* 52: 129–46

Restoration of Title IX: Implications for Higher Education. 1989. Washington: Association of American Colleges

Rich, Adrienne. 1979a. 'Toward a Woman-centered University (1973–74).' In *On Lies, Secrets, and Silence: Selected Prose (1966–1978)*, 125–55. New York: W.W. Norton

– 1979b. 'Claiming an Education (1977).' In *On Lies, Secrets, and Silence*, 231–5

– 1979c. 'Taking Women Students Seriously (1978).' In *On Lies, Secrets, and Silence*, 237–45

Richards, Mary P. (Acting Associate Dean, College of Liberal Arts, University of Tennessee). 1986. Letter, cited by Sandler with Hall, *The Campus Climate Revisited*

Richardson, Betty. 1974. *Sexism in Higher Education*. New York: Seabury Press

Ricks, Frances A., Sandra W. Pyke, Elinor W. Ames, Penny Parry, and Pam Duncan. 1980. 'The Status of Women and Men in Canadian Psychology Academia.' *Canadian Psychology/Psychologie Canadienne* 20: 109–15

Riesman, David. 1964. Introduction to Jessie Bernard's *Academic Women*. New York: New American Library

Robbins, Lillian, and Ethel D. Kahn. 1985. 'Sex Discrimination and Sex Equity for Faculty Women in the 1980s.' *Journal of Social Issues* 41: 1–15

Rose, Suzanna, ed. 1986. *Career Guide for Women Scholars*. New York: Springer

– 'Building a Professional Network.' In Rose, ed., *Career Guide for Women Scholars*, 46–56

Rosenfelt, Deborah, and Rhonda Williams. 1992. 'Learning Experience.' *Women's Review of Books* 9(5): 33–5

Rosser, S.V., ed. 1988. *Feminism within the Science and Health Care Professions: Overcoming Resistance*. New York: Pergamon Press

Rossi, Alice, and A. Calderwood, eds. 1973. *Academic Women on the Move*. New York: Russell Sage Foundation

Rothblum, Esther D. 1988. 'Leaving the Ivory Tower: Factors Contributing to Women's Voluntary Resignation from Academia.' *Frontiers* 10: 14–17

Ruddick, Sara, and Pamela Daniels. 1977. *Working It Out: Twenty-three Women Writers, Artists, Scientists, and Scholars Talk about Their Lives and Work*. New York: Pantheon

Russell, S. 1986. 'The Hidden Curriculum of School: Reproducing Gender and Class Hierarchies.' In *The Politics of Diversity*, R. Hamilton and M. Barrett, 343–60. Montreal: Book Centre, Inc.

Russell, S.H., R.S. Cox, C. Williamson, J. Boismier, H. Javitz, and J. Fairweather. 1988. *Faculty in Higher Education Institutions*. Washington: U.S. Department of Education, Office of Educational Research and Improvement

Salancik, Gerald R. 1987. 'Power and Politics in Academic Departments.' In *The Compleat Academic: A Practical Guide for the Beginning Social Scientist*, Mark P. Zanna and John M. Darley, eds, 61–84. New York: Random House

Sandler, Bernice Resnick. 1991. 'Women Faculty at Work in the Classroom, or, Why It Still Hurts to Be a Woman in Labor.' *Communication Education* 40: 6–15

– 1981. 'Strategies for Eliminating Sex Discrimination: Times That Try Men's Souls.' In *Sex Discrimination in Higher Education: Strategies for Equality*, Jennie Farley, ed., 66–89. Ithaca, NY: New York State School of Industrial and Labor Relations

Sandler, Bernice, with Roberta M. Hall. 1986. *The Campus Climate Revisited: Chilly for Women Faculty, Administrators, and Graduate Students*. Washington: Association of American Colleges

Sandler, Bernice R., Jean O'Gorman Hughes, and Mary DeMouy. 1988. 'It's All in What You Ask: Questions for Search Committees to Use.' Washing-

ton: Project on the Status and Education of Women, Association of American Colleges

Sanford, Linda Tschirhart, and Mary Ellen Donovan. 1984. *Women and Self-
esteem: Understanding and Improving the Way We Think and Feel about Ourselves*. New York: Penguin

Schwartz, Pepper, and Janet Lever. 1973. 'Women in the Male World of
Higher Education.' In *Academic Women on the Move*, A.S. Rossi and A.
Calderwood, eds, 57–77. New York: Russell Sage Foundation

Science. 1992. Special section on women in science. 255: 1365–88

Scott, Patricia Bell. 1982. 'Debunking Sapphire: Toward a Non-racist and
Non-sexist Social Science.' In *All the Women Are White, All the Blacks Are
Men, But Some of Us Are Brave*, Gloria T. Hull, Patricia Bell Scott, and Bar-
bara Smith, eds, 85–92. Old Westbury, NY: Feminist Press

Scott, Sue, and Mary Porter. 1983. 'On the Bottom Rung: A Discussion of
Women's Work in Sociology.' *Women's Studies International Forum* 6:
211–22

Selleck, Laura J., and Helen J. Breslauer. 1989. 'The Increasingly Female
Clientele for University Education in Canada.' Paper presented at Canadian
Society for the Study of Higher Education / La Société canadienne pour
l'étude de l'enseignement supérieur, Laval University, Quebec

Selvin, Paul. 1992. 'Profile of a Field: Mathematics – Heroism is Still the
Norm.' *Science* 255: 1382–3

Shapiro, Eileen. 1982. 'A Survival Guide.' In Spencer, Kehoe, and Speece,
eds, *Handbook for Women Scholars*, 121–22

Shavlik, Donna (Director, Office of Women in Higher Education, American
Council on Education). 1986. Conversation, March. Cited by Sandler with
Hall, *The Campus Climate Revisited* (see above)

Sheinin, Rose. 1989. 'Review of the Implementation of the Recommendations
of the Report on the "Status of Women in Ontario Universities." ' In *Proceedings of a Conference on Women in Graduate Studies in Ontario*, Carolyn
Filteau, ed., 90–113. Toronto: Ontario Council on Graduate Studies

– 1987. 'The Monastic Origins of the University.' Presented to Canadian Association of University Teachers' Status of Women workshop, Fredericton,
NB

Silvia, Evelyn M. 1990. *Collegial Advice for Assistant Professors: Hints for Success and Stress Reduction as an Assistant Professor at UC Davis*. Davis, Calif.:
University of California

Simeone, Angela. 1987. *Academic Women: Working toward Equality*. South
Hadley, Mass.: Bergin & Garvey

Smith, D.E., A.J. Cohen, P.A. Staton, J. Drakich, D. Rayside, and G.E. Burt.
n.d. *A Future for Women at the University of Toronto: The Report of the Ad*

Hoc Committee on the Status of Women. Occasional Papers Series no. 13, Centre for Women's Studies in Education. Toronto: Ontario Institute for Studies in Education

Smith, Kenwyn K., Valerie M. Simmons, and Terri B. Thames. 1989. ' "Fix the Women": An Intervention into an Organizational Conflict Based on Parallel Process Thinking.' *Journal of Applied Behavioral Science* 25:`11–29

Smye, Marti Diane, Jeri Dawn Wine, and Barbara Moses. 1980. 'Sex Differences in Assertiveness: Implications for Research and Treatment.' In *Sex Roles: Origins, Influences, and Implications for Women*, Cannie Stark-Adamec, ed., 164–75. Montreal: Eden Press

Spanier, Bonnie, Alexander Bloom, and Darlene Boroviak, eds. 1984. *Toward a Balanced Curriculum: A Sourcebook for Initiating Gender Integration Projects.* Cambridge, Mass.: Schenkman Publishing Co.

Spatta, Carolyn D. 1984. *White Faculty, Black Students: Exploring Assumptions and Practices*. Washington: Association of American Colleges

Spencer, Mary L., Monika Kehoe, and Karen Speece, eds. 1982. *Handbook for Women Scholars: Strategies for Success*. San Francisco: Center for Women Scholars, Americas Behavioral Research Corporation

Spender, Dale. 1990. *Manmade Language*. 2nd ed. London: Pandora

– 1982. *Invisible Women: The Schooling Scandal*. London: Writers and Readers Cooperative

– 1981. 'The Gatekeepers: A Feminist Critique of Academic Publishing.' In *Doing Feminist Research*, H. Roberts, ed., 186–202. London: Routledge and Kegan Paul

Stafford, S.G., and G.B. Spanier. 1990. 'Recruiting the Dual-Career Couple: The Family Employment Program.' *Initiatives* 53(2): 37–44

Stake, Jayne E. 1986. 'When It's Publish or Perish: Tips on Survival.' In *Career Guide for Women Scholars*, Suzanna Rose, ed., 57–65. New York: Springer

Stark-Adamec, Cannie. 1991. 'Coping with Fear and Loathing of Academia: or, If I Knew Then What I Know Now ...' Presented at Section on Women and Psychology symposium, 'Fear and Loathing in Academia.' Canadian Psychological Association convention, Calgary

Statistics Canada. 1992. *Universities: Enrolment and Degrees / Universités: Inscription et grades décernés*. Ottawa

– 1991a. *Education in Canada / L'éducation au Canada*. Ottawa

– 1991b. *Teachers in universities / Enseignants dans les universités. 1987–88.* Ottawa

Statistics Canada. Education, Culture, and Tourism Division. 1990. *Teachers and Universities 1986–7*. Ottawa

Status of Women Committee, Ontario Confederation of University Faculty

Associations. 1992. *Responding to Women's Concerns: A Primer for Faculty Associations.* Toronto: OCUFA

– 1990. Status of Women Committee Report. *OCUFA Forum* 6, October: 4

Stecklein, John E., and Gail E. Lorenz. 1986. 'Academic Woman: Twenty-four Years of Progress?' *Liberal Education* 72: 63–71

Stein, Sandra L., and Marlaine E. Lockheed. 1983. 'Women's Studies and Men's Careers: How the "Social Problem" of Women in Education Maintained the Academic Status of Men in the 1970s.' *Women's Studies International Forum* 6: 203–10

Stoppard, Janet. 1988. 'Depression in Women: Psychological Disorder or Social Problem?' *Atlantis: A Women's Studies Journal* 14: 38–44

Sutherland, Margaret B. 1985. 'The Situation of Women Who Teach in Universities: Contrasts and Common Ground.' *Comparative Education* 21: 21–8

Symons, Douglas K. 1992. 'The Ethics of Faculty Searches Revisited.' *Canadian Psychology / Psychologie Canadienne* 33: 116–18

Symons, Thomas H.B., and James E. Page. 1984. 'Some Questions of Balance: Human Resources, Higher Education and Canadian Studies.' In *To Know Ourselves: The Report of the Commission on Canadian Studies* 3: 188–214. Ottawa: Association of Universities and Colleges of Canada

Tancred-Sheriff, Peta. 1988. ' "Demi-nationalism" in Higher Education: Women in Canadian and Australian Universities.' *Australian Universities Review* 32: 14–19

Taylor, Shelley E., and Joanne Martin. 1987. 'The Present-minded Professor: Controlling One's Career.' In *The Compleat Academic: A Practical Guide for the Beginning Social Scientist*, Mark P. Zanna and John M. Darley, eds, 23–60. New York: Random House

Thielens, Wagner, Jr. 1984. 'Women Professors and Lecturing.' Paper presented at International Conference on Improving University Teaching

Tidball, Elizabeth. 1976. 'Of Men and Research.' *Journal of Higher Education* 47: 373–90

Tidball, M.E. 1974. 'Perspective on Academic Women and Affirmative Action.' *Educational Record* 54 (1973): 130–5

Tolpin, Martha. 1981. *A Wo/man's Guide to Academe: Moving in, Moving up, Moving over.* Higher Education Resource Services (HERS)–New England

Touchton, Judith G., and Lynne Davis, with Vivian Parker Makosky. 1991. *Fact Book on Women in Higher Education.* New York: American Council on Education and Macmillan Publishing Company

Tuckman, Barbara, and Howard Tuckman. 1981. 'Women as Part-time Faculty Members.' *Higher Education* 10: 169–79

United States Department of Education, Office of Educational Research and

Improvement. 1990a. *The Condition of Education, 1990, Vol. 2, Postsecondary Education*. Washington: U.S. Government Printing Office

– 1990b. *Faculty in Higher Education Institutions, 1988*. Washington: U.S. Government Printing Office

– 1988. *Digest of Education Statistics, 1988*. Washington: U.S. Government Printing Office

University of Western Ontario's Caucus on Women's Issues and The President's Standing Committee for Employment Equity, University of Western Ontario. 1991. *The Chilly Climate for Women in Colleges and Universities: Warming the Environment*. (Facilitator's manual for videotape of that name)

University of Wisconsin. 1988. *Achieving Faculty Diversity*. Madison: University of Wisconsin

Vandell, Kathy, and Lauren Fishbein. 1989. 'Women and Tenure: The Opportunity of a Century.' Washington: American Association of University Women

Vetter, Betty M. 1976. 'Minority Women in Science and Engineering.' Paper presented to American Association for the Advancement of Science Conference. In *The Double Bind: The Price of Being a Minority Woman in Science*. AAAS Report no. 76-R-3. Washington: AAAS

Vetter, B.M., and E.L. Babco. 1987. *Professional Women and Minorities: A Manpower Data Resource Service*. Washington: Commission on Professionals in Science and Technology

Vickers, Jill McCalla, and June Adam. 1977. *but can you type? Canadian Universities and the Status of Women*. Clarke, Irwin and Co. in association with Canadian Association of University Teachers

Walsh, Mary Roth. 1985. 'Academic Professional Women Organizing for Change: The Struggle in Psychology.' *Journal of Social Issues* 41: 17–28

Weis, L. 1987. 'Academic Women in Science 1977–1984.' *Academe* 73 (Jan./ Feb.): 43–7

Weisstein, Naomi. 1977. ' "How can a little girl like you teach a great big class of men?" the Chairman said, and Other Adventures of a Woman of Science.' In *Working It Out: 23 Women Writers, Artists, Scientists and Scholars Talk about Their Lives and Work*, Sara Ruddick and Pamela Daniels, eds, 241–50. New York: Pantheon Books

Weitzman, Lenore J. 1973. 'Affirmative Action Plans for Eliminating Sex Discrimination in Academe.' In *Academic Women on the Move*, A.S. Rossi and A. Calderwood, eds, 463–504. New York: Russell Sage Foundation

White, Georgina. 1980. 'Attributions about Women.' *Resources for Feminist Research / Documentation sur la recherche féministe* 9: 9

Williams, J.D., J.A. Williams, V.T. Anderson, and S.J. Roman. 1987. 'A Ten-year Study of Salary Differential by Sex through a Regression Methodology.' Paper presented at annual meeting of American Educational Research Association, Washington

Williams, Tannis MacBeth, Merle L. Zabrack, and Linda F. Harrison. 1980. 'Some Factors Affecting Women's Participation in Psychology in Canada.' *Canadian Psychology / Psychologie Canadienne* 21: 97–108

Wilson, D., and K.O. Doyle, Jr. 1976. 'Student Ratings of Instruction.' *Journal of Higher Education* 47(4): 465–9

Wine, Jeri Dawn, Barbara Moses, and Marti Smye. 1980. 'Female Superiority in Sex Difference Competence Comparisons: A Review of the Literature.' In *Sex Roles: Origins, Influences, and Implications for Women*, Cannie Stark-Adamec, 176–86. Montreal: Eden Press

Women's Caucus, Political Science Department, University of Chicago. 1970. 'The Halls of Academe.' In *Sisterhood Is Powerful*, Robin Morgan, ed., 101. New York: Vintage

The Women's Review of Books. 1992. 'Revolution and Reaction.' February: 13

Women Students' Coalition. 1980. *The Quality of Women's Education at Harvard University: A Survey of Sex Discrimination in the Graduate and Professional Schools.* Cambridge, Mass.: Harvard University

Yoder, Janice D. 1986. 'Challenges during the Transition from Graduate Student to Assistant Professor.' In *Career Guide to Women Scholars*, Suzanna Rose, ed., 81–8. New York: Springer

– 1985. 'An Academic Woman as a Token: A Case Study.' *Journal of Social Issues* 41: 61–72

Zanna, Mark P., and John M. Darley, eds. 1987a. *The Compleat Academic: A Practical Guide for the Beginning Social Scientist.* New York: Random House

– 1987b. 'On Managing the Faculty–Graduate Student Research Relationship.' In *The Compleat Academic*: 139–49

Zimmerman, Bonnie. 1983. 'Is "Chloe liked Olivia" a Lesbian Plot?' *Women's Studies International Forum* 6: 169–76

A Graduate students

Adler, Nancy E. 1976. 'Women Students.' In *Scholars in the Making: The Development of Graduate and Professional Students*, Joseph Katz and Rodney T. Hartnett, eds, 197–225. Cambridge, Mass.: Ballinger

Barnett, Sharon. 1982. 'New Brains for Old: The Impact of Emotional and Physical Stress during the Ph.D. Period.' In *The Ph.D. Experience: A Woman's Point of View*, Sue Vartuli, ed., 61–9. New York: Praeger

Bolig, Rosemary. 1982. 'The Ambivalent Decision.' In *The Ph.D. Experience: A Woman's Point of View*, Sue Vartuli, ed., 15–26. New York: Praeger

Carter, Mae R. 1985. 'Improving the Learning Environment for Women Students.' Panel on climate issues, Association of American Colleges annual meeting, Washington

Committee on the Status of Women. 1991. *The Status of Women Graduate Students*. Toronto: Council of Ontario Universities

– 1988. *Attracting and Retaining Women Students for Science and Engineering*. Toronto: Council of Ontario Universities

Dagg, Anne Innis. 1989. 'Women as Graduate Students: Discrimination and Accessibility.' In *Proceedings of a Conference on Women in Graduate Studies in Ontario*, Carolyn Filteau, ed., 28–31. Toronto: Ontario Council on Graduate Studies

Delisle, G.J. 1989. 'Issues Affecting the Quality of the Graduate Experiences for Women in Science and Engineering.' In *Proceedings of a Conference on Women in Graduate Studies in Ontario*, Carolyn Filteau, ed., 72–4. Toronto: Ontario Council on Graduate Studies

Dudovitz, Resa L., Ann Russo, John Duvall, and Patricia Cramer. 1983. 'Survival in the "Master's House": The Role of Graduate Teaching Assistants in Effecting Curriculum Change.' *Women's Studies International Forum* 6: 149–58

Eichler, Margrit. 1989. 'The Supervision of Theses Adopting Feminist Perspectives, or: Jane's Search for a Feminist Supervisor.' In *Proceedings of a Conference on Women in Graduate Studies in Ontario*, Carolyn Filteau, ed., 75–7. Toronto: Ontario Council on Graduate Studies

Filteau, Carolyn, ed. 1989. *Proceedings of a Conference on Women in Graduate Studies in Ontario*. Toronto: Ontario Council on Graduate Studies

Fox, G.L. 1970. 'The Woman Graduate Student in Sociology.' Presented at 'Women on Campus: 1970, A Symposium,' Center for Continuing Education of Women, University of Michigan, Ann Arbor

Girves, J., and V. Wemmerus, 1988. 'Developing Models of Graduate Student Degree Programs.' *Journal of Higher Education* 59(2): 163–89

Haley, Ella. 1989. 'Support Systems for Women in Graduate School.' In *Proceedings of a Conference on Women in Graduate Studies in Ontario*, Carolyn Filteau, ed., 32–41. Toronto: Ontario Council on Graduate Studies

– 1985. 'Exploratory Study of Factors Affecting Graduate Students' Performance.' Master's research paper, University of Waterloo

McConnell, Mary Ann. 1982. 'High Noon: Surviving the Comprehensive Exams.' In *The Ph.D. Experience: A Woman's Point of View*, Sue Vartuli, ed., 27–34. New York: Praeger

McCurdy-Myers, Joan. 1991. 'The Status of Women in Ontario Universities: Graduate Students.' Unpublished paper, Ontario Institute for Studies in Education

Menges, Robert J., and William H. Exum. 1983. 'Barriers to the Advancement of Women and Minority Faculty.' *Journal of Higher Education* 54(2): 123–44

Nevitte, N., R. Gibbins, and P.W. Codding. 1988. 'The Career Goals of Female Science Students in Canada. *Canadian Journal of Higher Education* 18: 31–48

Newsletter of the Teaching Resource Office. 1981. Cited by Haley, 'Exploratory Study of Factors' (see above)

Pyke, Sandra W. 1991. 'Gender Issues in Graduate Education.' Trevor N.S. Lennam Memorial Lecture, University of Calgary, 27 March

Roby, Pamela. 1973. 'Institutional Barriers to Women Students in Higher Education.' In *Academic Women on the Move*, A.S. Rossi and A. Calderwood, eds, 37–56. New York: Russell Sage Foundation

Rogers, Linda. 1986. 'The Graduate School Experience.' In *Career Guide for Women Scholars*, Suzanna Rose, ed., 94–101. New York: Springer

Rothblum, Esther D., and Ellen Cole. 1991. *Professional Training for Feminist Therapists: Personal Memoirs*. (Special issue of *Women and Therapy* 11.) New York: Haworth Press

School of Graduate Studies, University of Toronto. 1990. *Report of the Committee on Eligibility and Distribution of University of Toronto Open Fellowships*. July

Sethna, Christabelle. In press. 'Desperately Seeking Sisterhood: Diversity, Deception, Divisiveness.' *Journal of Social and Political Action*.

Smedick, Lois. 1989. 'Response to "Status of Women" Report.' In *Proceedings of a Conference on Women in Graduate Studies in Ontario*, Carolyn Filteau, ed., 80–2. Toronto: Ontario Council on Graduate Studies

Smith, Bernice D. 1982. 'Taking the Giant Step: Writing the Dissertation.' In *The Ph.D. Experience: A Woman's Point of View*, Sue Vartuli, ed., 35–44. New York: Praeger

Symons, Gladys. 1977. 'Stress in Graduate School: Some Male-female Comparisons.' Paper presented at Canadian Sociological and Anthropological Association annual meeting, Fredericton

Tracey, Katherine O. 1982. 'The Diary of a Web Spinner.' In *The Ph.D. Experience: A Woman's Point of View*, Sue Vartuli, ed., 71–8. New York: Praeger

Trofimenkoff, Susan Mann. 1989. 'A Woman Administrator Looks at Life and Love in the Graduate School.' In *Proceedings of a Conference on Women in Graduate Studies in Ontario*, Carolyn Filteau, ed., 114–18. Toronto: Ontario Council on Graduate Studies

Vartuli, Sue, ed. 1982. *The Ph.D. Experience: A Woman's Point of View*. New York: Praeger

Wells, Mary Cay. 1982. 'Grandma! What Big Plans You've Got!' In *The Ph.D.*

Experience: A Woman's Point of View, Sue Vartuli, ed., 105–14. New York: Praeger

Williams, Rosalind. 1982. 'In and Out of Relationships: A Serious Game for the Woman Doctoral Student.' In *The Ph.D. Experience: A Woman's Point of View*, Sue Vartuli, ed., 79–92. New York: Praeger

Wise, Sydney, 1989. 'Response to "Status of Women" Report.' In *Proceedings of a Conference on Women in Graduate Studies in Ontario*, Carolyn Filteau, ed., 86–9. Toronto: Ontario Council on Graduate Studies

Yeates, Maurice. 1989. 'Preface.' In *Proceedings of a Conference on Women in Graduate Studies in Ontario*, Carolyn Filteau, ed., iv–vii. Toronto: Ontario Council on Graduate Studies, 1989

Yoder, Janice D. 1986. 'Challenges during the Transition from Graduate Student to Assistant Professor.' In *Career Guide to Women Scholars*, Suzanna Rose, ed., 81–8. New York: Springer

York University Task Force on the Status of Women Graduate Students. 1992. *Not Satisfied Yet: Report of the Task Force on the Status of Women Graduate Students*. North York, Ont.: York University

Zanna, Mark P., and John M. Darley. 1987a. 'Everything You Always Wanted to Know about Research but Were Afraid to Ask (Your Advisor).' In Zanna and Darley, eds., *The Compleat Academic: A Practical Guide for the Beginning Social Scientist*, 115–37. New York: Random House

– 1987b. 'On Managing the Faculty–Graduate Student Research Relationship.' In Zanna and Darley, eds., *The Compleat Academic*, 139–49

Zappert, L., and K. Stansbury. 1985. 'Graduate Women and Men in Science and Engineering at Stanford: Very Different Experiences.' Excerpt from Association of American Colleges, *Project on the Status and Education of Women* 14: 8–9

B Grievances and legal proceedings

Boring, Phyllis Zatlin. 1982. 'Filing a Faculty Grievance.' In Spencer, Kehoe, and Speece, eds, *Handbook for Women Scholars*, 124–6

Davies, Helen C., and Robert E. Davies, 1981. 'Grievances and Their Redress in the Eighties.' In *Sex Discrimination in Higher Education: Strategies for Equality*, Jennie Farley, ed., 34–65. Ithaca: New York State School of Industrial and Labor Relations

Drainie, Bronwyn. 1991. 'Trials and Errors: In the Case of the Women vs. the Men at Osgoode Hall Law School, the Jury Is Still out.' *Toronto Life*, August: 27–31, 44–48

Gray, Mary W. 1985a. 'Legal Perspectives on Sex Equity in Faculty Employment.' *Journal of Social Issues* 41: 121–34

– 1985b. 'The Halls of Ivy and the Halls of Justice: Resisting Sex Discrimination against Faculty Women.' *Academe* 71: 33–41

Hill, Anita. 1992. 'The Nature of the Beast.' *Ms.*, January/February: 32–3

LaNoue, George R., and Barbara A. Lee. 1987. *Academics in Court: The Consequences of Faculty Discrimination Litigation*. Ann Arbor: University of Michigan

Leonard, E.L. 1986. 'Faculty Women for Equity: A Class-action Suit against the State of Oregon.' *Affilia* (Summer): 6–19

Rumbarger, Margaret L. 1973. 'Internal Remedies for Sex Discrimination in Colleges and Universities.' In *Academic Women on the Move*, A.S. Rossi and A. Calderwood, eds., 425–38. New York: Russell Sage Foundation

Sandler, Bernice. 1973. 'A Little Help from Our Government: WEAL and Contract Compliance.' In *Academic Women on the Move*, A.S. Rossi and A. Calderwood, eds., 439–62. New York: Russell Sage Foundation

Steinschneider, Janice. 1990. *Federal Laws and Regulations Prohibiting Sex Discrimination in Educational Institutions* (chart). Washington: Association of American Colleges

Taub, Nadine. 1985. 'Dealing with Employment Discrimination and Damaging Stereotypes: A Legal Perspective.' *Journal of Social Issues* 41: 99–10

Theodore, Athena. 1986. *The Campus Troublemakers: Academic Women in Protest*. Houston: Cap and Gown Press

Vladeck, Judith P. 1981. 'Litigation: Strategy of the Last Resort. In *Sex Discrimination in Higher Education: Strategies for Equality*, Jennie Farley, ed., 1–22. New York State School of Industrial and Labor Relations

c Job search and hiring

Breslauer, Helen, and Leigh West. 1989. 'Hiring Women into Tenure-stream Faculty Positions.' *OCUFA Forum* ('Supplement') 6(18): 3–4

Bronstein, Phyllis. 1986. 'Applying for Academic Jobs: Strategies for Success.' In *Career Guide for Women Scholars*, Suzanna Rose, ed., 3–26. New York: Springer

Bronstein, Phyllis, Leora Black, Joyce Pfennig, and Adele White. 1986. 'Getting Academic Jobs: Are Women Equally Qualified – and Equally Successful?' *American Psychologist* 41: 318–22

Darley, John M., and Mark P. Zanna. 1987. 'The Hiring Process in Academia.' In *The Compleat Academic: A Practical Guide for the Beginning Social Scientist*, Zanna and Darley, eds, 3–21. New York: Random House

Heiberger, Mary Morris, and Julia Miller Vick. 1992. *The Academic Job Search Handbook*. University of Pennsylvania Press

McNairy, Marion R. 1982. 'The Job Hunt.' In ed., *The Ph.D. Experience: A Woman's Point of View*, Sue Vartuli, ed., 115–26. New York: Praeger

Minority Faculty Registry. 1992. c/o Dr William B. Jones, Southwestern University, Georgetown, Tex. 78626. Printed in *Chronicle of Higher Education* 8 January: B19

Ontario Confederation of University Faculty Associations. 1989. 'The Hiring and Retention of Female Faculty: An Introduction to Resource Materials.' *OCUFA Forum* ('Supplement') 6

Parr, Joy. 1989. 'Chilly Climate – the Systemic Dilemma.' *OCUFA Forum* ('Supplement') 6(18): 1–2

D Mentors, supervisors, and role models

Eichler, Margrit. 1989. 'The Supervision of Theses Adopting Feminist Perspectives, or: Jane's Search for a Feminist Supervisor.' In *Proceedings of a Conference on Women in Graduate Studies in Ontario*, Carolyn Filteau, ed., 75–7. Toronto: Ontario Council on Graduate Studies, 1989

Gibbons, Ann. 1992a. 'Key Issue: Mentoring.' *Science* 255: 1368

– 1992b. 'Creative Solutions: Electronic Mentoring.' *Science* 255: 1369

Goldstein, E. 1979. 'Effect of Same-sex and Cross-sex Role Models on the Subsequent Academic Productivity of Scholars.' *American Psychologist* 34: 407–10

Hall, Roberta M., and Bernice R. Sandler. 1983. *Academic Mentoring for Women Students and Faculty: A New Look at an Old Way to Get Ahead.* Washington: Project on the Status and Education of Women, Association of American Colleges

Laurence, Martha Keniston. 1989. 'Role Models – Importance and Availability. In *Proceedings of a Conference on Women in Graduate Studies in Ontario*, Carolyn Filteau, ed., 60–7. Toronto: Ontario Council on Graduate Studies

Moore, Kathryn M. 1982. 'The Role of Mentors in Developing Leaders for Academe.' *Educational Record* 63: 23–8

Project on the Status and Education of Women, Association of American Colleges. 1983. *Academic Mentoring for Women Students and Faculty: A New Look at an Old Way to Get Ahead.* Washington: Association of American Colleges

Rowe, Mary P. 1981. 'Building Mentorship Frameworks as Part of an Effective Equal Opportunity Ecology.' In *Sex Discrimination in Higher Education: Strategies for Equality*, Jennie Farley, ed., 23–33. Ithaca: New York State School of Industrial and Labor Relations

E Non-dominant groups

Aguirre, Adalberto. 1985. 'Chicano Faculty at Post-secondary Educational Institutions in the Southwest.' *Journal of Educational Equity and Leadership* 5: 133–44

– 1987. 'An Interpretative Analysis of Chicano Faculty in Academe.' *Social Science Journal* 24(1): 71–81

American Association for the Advancement of Science. 1976. *The Double Bind: The Price of Being a Minority Woman in Science.* Washington: AAAS

Arcienega, Tomas (chair). 1985. *Hispanics and Higher Education: A CSU Imperative.* Final report of Commission on Hispanic Underrepresentation. Long Beach: Office of the Chancellor, California State University

Astin, Helen, and Cecilia Burciaga. 1981. *Chicanos in Higher Education: Process and Attainment.* Los Angeles: Higher Education Research Institute, Inc.

Banks, Martha E. 1986. 'Black Women Clinicians: Survival against the Odds. In *Career Guide for Women Scholars*, Suzanna Rose, ed., 108–14. New York: Springer

Bannerji, Himani, Linda Carty, Kari Delhi, Susan Heald, and Kate McKenna, eds. 1991. *Unsettling Relations: The University as a Site of Feminist Struggles.* Toronto: Women's Press

Barale, M.A. 1988. 'The Lesbian Academic: Negotiating New Boundaries.' *Women and Therapy* 8: 183–94

Barnes, Denise R. 1986. 'Transitions and Stresses for Black Female Scholars.' In *Career Guide for Women Scholars*, Suzanna Rose, ed., 66–77. New York: Springer

Bell-Scott, Patricia, and Beverly Guy-Sheftall. 1987. *Black Women in Higher Education: Struggling to Gain Visibility.* New York: Garland

Black, Albert. 1981. 'Affirmative Action and the Black Academic Situation.' *Western Journal of Black Studies* 5: 87–94

Brown, Peggy Ann. 1985. *Helping Minority Students Succeed.* Washington: Association of American Colleges

Carroll, Constance M. 1973. 'Three's a Crowd: The Dilemma of the Black Woman in Higher Education.' In *Academic Women on the Move*, A.S. Rossi and A. Calderwood, eds., 173–85. New York: Russell Sage Foundation

Carty, Linda. 1991. 'Black Women in Academia: A Statement from the Periphery.' In Himani Bannerji, Linda Carty, Kari Delhi, Susan Heald, and Kate McKenna, *Unsettling Relations: The University as a Site of Feminist Struggles*, 13–44. Toronto: Women's Press

Chavers, Dean. 1980. 'Isolation and Drainoff: The Case of the American Indian Educational Researcher.' *Educational Researcher* 9: 12–16

Chayat, Sherry. 1987. 'JAP-baiting on the College Scene.' *Lilith* 17 (Fall): 6–7

Clarke, L. 1989. 'Academic Aliens.' *Psychology of Women Section Newsletter* 4: 3–8

Collins, Sharon. 1979. 'Making Ourselves Visible: Evolution of Career Status and Self-image of Minority Professional Women.' In *The Minority Woman in America: Professionalism at What Cost?* San Francisco: University of California

Comely, Louise, Celia Kitzinger, Rachel Perkins, and Sue Wilkinson. 1992. 'Lesbian Psychology in Britain: Back into the Closet.' *Feminism and Psychology* 2(2): 265–8

Committee on Women in Psychology, American Psychological Association. 1992. *Survival Guide to Academe for Women and Ethnic Minorities.* Washington: American Psychological Association

Crew, L., and R. Norton. 1974. 'The Homophobic Imagination: An Editorial.' *College English* 36: 272–90

D'Augelli, A. 1989. 'Lesbians' and Gay Men's Experiences of Discrimination and Harassment in a University Community.' *American Journal of Community Psychology* 17: 317–21

Davenport, Doris. 1982. 'Black Lesbians in Academia: Visible Invisibility.' In *Lesbian Studies: Present and Future*, Margaret Cruikshank, ed., 9–12. New York: Feminist Press

Elmore, Charles, and Robert Blackburn. 1983. 'Black and White Faculty in White Research Universities.' *Journal of Higher Education* 54: 1–15

Escobedo, Theresa. 1980. 'Are Hispanic Women in Higher Education the Non-existent Minority?' *Educational Researcher* 9: 7–12

Evans, Gaynelle. 1986. 'Graduates of Traditionally Black Colleges Learn How to Operate within the System.' *Chronicle of Higher Education*, 24 September

Farrell, W., and C. Jones. 1988. 'Recent Racial Incidents in Higher Education.' *Urban Review* 20(3): 211–26

Fikes, Robert. 1978. 'Control of Information: Black Scholars and the Academic Press.' *Western Journal of Black Studies* 2: 219–21

Fine, Michelle, and Adrienne Asch, eds. 1988. *Women with Disabilities: Essays in Psychology, Culture, and Politics.* Philadelphia: Temple University Press

Giddings, Paula. 1984. *When and Where We Enter: The Impact of Black Women on Race and Sex in America.* New York: Mirror

Hall, Lisa Hahaleole Change. 1992. 'Trapped in the Ivory Tower?' *Women's Review of Books* 9(5): 25 (about racialized women)

Hall, Marny, Celia Kitzinger, JoAnn Loulan, and Rachel Perkins. 1992. 'Lesbian Psychology, Lesbian Politics.' *Feminism and Psychology* 2: 7–25

Hall, Roberta M., and Bernice R. Sandler. 1983. *Academic Mentoring for Women Students and Faculty: A New Look at an Old Way to Get Ahead.* Washington: Project on the Status and Education of Women, Association of American Colleges

Harris, Michael. 1986. 'Black Professors Still a Rarity at UC and Stanford.' *San Francisco Chronicle*, 2 June: 6

Harvey, William. 1986. 'Where Are the Black Faculty: In the Lingering Climate of Institutional Racism, They Are Not the Only Losers.' *Chronicle of Higher Education*, 22 January

Heller, Scott. 1986. 'Language, Politics, and Chicano Culture Spark Battle at U. of Arizona.' *Chronicle of Higher Education*, 12 February

Hensel, Nancy. 1991. *Realizing Gender Equality in Higher Education: The Need to Integrate Work/Family Issues.* ASHE-ERIC Higher Education Research Report no. 2. Washington: George Washington School of Education and Human Development

Heth, Charlotte, and Susan Guyette. 1985. *Issues for the Future of American Indian Studies.* Los Angeles: American Indian Studies Center, University of California

hooks, bell. 1990. *YEARNING: race, gender, and cultural politics.* Toronto: Between the Lines

Ihle, Elizabeth L., ed. 1992. *Black Women in Higher Education: An Anthology of Essays, Studies, and Documents.* New York: Garland

Jacobs, Lucy. 1981. 'Problems Encountered by Women and Minority Students at Indiana University.' *Indiana Studies in Higher Education* (ERIC document no. ED210-996)

Justus, Joyce Bennett, Sandria B. Freitag, and L. Leann Parker. 1987. *The University of California in the Twenty-First Century: Successful Approaches to Faculty Diversity*

Kitzinger, Celia. 1990. 'Heterosexism in Psychology.' *The Psychologist*: 391–2
– In press. 'Beyond the Boundaries: Lesbians in Academe.' In *Storming the Tower: Women in the Academic World*, S. Lie and V. O'Leary, eds. London: Kogan Page

Levy, Phyllis Saltzman. 1982. 'Surviving in a Predominantly White Male Institution.' In *The Ph.D. Experience: A Woman's Point of View*, Sue Vartuli, ed., 45–59. New York: Praeger

McCombs, H.G. 1989. 'The Dynamics and Impact of Affirmative Action Processes on Higher Education, the Curriculum, and Black Women.' *Sex Roles* 21: 127–44

McDaniel, J. 1982. 'We Were Fired: Lesbian Experiences in Academe.' *Sinister Wisdom* 20: 30–43

McKay, Nellie. 1983. 'Black Woman Professor – White University.' *Women's Studies International Forum* 6(2): 143–7

McMillen, Liz. 1986. 'Women Flock to Graduate School in Record Numbers, but Fewer Blacks Are Entering the Academic Pipeline: Women.' *Chronicle of Higher Education*, 10 September

McNaron, Toni A.H. 1992. 'Life on the Faultline.' *Women's Review of Books* 9(5): 29–30 (about lesbians)

Mahdesian, Lina. 1992. 'The Minority Deficit.' *Brown Alumni Monthly*, November: 27–31

Minority Faculty Registry. 1992. c/o Dr William B. Jones, Southwestern University, Georgetown, Tex. 78626. Printed in *Chronicle of Higher Education*, 8 January: B19

Mohanty, Chandra Talpade. 1983. 'On Salvaging Difference: The Politics of Black Women's Studies.' *Women's Studies International Forum* 6: 243–8

Moses, Yolanda T. 1989. *Black Women in Academe: Issues and Strategies.* Washington: Association of American Colleges

Mosley, Myrtis Hall. 1982. 'Black Women Administrators in Higher Education: An Endangered Species.' *Ivy Leaf* (Spring): 21; reprinted from *Journal of Black Studies* 10 (1980)

Mulvey, Anne, Marg Schneider, Meg A. Bond, and Bill Berkowitz. 'Feminism and Community Psychology in Diverse Classrooms.' Paper presented at Northeast Regional Community Psychology conference, New Britain, Conn.

Nadasen, Pam. 1992. 'United We Stand.' *Women's Review of Books* 9(5): 31 (about racialized women)

New York Times 1991. 'Race and Sex Tied to Disparities in Professors' Pay.' 8 December: 771–2

Noonan, John F. 1980. 'White Faculty and Black Students: Examining Assumptions and Practices.' Cited by Hall and Sandler, 1982 (see 'General' section, above)

Office of Minority Concerns. 1985. *Minorities in Higher Education.* 4th annual status report. Washington: American Council on Education

O'Toole, J. Corbett, and CeCe Weeks. 1978. *What Happens after School? A Study of Disabled Women and Education.* Available through Library of Congress, National Library Service for the Blind and Physically Handicapped, 1291 Taylor St. N.W., Washington 20542

Preer, Jean. 1981. *Minority Access to Higher Education.* ASHE-ERIC / Higher Education Research Report 1. Washington: ERIC Clearinghouse on Higher Education (ERIC document no. ED207–474)

Program for Women in Health Sciences. 1979. *The Minority Woman in America: Professionalism at What Cost?* San Francisco: University of California

Ramcharan, Subhas, with James Chacko and Roxanne Baker. 1991. *An Attitudinal Study of Visible Minority Students at the University of Windsor.* Windsor, Ont.: University of Windsor

Rendon, Linda. 1981. 'The Three Rs for Hispanics in Higher Education: Retention, Recruitment, and Research.' Paper presented to College Recruitment Association for Hispanics, Lansing, Mich. (ERIC document no. ED210-075)

Rohrbaugh, Joanna Bunker. 1986. 'Issues Confronting Lesbian Academics.' In *Career Guide for Women Scholars*, Suzanna Rose, ed., 115–20. New York: Springer

Romero, Dan. 1977. 'The Impact and Use of Minority Faculty within a University.' Paper presented at annual meeting of American Psychological Association, San Francisco (ERIC document no. ED146-240)

Rosenfelt, Deborah, and Rhonda Williams. 1992. 'Learning Experience.' *Women's Review of Books* 9(5): 33–5 (about racialized women)

Rothblum, Esther D. n.d. 'Lesbians and Gay Men in Academia: Examples from the Social Sciences.' Burlington: University of Vermont

Rubenstein, Judith Allen. 1987. 'Graffiti Wars.' *Lilith* 17 (Fall): 8–9

Russell, S. 1986. 'The Hidden Curriculum of School: Reproducing Gender and Class Hierarchies.' In R. Hamilton and M. Barrett, *The Politics of Diversity*, 343–60. Montreal: Book Centre, Inc.

Schnur, Susan. 1987. 'Blazes of Truth: When Is a JAP Not a Yuppie?' *Lilith* 17 (Fall): 10–11

Scott, Patricia Bell. 1982. 'Debunking Sapphire: Toward a Non-racist and Non-sexist Social Science.' In *All the Women Are White, All the Blacks Are Men, But Some of Us Are Brave*, Gloria T. Hull, Patricia Bell Scott, and Barbara Smith, eds, 85–92. Old Westbury, NY: Feminist Press

Siegel, Rachel Josefowitz. 1986. 'Antisemitism and Sexism in Stereotypes of Jewish Women.' *Women and Therapy* 5: 249–57

Simpson, Adelaide. 1979. 'A Perspective on the Learning Experiences of Black Students at VCU.' Unpublished paper, Center for Improving Teaching Effectiveness. Richmond: Virginia Commonwealth University

Spatta, Carolyn D. 1984. *White Faculty, Black Students: Exploring Assumptions and Practices*. Washington: Association of American Colleges

Spencer, Gary, Sherry Chayat, and Judith Allen Rubenstein. 1987. 'JAP-baiting: How to Fight Back.' *Lilith* 17 (Fall): 3

Staples, Brent. 1986. 'The Dwindling Black Presence on Campus.' *New York Times Magazine*, 27 April: 46–52, 62

Thomas, Susan, Mary L. Spencer, and Margine Sako, comps and eds. 1982. 'Conversations with Minority Women Scholars.' In Spencer, Kehoe, and Speece, eds, *Handbook for Women Scholars*, 41–59

Tidwell, Romeria. 1981. 'University Efforts to Promote Minorities and Women: Three Realities.' *Journal of Educational Equity and Leadership* 1: 115–25

Tyler, Tracey. 1992. 'Black Law Students Unite to Fight Racism: Group Fears Backlash against Minority Hiring.' *Toronto Star*, 24 February: B11

University of Western Ontario. 1989. *Report of the President's Advisory Committee on Race Relations*. Windsor, Ont.: University of Windsor

University of Wisconsin. 1988. *Achieving Faculty Diversity*. Madison: University of Wisconsin

Valverde, Leonard. 1980. 'Development of Ethnic Researchers and the Education of White Researchers.' *Educational Researcher* 9: 16–20

Vetter, Betty M. 1976. 'Minority Women in Science and Engineering.' Paper presented to American Association for the Advancement of Science conference. In *The Double Bind: The Price of Being a Minority Woman in Science*. AAAS Report no. 76-R-3. Washington: AAAS

Vetter, Betty, and Eleanor Babco. 1986. *Professional Women and Minorities: A Manpower Data Resource Service*. Washington: Commission on Professionals in Science and Technology

Washington, V., and W. Harvey. 1989. *Affirmative Rhetoric, Negative Action: African-American and Hispanic Faculty at Predominantly White Institutions*. ASHE-ERIC Higher Education Research Report no. 2. Washington: School of Education and Human Development, George Washington University

Wilkerson, Margaret B. 1979. 'Minority – Professional – Woman: The Creative Tension.' Keynote address to University of California at San Francisco Program for Women in Health Sciences conference, 'The Minority Woman in America: Professionalism at What Cost?' San Francisco

Wine, Jeri Dawn. 1988. 'On Prejudice and Possibility: Lesbians in Canadian Academe.' *Atlantis* 14: 45–55

Wiseman, Paul. 1991. 'Blacks More Likely to Face Loan Rejection.' *USA Today*, 22 October: A1

Wyche, Karen Fraser, and Sherryl Browne Graves. 1992. 'Minority Women in Academia: Access and Barriers to Professional Participation.' *Psychology of Women Quarterly* 16: 429–37

Yeskel, Felice, 1992. 'The Price of Progress.' *Women's Review of Books* 9(5): 21 (about lesbian and bisexual women)

York University. 1986. *Report of the Committee on Race and Ethnic Relations*. Toronto

Zimmerman, Bonnie. 1983. 'Is "Chloe liked Olivia" a Lesbian Plot?' *Women's Studies International Forum* 6: 169–76

F **Non-regular instructional personnel**

Clapp, Patricia. 1987. 'Part-time Teaching as Career Development.' Unpublished paper, University of Calgary

Committee on the Status of Women. 1991. *Non-regular Instructional Personnel in Ontario Universities*. Toronto: Council of Ontario Universities

Conseil des universités, Québec. 1989. *Les Chargés de cours dans les universités québécoises*. Sainte-Foy, Qué.: Gouvernement du Québec

Gordon, Jane. 1987. 'We Tried: A Case Study of Ideology and Inertia.' Paper
    prepared for Conference on Part-time Teaching in the University. York
    University, Toronto
Jones, Paul. n.d. 'The Situation of Chargé-e-s de cours in Quebec.' Unpub-
    lished paper, Fédération nationale des enseignants et des enseignantes du
    Québec
Lundy, K.L.P., and B.D. Warme, 1986. 'Part-time Faculty: Institutional Need
    and Career Dilemma. In *Work in the Canadian Context*, Lundy and Warme,
    eds, 132–148. Toronto: Butterworths
Professional Women's Association. 1986. Report of a Study on Part-time Fac-
    ulty and Staff. Waterloo, Ont.: University of Waterloo
Rajagopal, Indhu, and William D. Farr. 1990. 'Part-time Faculty in Ontario
    Universities.' In Committee on the Status of Women. *Non-regular Instruc-
    tional Personnel in Ontario universities*, 1–15. Toronto: Council of Ontario
    Universities
Weis, Lyle. n.d. 'Falling through the Cracks: Sessionals in Alberta.' Unpub-
    lished paper, University of Alberta
Zeytinoglu, Isik Urla, and Maroussia Ahmed. 1989. 'Results of a Survey on
    Part-time Faculty at McMaster University.' Hamilton, Ont.: Committee on
    the Status of Women, McMaster University Faculty Association

G Older women

Ackerman, Rosalie J. 1986. 'Middle-aged Women and Career Transitions.' In
    Career Guide for Women Scholars, Suzanna Rose, ed., 102–7. New York:
    Springer
Re-entry packets I, II, and III. 1980–81. Washington: Association of American
    Colleges
Siegel, Rachel Josefowitz. 1990a. 'Love and Work after Sixty: An Integration
    of Personal and Professional Growth within a Longterm Marriage.' In
    Women, Aging, and Ageism, Evelyn Rosenthal, ed., 69–79. New York: Ha-
    worth
– 1990b. 'We Are Not Your Mothers.' In *Women, Aging, and Ageism*, Evelyn
    Rosenthal, ed., 81–9. New York: Haworth
– 1990c. 'Old Women as Mother Figures.' In *Woman-defined Motherhood*, Jane
    Price Knowles and Ellen Cole, eds, 89–97. New York: Haworth
Wells, Mary Cay. 1982. 'Grandma! What Big Plans You've Got! In *The Ph.D.
    Experience: A Woman's Point of View*, Sue Vartuli, ed., 105–14. New York:
    Praeger

H Research, writing, publishing, obtaining grants

Baron, Robert A. 1987. 'Research Grants: A Practical Guide.' In *The Compleat Academic: A Practical Guide for the Beginning Social Scientist*, Mark P. Zanna and John M. Darley, eds, 151–69. New York: Random House

Bem, Daryl J. 1987. 'Writing the Empirical Journal Article.' In *The Compleat Academic: A Practical Guide for the Beginning Social Scientist*, Mark P. Zanna and John M. Darley, eds, 171–201. New York: Random House

Bleier, Ruth. 1988. 'Science and the Construction of Meaning in the Neurosciences.' In *Feminism within the Sciences and Health Care Professions*, S.V. Rosser, ed., 91–104. New York: Pergamon

– 1987. Presentation in symposium on 'Bias in Sex Differences Research.' American Association for the Advancement of Science convention, Chicago

Daniels, Arlene Kaplan. 1982. 'Acquiring Skills for the Funding Search.' In Spencer, Kehoe, and Speece, eds, *Handbook for Women Scholars*, 97–105

Fox, M.F., ed. 1985. *Productive Scholarship: Issues, Problems, Solutions.* Boulder, Colo.: Westview Press

Henson, Kenneth T. 1991. 'Writing for Successful Publication.' Bloomington, Ind.: National Educational Service

Patai, Daphne. 1983. 'Beyond Defensiveness: Feminist Research Strategies.' *Women's Studies International Forum* 6: 177–90

Project on the Status and Education of Women. 1980. 'Sexist Biases in Sociological Research: Problems and Issues.' Washington: Association of American Colleges

Richardson, Mary Frances. 1991. 'Support for Women Researchers in Small Universities.' Presented at Sixth Conference on Research at Small Universities, Trent University, Peterborough, Ont.

Spender, Dale. 1981. 'The Gatekeepers: A Feminist Critique of Academic Publishing.' In *Doing Feminist Research*, H. Roberts, ed., 186–202. London: Routledge and Kegan Paul

Stake, Jayne E. 1986. 'When It's Publish or Perish: Tips on Survival.' In *Career Guide for Women Scholars*, Suzanna Rose, ed., 57–65. New York: Springer

Stark-Adamec, Cannie, and Robert Adamec. 1981. 'Breaking into the Grant Proposal Market: Or, the Trials, Tribulations, Tears, Rage and Fun(?) of Acquiring a Quarter of a Million Dollars and Still Being Left Wondering How You're Going to Pay the Rent.' *International Journal of Women's Studies* 4: 105–17

Taylor, Shelley E., and Joanne Martin. 1987. 'The Present-minded Professor:

Controlling One's Career.' In *The Compleat Academic: A Practical Guide for the Beginning Social Scientist*, Mark P. Zanna and John M. Darley, eds, 23–60. New York: Random House

1 Sexual harassment and safety

Barickman, R., S. Korn, B. Sandler, Y. Gold, A. Ormerod, and L. Weitzman. 1990. An Ecological Perspective to Understanding Sexual Harassment.' In *Ivory Power: Sexual Harassment on Campus*, M. Paludi, ed., xi–xix. Albany: State University of New York Press
Burger, Anne. 1986. *Report on Sexual Harassment and Sexual Assault at Simon Fraser University*. Vancouver: British Columbia Public Interest Research Group
Cammaert, Lorna P. 1985. 'How Widespread Is Sexual Harassment on Campus?' *International Journal of Women's Studies* 8(4): 388–97
Fisher, Gina. 1989. *Sexual Harassment of Students in a University Setting*. Unpublished doctoral dissertation, University of Toronto
Fitzgerald, L.F., L.M. Weitzman, Y. Gold, and M. Ormerod. 1988. 'Academic Harassment: Sex and Denial in Scholarly Garb.' *Psychology of Women Quarterly* 12: 329–40
Franklin, Phyllis, et al. 1981. *Sexual and Gender Harassment in the Academy: A Guide for Faculty, Students and Administrators*. Commission on the Status of Women in the Profession, Modern Language Association of America, New York
Glaser, R.D., and J.S. Thorpe. 1986. 'Unethical Intimacy: A Survey of Sexual Contact and Advances between Psychology Educators and Female Graduate Students.' *American Psychologist* 41: 43–51
Govier, Katherine. 1990. 'Shocked into Awareness: Sexism at Queen's.' *Whig-Standard Magazine*, 5 May: 4–8
'Harvard Releases Sexual Harassment Report.' 1984. In *On Campus with Women* 13 (Winter): 1. Project on the Status and Education of Women, Association of American Colleges, Washington
Hill, Anita. 1992. 'The Nature of the Beast.' *Ms.*, January/February: 32–3
Hughes, Jean O'Gorman, and Bernice R. Sandler. 1988. *Peer Harassment: Hassles for Women on Campus*. Washington: Project on the Status and Education of Women, Association of American Colleges
– 1986. *In Case of Sexual Harassment ... A Guide for Women Students*. Washington: Association of American Colleges
Johnston, Nancy, and Claire Polster. 1992. 'Report on the Safety and Security of Graduate Women at York University.' In York University Task Force on the Status of Women Graduate Students. *Not Satisfied Yet: Report of the*

Task Force on the Status of Women Graduate Students, 75–91. North York, Ont.: York University

Landsberg, M. 1990. 'Dean's Silence Worst Response to Sexist Slurs.' *Toronto Star*, 20 April

McCann, W. 1989. 'Law School Students Complain of Harassment, Discrimination.' *London Free Press*, 24 October: 50–1

MacKenzie, M., and T. Lussier. 1988. *Sexual Harassment: Report on the Results of a Survey of the University of Manitoba Community*. Winnipeg: University of Manitoba

Malette, L., and M. Chalouh, eds. 1991. *The Montreal Massacre*. Charlottetown, PEI: Gynergy Books

METRAC (Metro Action Committee on Public Violence Against Women and Children) and Council of Ontario Universities Committee on the Status of Women. 1991. *Women's Campus Safety Audit Guide*. Toronto

Morris, Ramona. 1989. 'Safety Problems and Sexual Harassment on Campus.' In *Women in Graduate Studies in Ontario: Proceedings of a Conference on Women in Graduate Studies in Ontario*, C. Filteau, ed., 13–27. Toronto: Ontario Council on Graduate Studies

Paludi, Michele A, ed. 1990. *Ivory Power: Sexual Harassment on Campus*. Albany: State University of New York Press

Ramazanoglu, C. 1987. 'Sex and Violence in Academic Life, or, You Can Keep a Good Woman Down.' In *Women, Violence and Social Control*, J. Hanmer and M. Maynard, eds, 61–74. London: MacMillan

Randall, M. 1987. *Sexual Harassment*. Women's Directorate: Toronto

Reed, Carole-Ann, Leslie Russell, June Larkin, and Marian Beauregard. 1991. 'Shrews Unite.' *Canadian Woman's Studies* 12: 60–2

Sexual Harassment Packet. 1979–87. Washington: Association of American Colleges

Till, Frank J. 1980. *Sexual Harassment: A Report on the Sexual Harassment of Students*. Washington: National Advisory Council on Women's Educational Programs

Wiggins, Lee. 1992. 'Sexual and Gender Harassment.' In York University Task Force on the Status of Women Graduate Students, *Not Satisfied Yet: Report of the Task Force on the Status of Women Graduate Students*, 93–109. North York, Ont.: York University